AF568053

Rocketing Through the Skies

'G. Madhavan Nair is India's rocket science prodigy, and the story of his life embodies the history of ISRO in its difficult years when it had to brave all kinds of odds in its bid to conquer space. I found [his] autobiography to be a compelling read because his and ISRO's evolution are so intimately intertwined. The book reads like a sequel to Abdul Kalam's *Wings of Fire*, and I think it is a must read for all those who are keen to know everything about those fascinating machines called rockets.'

—S.K. Das
IAS (Retd), Former Member (Finance), Department of Space

'I have a common link with Madhavan Nair through the BARC training school. We worked on cutting-edge technologies in atomic energy and space, ultimately getting the opportunity to lead the respective organizations. We could work together in formulating policies related to science and technology and strive for self-reliance in high technology for our country and also for improving the remuneration for scientists and other staff working in high-tech R&D fields. Madhavan Nair has played a pivotal role in India's evolution as a space power [to ensure that] space technology benefits every Indian and in defining a future roadmap. The book is not only his autobiography but depicts the history of rocketry in India. It is quite informative and makes compelling reading for youth aspiring to take up challenges in advanced technologies.'

—Dr Anil Kakodkar
Former Chairman of the Atomic Energy Commission of India and Secretary to the Department of Atomic Energy

'Like other chairpersons before him, Shri Madhavan Nair carried forward the vision of Dr Vikram Sarabhai, who believed that technology must alleviate the hardships of the common Indian. Madhavan Nair's contribution in this direction has been immense during ISRO's growth. His personal journey, from humble beginnings to ISRO's highest office will motivate many who are about to embark on their chosen careers. It is a story that proves that it is possible to positively influence the lives of an entire country using space technology.'

—Wg Cdr Rakesh Sharma, AC (Retd)
Research Cosmonaut, India

'I was privileged to work with Shri G. Madhavan Nair during the developmental phase of the PSLV and until the realization of the LVM-3. I always awed by his ability to quickly decipher technical issues and provide solutions and guidance to the team members. Remarkable was his leadership and mentoring abilities. The birth pangs of rocketry in India have been narrated along with his own personal life history. It projects the complexity of the rocket and space technology in simple language and makes for interesting reading.'

—S. Somanath
Secretary to the Department of Space and Chairman, ISRO

Rocketing Through the Skies

AN EVENTFUL LIFE AT ISRO

G. MADHAVAN NAIR

RUPA

Published by
Rupa Publications India Pvt. Ltd 2023
7/16, Ansari Road, Daryaganj
New Delhi 110002

Sales centres:
Prayagraj Bengaluru Chennai
Hyderabad Jaipur Kathmandu
Kolkata Mumbai

Copyright © G. Madhavan Nair 2023
Translated and updated by Jaya G. Nair based on G. Madhavan Nair's
original autobiography in Malayalam.

The views and opinions expressed in this book are the author's own and the facts are as reported by him which have been verified to the extent possible, and the publishers are not in any way liable for the same.
All rights reserved.

No part of this publication may be reproduced, transmitted, or stored in a retrieval system, in any form or by any means, electronic, mechanical, photocopying, recording or otherwise, without the prior permission of the publisher.

P-ISBN: 978-93-5702-472-3
E-ISBN: 978-93-5702-488-4

First impression 2023

10 9 8 7 6 5 4 3 2 1

The moral right of the author has been asserted.

Printed in India

This book is sold subject to the condition that it shall not, by way of trade or otherwise, be lent, resold, hired out, or otherwise circulated, without the publisher's prior consent, in any form of binding or cover other than that in which it is published.

I dedicate this book to the ISRO family,
who made me who I am.

Contents

Foreword

The space cooperation between France and India started with scientific work dating back to 1963 between Professor Jacques Blamont (Centre National d'Études Spatiales [CNES]) and Dr Vikram Sarabhai (founder of Indian Space Research Organisation [ISRO]), which created the foundation for a successful, amicable and long-lasting partnership. The first intergovernmental agreement for space cooperation in 1977, followed by another signed on 30 September 2008, during the Franco-Indian summit in Paris, sealed the strong desire to strengthen the cooperation between France and India. The launch of numerous Indian telecommunication and meteorology satellites starting from 1981 from French Guiana by the Ariane launch vehicle is a perfect example of the strength of the Franco-Indian cooperation.

Madhavan Nair and I became chairmen of ISRO and the CNES, respectively, in 2003, and we very quickly focussed on the development of space collaboration between our two countries.

There was a 'spark' at a personal and professional level that developed quickly, which allowed us to work in an environment of trust and friendship. We had the same strategic vision: to put space at the service of the needs of all humankind. At that time, I took a new slogan for the CNES: 'Space for Earth'.

Indeed, we shared the vision that space applications are bound to develop extensively, thanks to the tremendous advancements made in the field of space technologies (satellites, launchers, scientific instruments, telecommunications, navigation, etc.) and by conjugating with the Internet world and the digital revolution. Working together compounds the benefits for both nations. It could be used anywhere in the world, serving both public policy, scientific knowledge and the development of space services and related industries: fixed and mobile telephony, television, broadband Internet, positioning, Earth observation, meteorology, oceanography, hydrology, climate and the fight against climate change, 3D cartography, tele-education, tele-medicine, agriculture and forests, fishing, tourism, prevention and management of natural disasters, search and rescue, etc.

It is from this perspective that Madhavan Nair and I decided to jointly develop two scientific Earth observation satellites. First, Megha Tropiques for the study of meteorological and climatic phenomena in tropical zones (*megha* means cloud in Sanskrit), and second, Saral, an oceanographic altimetry satellite. Saral, which was under construction at the ISRO centre in Bengaluru (earlier known as Bangalore), had the privilege to be presented to the then president of the French Republic, Nicolas Sarkozy, during the first stop of his State visit to India in 2010, highlighting the strength of the Franco-Indian partnership. Both satellites were launched from the Satish Dhawan Space Centre by the Polar Satellite Launch Vehicle (PSLV). We also embarked the French instrument Argos-4 on the Indian satellite Oceansat-3.

Madhavan Nair and I pushed our cooperation to grow. We received support from our directors, and, at the CNES, Dr Sylvie Callari was instrumental in the coordination.

The joint work done by our teams, driven by a common passion for space and the strong desire to succeed together, produced excellent results in the rewarding context of different working methods and reciprocal cultures.

I valued the high proficiency of Indian scientists, engineers and technicians, and their achievements. I remember the achievement of the Chandrayaan-1 lunar probe in 2008, which notably discovered the presence of water as well as recent volcanism on the Moon, after which media started referring to Madhavan Nair as the 'Moon Man'.

We had the privilege to collaborate in person as I travelled to India very often to visit ISRO centres and hosted Madhavan and his team in Paris, Toulouse and Kourou, French Guiana. The International Academy of Astronautics was also a place where we had the opportunity to work together when Madhavan Nair was its president and I was its vice-president.

I remember our discussions on space and science, but we also shared our thoughts on the fabulous history of India, on Indian and Western culture and gastronomy!

We also shared a common passion for teaching. Madhavan Nair has done a lot for education (notably at the Indian Institute of Space Science and Technology [IIST] in Thiruvananthapuram) and for science and technology outreach.

The memories and successes achieved working with ISRO left a lasting impression on my career in terms of international cooperation. I gained an extraordinary wealth of experience both professionally and personally, and I am happy and proud to have served with Madhavan Nair, working towards the space cooperation between our two countries.

I am happy to introduce the autobiography of Madhavan Nair, *Rocketing through the Skies*, in which he has narrated his life experiences starting from a remote village in Kanyakumari district, the southernmost tip of India, to the topmost position in ISRO. Nearly half a century of his association with the Indian space programme, starting from its inception, means most of his story is that of ISRO as well.

Yannick d'Escatha
Chairman and CEO (2003–13)
Centre National d'Études Spatiales

Preface

I have grown up and lived for the most part in independent India. I have enjoyed the freedom and benefitted from the opportunities in the largest democracy in the world. That is how a village boy like me could rise to the highest position in the Indian space programme. I stepped down as the chairman of ISRO in 2009 after taking its glory to the pinnacle by placing the Indian national flag on the Moon.

Afterwards, wherever I went, several people asked me why I did not write my autobiography, just as my guru Dr Kalam had done through *Wings of Fire*. I used to brush aside such suggestions, saying that I cannot be compared with Dr Kalam, the national icon! The fact was that Dr Kalam was meticulous in keeping daily notes of events in his notebook, whereas I had to comb through my memory. Writing was never my cup of tea. It was during a flight from Delhi that Ravi Deecee, the CEO of DC Books, convinced me about the need for such a book. He said that he would organize a scribe for me and I had to only narrate my story. I was lucky that he recommended P.V. Alby, who had translated *Wings of Fire* to Malayalam. We spent nearly a month together, and Alby absorbed every word of mine like a sponge. The result was my autobiography in Malayalam titled *Agniparikshakal*, published by DC Books in 2017.

There was a lot of demand for an English version. I was hesitant to undertake that arduous task. One evening, my friends Dr Unnikrishnan and Jaya dropped in for a chat. I was impressed with the literary activity Jaya had been pursuing after voluntary retirement from ISRO. Not only that, she is the grand-niece of Rama Kurup, who was my teacher at what is now known as Raja Kesavadas N.S.S. Higher Secondary School and is my role model. I told her that I expect a re-narration rather than a literal translation of the Malayalam version. She did a wonderful job, and the end product is *Rocketing through the Skies*. In addition, my office staff and several of my close friends assisted me in this venture. I acknowledge the contributions of all those with gratitude.

I do not want to repeat what is written in this book. My life story and ISRO's history are intimately intertwined. I have tried to include several incidents—both happy and unpleasant ones. My destiny was not moulded deliberately by any individual but is the result of a series of events that may look like accidents. The cumulative effect of all the events has made me who I am. I have faced failures, successes, blames and praises. Failures have taught me more than path-breaking successes. I do not claim any credit to myself because I stood on the shoulders of my ISRO family while placing the tricolour on the Moon. The credit goes to them.

Prologue

A Golden Day in Pursuit of the Moon

It was 14 November 2008, one of the most memorable days of my life. The day when the Indian space programme made history by placing the Indian national flag on the Moon, Earth's nearest neighbour in space.

Just three weeks before, on 22 October, a Polar Satellite Launch Vehicle (PSLV) had blasted off from the launch pad at Sriharikota, commencing the journey of the spacecraft Chandrayaan-1 to the Moon. The PSLV placed the spacecraft initially into a highly elliptical orbit around the Earth. To traverse the nearly 400,000 km to the Moon, escaping Earth's gravity, was the most challenging feat ISRO had accomplished until then. That journey was undertaken cautiously, raising the apogee—the farthest point from the Earth—step by step using rocket engines built into the spacecraft.

Chandrayaan-1 zoomed through outer space with a velocity of nearly 3 km/s, around 30 times faster than a racing car. This velocity had to nearly halve (around 1.6 km/s) to enable the spacecraft to be pulled into an orbit around the Moon. To accomplish this, the spacecraft had to be turned in the opposite direction and engines fired for a predetermined duration. That was an extremely anxious moment for all of us. Had the timing not been correct or the velocity not precise enough, Chandrayaan-1 would have been lost in space forever. However, the operations were carried out successfully, and finally, after 21 days, Chandrayaan-1 dropped into an elliptical orbit around the Moon, where it was 500 km from the Moon at the closest point and 10,000 km away at the farthest.

The next two days were spent in carrying out detailed tests to ensure that all the spacecraft subsystems were operating correctly. Chandrayaan-1 was then lowered into a circular orbit around the poles of the Moon at an altitude of 200 km.

The Moon has enthralled humankind from time immemorial. Poets have compared it with beautiful faces of women. The Puranas have revered it as a god, a deva. Any new knowledge about the Moon has always been important for us earthlings. In that spirit, when the whole of India was waiting with bated breath for news about the progress of Chandrayaan-1, ISRO declared to the nation that its maiden attempt to take the spacecraft to a precise orbit around the Moon was a complete success.

Chandrayaan-1 carried a module called Moon Impact Probe (MIP), which was to be put on the surface of the Moon as proof of India's arrival. The module had the Indian tricolour inscribed on it and contained a high-resolution mass spectrometer, a video camera and an S-band altimeter, among others, for uncovering hitherto unknown details about the tenuous atmosphere of the Moon.

D-DAY

At last, the D-day for the MIP to touch the Moon's surface dawned: 14 November 2008. Like every day, I reached my office at the ISRO headquarters (HQ) in Bengaluru (earlier known as Bangalore) at 9.00 a.m. After some urgent meetings regarding future activities, I reached the specially set-up control centre in Peenya, Bengaluru, which was in charge of the mission operations of Chandrayaan-1. S.K. Shivakumar, the director of the spacecraft tracking station, and M. Annadurai, mission director of Chandrayaan-1, received me and took me to the control room. They briefed me about the current status of the spacecraft and the operations to be conducted later that day. We then had to wait for the scheduled time for the Moon impact.

An hour before the MIP was to be detached from the Chandrayaan-1 spacecraft, Dr A.P.J. Abdul Kalam, former president of India and my guru, strode into the control room flashing his trademark smile. He had not been able to come to Sriharikota for the launch of Chandrayaan-1 but kept his word to be with us to witness the landing of the MIP on the surface of the Moon.

I arranged spiced buttermilk—his favourite—for him and explained the details of the mission. He went around the newly built control room and appreciated the internal architecture as well as the sophisticated instrumentation. The control room was as big as a tennis court and as high as a two-storied building, fitted with the latest facilities. A giant display screen on the wall continuously showed the status of each of the instruments aboard Chandrayaan-1. The schedule of the upcoming operations was being projected on another screen. More than a hundred computers and an equal number of scientists were engrossed in work all around the room. Professor U.R. Rao, former chairman of ISRO, also joined us.

Maintaining communication with the spacecraft at the distance of the Moon is indeed a very challenging task. A giant dish antenna with a diameter of 30 m and a very sensitive receiver had been set up to capture the weak signals arriving from the distance of 400,000 km. Using completely home-grown technology, the receiving centre was able to accurately follow the spacecraft to collect data from it and relay it to the mission control centre in Peenya within seconds. Dr Kalam was excited to see the most modern set-up and remarked that he felt as if he was in a wonderland!

At exactly six minutes past 8.00 p.m., the command to initiate the Moon impact sequence was transmitted to Chandrayaan-1. As the command was executed by the spacecraft, the MIP was severed from the mother craft. The final journey of the MIP started from an altitude of 200 km above the Moon. The speed of the MIP had to be reduced, so that it descended to the lunar surface by gravitational pull. To commence the free fall, the velocity of the MIP was reduced by firing the small solid rocket attached to it. As we looked anxiously at the screens in the control room, the MIP descended on the Moon and finally impacted at a spot near the pole, beside the Shackleton crater. The Indian flag on the MIP inscribed India's presence on the Moon forever, heralding the nation's entry into the elite club of the countries that had earlier placed national flags on the Moon (the USA, Russia and China).

Thus, the dream mission, announced on Independence Day, 15 August 2003, by the then Prime Minister Atal Bihari Vajpayee, became a reality five years later, on 14 November, the birthday of the first prime minister of India, Pandit Jawaharlal Nehru. It was heartening that this historic moment was witnessed by Dr Kalam, who had originally put forth the idea that India must also place its flag on the Moon. We joined in the joyous uproar of hundreds of scientists in the control centre.

MAKING INDIA PROUD

After carefully verifying the data related to mission management and confirming that the impact had taken place successfully, I went out with my colleagues to meet the national press and media assembled in the Press Gallery. An Indian spacecraft had reached the Moon in its first attempt, that too at one-fifth the expense usually incurred by the developed countries! All the payloads in the spacecraft had been made operational, including the six payloads from other countries. Volumes of data had been received and provided valuable information about the Moon.

All the faces in the room beamed with joy and satisfaction when we announced to the world that India had once again proved herself in the arena of space through this Chandrayaan mission. I presented Dr Kalam with a model of the Moon with the exact landing place of MIP marked on it and another of the Chandrayaan-1 spacecraft. He patted me on the back and said in his characteristic style: 'You, buddy, you have done it!' To the entire control room, he announced, 'Today is a historic day as India has accomplished this fantastic mission. I congratulate each and every one of you!' He made a suggestion before returning to New Delhi—to name the impact location after Pandit Nehru. This declaration was made later with the permission of the Government of India and the place was christened 'Jawahar Sthal', meaning 'the place of Jawahar'.

Those were moments of pride and satisfaction for every Indian, and especially for the entire ISRO fraternity. The position of India as a space power had been affirmed. The international space community applauded the success achieved by India on the very first attempt in such a complex mission.

After announcing the success of the Chandrayaan-1 mission, I went back to the control room and shared my happiness with my colleagues there. They were only a small cross-section of the ISRO family, which had orchestrated the historic accomplishment. The dedication and hard work of the ISRO employees and the sacrifices and support of their families had crafted the mission's success. There were simultaneous celebrations across all centres of ISRO.

The accomplishment was indeed a result of the hard work of thousands of people and the staunch support of all Indians.

1

Evergreen Memories

After seeing off the dignitaries after the landing, as I returned from the industrial centres of Peenya, I found myself in a daze, with several scenes of the past passing through my mind. India had undeniably made another giant stride in space technology. But I knew there was still a long way to go and many more missions to accomplish—going to Mars, sending humans to space and so on—to fulfil great hopes of the Indian people and the dreams of our founding father Dr Vikram Sarabhai.

Watching the moon rise through the car window, my thoughts wandered back in time, to 60 years earlier. The sight of the Moon looking like a big, orange-tinted ball ascending over the hills at Mukaliyadimala at the southernmost part of Western Ghats in erstwhile Travancore, where I had spent my infancy and childhood, came vividly to mind. How many nights had I sat entranced on the stone steps of Erathuveedu (my ancestral property) in Thirunandikkara, looking at the full moon! I wondered whether those moonbeams had first enticed me into the wonders of the sky and into dreams about the universe. I could feel myself as the child Madhavankutty, who used to walk across the wide paddy fields near the ancient temple of Nandeeswara, clutching the fingers of his dear grandfather—his role model in life.

SOME PERSONAL HISTORY

My grandfather M.K. Kesava Pillai was among the respected elders in the village of Thirunandikkara. A contractor for road construction works in the old Travancore state, he was called 'road-mestry' by everyone—a noble soul, always clad in a white dhoti and shirt, with a long shawl thrown around his neck. He was a decisive man of action, with a lot of compassion for the people around. My mother was born to my grandparents after many still-births. She was named Sarojam but was called by her pet name 'Baby'. Born after so much anticipation, no doubt Baby became the darling of the whole family. She was fair, a little plump and beautiful.

My father R. Gopalan Nair belonged to Neyyattinkara, which is now part of Thiruvananthapuram (earlier Trivandrum) District of Kerala. His father—my grandfather Balakrishnan Nair—was a *parvathyar* (village officer) in the Travancore revenue department. In spite of being a good student, my father could not afford college. Instead, he took a diploma in civil engineering and joined the Public Works Department (PWD). It was while he was working as the supervisor of Pechiparai Dam site, which is in Kanyakumari District today, that he married Sarojam of the Erathu family. In those days, as soon as a girl reached puberty, marriage proposals would start flowing in. Grandfather and others liked the handsome young engineer from Neyyattinkara who hailed from a good family. The young couple also liked each other, and the marriage was solemnized. My mother was only about 12 years old.

After the marriage ceremony, acting against the matrilineal custom of those days, my father took his young bride to live in his own house. He must have been influenced by his modern, English-based education and familiarity with the family life of British officers. His parents seemed to have wanted that too. However, it was a source of great anguish for my maternal grandfather, grandmother and other relatives. Usually, such a revolutionary act can lead to quarrels and create distance between the families. But the mature reaction of my grandfather prevented such things from happening. He must have realized that ultimately, it would be his daughter who would be affected by any rift between the two families. Hence, my childhood came to be divided between two places, which today are in two different but adjoining states—Tamil Nadu and Kerala.

My mother started living at her husband's family house at Neyyattinkara. My father could come home only during weekends, staying at the government quarters near the dam on weekdays.

Since there were no good roads or fast vehicles, it was not practical to commute the distance of 40 km between Perunchani and Neyyattinkara daily. I wonder if my mother felt lonely, being separated from her husband at such a young age. Her own relatives could visit only infrequently.

When my mother was seven months pregnant, my maternal grandparents arrived in Neyyattinkara, with other relatives, to take their daughter home. As per the custom, they presented her with gifts, including seven types of sweets and savouries, at an auspicious time. Once the ceremony was over and it was time to leave, it became clear that my father's parents did not want to send their daughter-in-law to her paternal home for her delivery. My paternal grandmother was very much worried about the availability of medical facilities in the remote village in case anything untoward happened during the childbirth.

Two more months passed, and my mother gave birth to me on 31 October 1943. I have heard my maternal grandmother remark often that the newborn was also fair like his mother. As promised, the mother and child were brought to Thirunandikkara, making everybody there extremely joyful.

I was the first grandchild born at Erathuveedu, my ancestral property. As may be expected, I was showered with boundless affection from my grandparents and the many servants present in the household.

As per the custom, my grandfather approached his astrologer to draw up my horoscope. However, the astrologer refused and said mercilessly, 'The casting of the horoscope can wait. Let the child reach the age of four. By that time, only one—either the mother or the child—is going to survive.' Grandfather returned home in deep anguish but kept the prediction a secret.

Months passed, and my mother became pregnant again. My little sister Ratnamma was born when I was one-and-a-half years old. She was born at Thirunandikkara as my mother had not yet gone back to Neyyattinkara after my birth. Following that second delivery, my mother's health began to decline. She was only 15 years old at that time. This was not at all unusual in those days of early marriage for girls. In spite of expert treatment, her health did not improve. As she became pregnant again, her health worsened. She was admitted to a hospital in Thycaud, Thiruvananthapuram, for her third delivery.

My mother may have had a premonition of death. She called my father to her side and told him about a wish, perhaps her last wish—in case she died, he must marry her sister Santha. She did not want her children to grow up with any unknown woman.

After a few days, my mother delivered a baby boy and breathed her last. Her funeral rites were performed as per the custom. On the third day, my little brother also passed away.

I was three years old and my sister Ratnamma was one-and-a-half. The responsibility of taking care of us naturally fell on my maternal grandparents. Thankfully, they were well-off and had many servants in the house. There were no children of my age there except my youngest uncle.

Thus, my grandmother effectively became my mother. We began calling her 'amma', emulating my uncles. But the loss of my mother always remained a raw pain inside me, as it still is. It seems that in the early days, I used to wander around the house searching for 'the other mother'. But the love of my grandparents must have brought down my grief to a large extent. My sister was too little to have felt the loss.

My father was still living in his official quarters at Cheruppalur. He would come every evening to spend some time with us and go back after tea. That we were living happily with our grandparents must have brought some relief to his own sorrow at the loss of his wife.

A LAND OF TEMPLES AND PADDY

As stated earlier, Thirunandikkara was in erstwhile Travancore, one of the four taluks in the district of Kanyakumari. The district was handed over to Tamil Nadu during the reorganization of states in independent India. What Kerala forfeited was a place of great historical significance, natural beauty, rivers and fertile lands. Vast green paddy fields, plantain groves and flower gardens decorated the countryside. Ancient temples like that of Adi Kesava as well as many prominent houses are situated there. An ancient university for Vedic studies was said to have been at Thiruvattar, around 5 km away from Thirunandikkara. In ancient times, Jain monks meditated in the hills near the Thirunandikkara Temple.

On most days, we children would go to the old Nandeeswara Temple nearby. After this morning visit, we would mostly be inside the house, sometimes going to the farms around the compound. The two-storeyed house was modelled after a British bungalow. A spacious drawing room on the ground floor was flanked by some more rooms and a kitchen. The ceiling had wide wooden planks connected to a large beam made from a single piece of wood nearly 20 m long. No concrete or cement was used in the construction. There was a large hall on the first floor. In spite of being very old, all these structures still exist. The current owner of the house is Shylaja Raveendran, my sister Ratnamma's eldest daughter. Indeed, with some modernization, the house has now become very convenient for all the relatives to spend time together.

The house faces the east, and a number of long stone steps are in the front. During my childhood, I used to sit on those steps and daydream about the big things in life. Beyond the house, one could see vast tree-lined yards and paddy fields spreading to the foot of the Mukaliyadimala Hill, which looks like a huge natural Shiva linga. On full moon nights, the Moon would rise from behind the hill. Watching it could have inspired me to embark upon my journey to space.

During the day, one could see huge abstract pictures made by light and shadow on the main rock at the peak of the hill. My grandmother had many enthralling stories to tell about them. One story was about a leopard and a hunter, who had strayed near the rock and were frozen onto it. The stories enticed me to stretch my imagination and daydream. At the same time, a deep curiosity developed in me to enquire further into the mysteries of celestial bodies. I consider it a divine grace that, much later, I had the opportunity to lead the Indian space programme at a time when the nation put its first signature on the Moon's surface by placing a flag there.

Today, those green paddy fields have been swallowed up by the ubiquitous rubber plantations. So much damage is caused to the environment because of human greed!

A small stream flowed in front of the house. I would lose track of time while looking at the little fishes swimming in it against the flow of water. During many times in my life when I had to swim against the flow and succeed, I could not help but remember those fishes. There was a rather big pond in the yard on the side of the house where I learnt how to swim. It used to be full of lotuses and water lilies. Lotus flowers bloom from seeds that are very tasty. As time passed, the pond became filled with soil. The beautiful ambal plants slid into oblivion and got replaced with the *kaitha* (screw pine) seen there today.

My grandfather owned many paddy fields adjoining the house. My greatest pleasure was walking on the small embankments along the paddy fields, holding onto his fingers. I would then ask him hundreds of doubts that would be haunting my little mind. Grandfather never showed even the slightest impatience while answering me. The images of those walks, with me sometimes touching the flowers alongside the fields or chasing after dragonflies, are still etched in my mind. The local people we met on our path would invariably show great respect to my grandfather. Seeing that, my own regard for him increased manifold. Gradually, he became enshrined in my mind as my role model with his cool, action-oriented and strong personality imbued with compassion for the needy.

Observing my curiosity, my grandfather would tell my grandmother, 'Narayani, this boy will become world famous when he grows up!' Everyone believed him, as grandfather had some knowledge of astrology. I think he loved me more than any of his own children. Perhaps he gave me special treatment because I was a motherless child. I could be quite stubborn, but he used to accede to all my demands.

My grandmother maintained a beautiful rose garden in front of the house. The fragrance was really pleasant. My own interest in gardening must have sprung from those childhood memories. During these years of my retired life, the memory of that garden still motivates me to grow plants and trees around and on the terrace of my house in Sasthamangalam, Thiruvananthapuram.

Our neighbourhood was full of thatched huts of the Dalits who were workers in the paddy fields. In those days, caste supremacy was held precious by the Nairs and other upper castes. We were not permitted to play with the children of the workers, even though we knew all of them, just because they were considered untouchable. Neither the national movement nor the reformation movements of different communities had made inroads into our village yet. The elders did not dare defy the prevalent customs. We children knew nothing other than the rules prescribed to us by the elders. Today, when I look back, I realize the many beautiful facets of life that we missed during our childhood due to such evil customs.

Our main entertainment was our grandmother's retelling of ancient myths. She was not very busy as she had servants to take care of household work. We could sit forever listening to her narrating the saga of Shri Rama and Shri Krishna with great piety. I understand now that the intention of those stories was to instil devotion to God and righteous conscience in us children. We became staunch admirers of Shri Rama and Shri Krishna. Pride in the great Indian culture also grew in me. Belief in an almighty God who leads one forward during hardships became deeply rooted in me. It continues to give me strength, even in the face of all the challenges that I have had to confront later in my life.

Many people have asked me how I am able to maintain a child-like devotion while working in the higher echelons of science and technology. But science and spirituality are two sides of the same coin, namely, the search for the ultimate truth. However much excellence one achieves in the realm of science and technology, one finds some things in this boundless universe that are beyond human understanding and control. How do all the seemingly chaotic universal phenomena follow systematic rules? Who or what is responsible for the origin of the universe and for defining the universal laws? Is it God? Even Albert Einstein and Stephen Hawking ultimately came to such a conclusion about God. People working in the high-tech areas of space research find this easy to understand. Dr Kalam was my guide in this matter as well. A great mind, he remained a true proponent of technology while being a strong believer of Indian culture and was deeply absorbed in the spirituality of Islam. I strongly pursue Hindu philosophy.

There was no electricity in our village back then. We depended on traditional oil lamps for lighting. Those were the days of the Second World War, and there was scarcity of rice, oil, etc., in the country. But the War did not affect us much, since our lives were based almost entirely on local village produce. I recall that during the harvest season, agents of the British Raj used to come to the village and take away a major chunk of the produce at throwaway prices.

Grandfather's birthday was the biggest event of the year at Erathuveedu. It falls on the day of Chathayam in the month of Medam (April/May) as per the Malayalam calendar. We children used to eagerly wait for that day. The preparations would commence at least a week before. Many of my grandfather's favourite fruits—plantains, pomegranates, mangoes, jackfruits, sapota (chiku)—would be ripened and made ready. Along with the rice and vegetables for the *sadya*—a traditional feast served on plantain leaves with rice and a variety of vegetarian dishes—spinach, cucumber, ash gourd, long beans and bitter gourd were grown in plenty around the house.

On the big day, special pujas would be conducted at Kumara Kovil, a temple at the foot of Veli Hills, a little beyond the palace in Padmanabhapuram. We would travel to Kumara Kovil in *villuvandi*, carts drawn by oxen. In those times, carts drawn by oxen and horses were a luxury, equivalent to the Audi or Benz cars of today.

We would begin our festive trip at night, immediately after dinner. I cannot describe the joy of those trips. Our journey would proceed around hills, paddy fields and ponds full of beautiful lotus flowers in full bloom. Once we reached the temple after a journey of eight hours, we children would be engrossed in games in the ground surrounding the temple. The adults would be busy with preparations for the puja and the feast. Many of the locals would join in the celebrations. Grandfather was particular that everyone must partake of the feast. According to him, giving food was the greatest work of charity, as food is God for the hungry.

When I turned four, my father and the other elders decided that it was time for me to be initiated into the world of letters. The ritual of initiation into learning or *vidyarambham* at the Devi Temple in Kanyakumari is very famous. Hence, it was decided to take me there for the ceremony. According to my grandmother,

Devi Kanyakumari was the deity who had presented her with her first offspring.

That particular trip by oxen cart through the luxuriant farmlands of Kanyakumari District was quite unforgettable. We reached the temple and had our *darshan* (glimpse) of the deity. The next day, I sat on my grandfather's lap while he was praying and, after his prayers, he guided my fingers to write my first letters on rice held in a bamboo tray, as per the custom: *Om Hari Sree Ganapathaye namah* (Pranaams to Lord Vishnu, Goddess Lakshmi and Lord Ganapathy).

The letters of knowledge that were initiated at the feet of Devi Kanyakumari became the guiding lamps of my life and led me to all my accomplishments. Let me prostrate myself mentally before the feet of the Devi, my mother, my forefathers and all my teachers.

2

Into the Learning Orbit

'*Bharat Mata ki jai!*' (Victory to Mother India!)

I, too, shouted along with the other students standing around the decorated flag staff in front of the lower primary school at Thirunandikkara. It was 15 August 1947, the day of India's independence. The dignitary hoisting the flag was none other than my own personal hero—my grandfather! It was the first time that I had stepped into that school, holding on to his fingers. Later, when I joined as a student in Class 1, I became a hero in front of the other children!

THE HEADMASTER'S MANY ROLES

At the school, a long, thatched shed was divided into classrooms for Classes 1 to 5 by using reed screens. The room in the middle was the 'office' of Headmaster Kurup. An endearing person, he was indeed the heart and soul of the school. The usually boisterous classrooms would become deathly silent when his shadow fell over them. Once urgent office matters and initial classes in the morning were attended to, he would change his white official attire and wear a faded *dhoti*. With a towel thrown over the shoulders, he would rush to the 'kitchen' to prepare lunch for the students. Oh, he had many things to do—light the firewood hearth, put rice to cook and so on. Lunch was *kanji* (rice gruel) and *chammathy* (scraped coconut ground with red chillies, salt and a little tamarind). I think most of the raw materials came from my generous grandparents' house. Once lunch was ready, Kurup Sir's identity would again be transformed—he would be back to the office in his white clothes.

With only reed partitions separating the classrooms, sounds of teachers from all the five classes would mingle. The noise of mischievous students added to it, and one had to sit with sharpened eyes and ears to catch the words of the class teacher. I was there in that school for only three or four months.

I vividly remember a natural calamity that occurred during my stint at that school. Classes had just resumed after lunch break. Most of the students were sleepy. Suddenly, a series of bright flashes of lightning was seen across the skies, followed by the deafening sound of thunder. We were frightened and gathered around the teachers. The thunder was followed by torrential rains. Within moments, the school grounds were flooded. The headmaster announced that classes were over for the day. But how could anyone go out? Thankfully, after about an hour, the skies cleared, and the rain stopped abruptly. Many parents arrived to take their children home. The real picture of the calamity was shocking. All the canals and paddy fields were inundated. There was water everywhere, even with the sun blazing above. A servant from my grandparents' house came to fetch me. He did something clever—he tied together a few banana stems that had fallen during the thunderstorm and made a small raft! With great joy, we rode that makeshift boat and reached home. I understood afterwards that we had experienced a 'cloud burst'. Later in my career, I used to invariably recall that incident whenever we got ready to launch a rocket. As part of getting clearance for the launch, many atmospheric parameters would be measured to ensure that such natural disasters did not affect the launch operations.

Meanwhile, there was an important event in the house—my father's remarriage. Everyone in the family eagerly anticipated it. Father kept the word given to mother on her death bed and married her sister Santha, my *kunjamma* (literally, 'younger mother'). Santha was then studying in Class 8 at the school in Thiruvattar. As per the custom in those days, the marriage was solemnized as soon as the bride attained puberty. I do not recall any great festivities—just a simple function in the family house with exchange of garlands and my father tying the auspicious *thali*, also known as *mangalsutra*—an auspicious pendant symbolizing marriage. Thus, Santha Kunjamma became mother to me and my sister Ratnamma.

We shifted to father's quarters in Cheruppalur, at a distance of about 3 km from Erathuveedu. Now there were just the four of us in our small family. Many of the officers and workers connected with the construction of the dam lived in Cheruppalur. Unlike the village of Thirunandikkara, Cheruppalur had many facilities like piped water, drainage facilities and 24x7 electricity supply. I continued my primary schooling at the fairly well-equipped government-run school there. I was also greatly interested in watching films at the theatre nearby, as they were—and still are—a blend of art and technology. My imagination took wings when I saw real-life scenes appearing on a stretch of white cloth inside the theatre.

As days passed, I could notice the decrease in attention I received in the new family set-up. That is quite natural when one changes from a joint family to a nuclear one. Parents who are busily immersed in daily chores must also find time to take care of the needs of the children! In a joint family, the kids would be mostly with grandparents or other seniors in the family who have all the time in the world to patiently deal with childish tantrums.

Soon we were once again back under the loving care of our dear grandparents at Erathuveedu. Kunjamma became pregnant, and father did not want to keep his wife away from her home during the confinement again. His mother also agreed. My mother's tragedy must have been still fresh in both their minds. Father brought my sister, along with Santha Kunjamma, to Erathuveedu while I had to stay with my father since I had already enrolled at Cheruppalur Government Lower Primary school.

THE MUSICIAN'S SCHOOL

My studies in that school came to an end by Class 5, and I joined the middle school in Puthenkada, Thiruvattar. The school was owned by the family of the famous singer Kamukara Purushothaman, and his father Kamukara Parameswara Kurup was the manager and headmaster. The *Kamukara tharavadu*—Purushottaman's family house—was nearby. Purushottaman had, by then, finished college education and become a famous singer. His sister Leela Omchery was also a well-known musician and dancer. Both were artists who appeared regularly on the radio—the most important medium for entertainment in those days. Both of them used to perform Carnatic music concerts during festivals at the nearby Adi Kesava Temple.

I, too, shifted to Erathuveedu soon. The school was nearly 4 km away, and there was no bus service, so I walked to and from school every day. Footwear was a luxury. Those barefoot walks became wonderful experiences for me. We friends would walk together, chatting and discussing life while relishing the lush-green nature around us. We ate packed lunches from home instead of kanji like at my old school. Lunch for me was hot rice mixed with fresh curd neatly packed in plantain leaves by my grandmother. It would be fresh even when I opened it at lunch time. There would be coconut chutney and mango pickle to go with the rice—the taste still lingers on my tongue.

I was in Class 6 when Kamukara Purushothaman started singing for films. His first film was *Harishchandra* (1955), which became a smash hit. Indeed, one of the main factors behind the success was the soulful and lyrical song 'Atmavidyalayame' sung by Kamukara. Once, when there was a need for a child actor for some film, my close friend Raveendran and I were sent from the school as candidates. Kamukara took us to Thiruvananthapuram for a voice test. Raveendran was selected. It is no wonder that I lost. Even today, singing or acting is totally alien to me! Later in life, Kamukara built a house in Thiruvananthapuram—at Pippinmoodu in Sasthamangalam. He was able to remain an active musician till his death in 1995. His daughter currently resides in that house.

The school used to maintain high standards. I loved mathematics, physics and drawing. I still remember our mathematics teacher Gangadharan. He showed special attention to me and would explain arithmetic tricks during free time. I am sure that those classes dealing with numbers, geometry and the principles of design nucleated logical thinking and a sound engineering methodology in me. He trained us to study mathematics and physics in an interrelated manner. Mathematical models help to define the physical phenomena of nature—adding the principle of design to these two leads to modern engineering.

Alas, the language classes were quite challenging for me. English was not too bad, but Malayalam proved insurmountable, especially the literature and poetry lessons! I put in extra effort and somehow got enough marks to pass. Since there was no electricity at home, we had to study and do our homework under the faint light of oil lamps.

My uncles did not pursue their education seriously, probably thinking it was a waste of time as they could make a good living just by looking after grandfather's properties. But many years later, the situation worsened due to changes in the economic system as well as land reforms. The realization of the need to become educated and acquire jobs came too late, only after losing most of the landed property.

It was while I was studying in middle school that electricity came to my village for the first time. What a revolution of light it brought! I was wonderstruck and greatly motivated to learn and know more about electricity. Around the same time, a bus service was started between Thiruvananthapuram and Pechiparai, touching my place. I could take the bus to school, but there was no transport available for my return. Thus, the long walks could be avoided, albeit only one way.

I used to observe with great interest the laying of electric posts and wires by workers under the guidance of engineers from the electricity department in order to bring electricity into our house. Whenever possible, I asked questions of the engineers.

I understood the basics of how electricity was transmitted as well as terms like 'live', 'neutral', 'earth' and 'fuse'. Then I thought—why not try to build a model by myself in the house? Immediately, I started working on the idea. I was too afraid to go near the high-voltage lines of the electric supply. So I tried to implement my model using batteries. I tied a few tiny rods onto a big rod to make a 'post'. Then I tied thin copper wires to simulate 'lines'. Now, to make electricity flow, batteries and small bulbs were required. But where was the money to buy them? I thought about several ways and suddenly remembered the paddy in my possession. It had been given as pocket money by my grandfather. He used to give us one *kutta* (wooden container) full of paddy each—not money—for keeping watch on the paddy brought for threshing. I sold off my savings of grain and bought torch batteries and bulbs.

Soon it was ready—my own electricity distribution system! As soon as I connected the batteries, the bulbs glowed. It was a miracle! Everybody heaped praises on me. But I was not fully satisfied. How could I turn the light on and off without a switch? Suddenly, one of the bulbs accidentally burst. The wires came out of the filament and lay next to each other. It was now possible to touch the wires together and make contact whenever required, and the bulbs would switch off! When the contact was released, the bulbs would switch on. I proudly demonstrated the new method to everyone. When I finally pulled the circuit off in this manner, I didn't realize that it had caused a short circuit across the batteries. By the next morning, all the batteries had gone bad! My endeavour had come to naught. If only I had known the difference between parallel and series connections, I could have averted the mishap! However, I learnt many lessons from that failure. In fact, it was indeed this kind of self-study, observation, experimentation, learning from mistakes and error correction that helped me to face many of the challenges during my stint with our space programme.

When I reached Class 7, another event once again divided our big family—the formation of the unified state of Kerala on 1 November 1956. Thirunandikkara and Pechippara in Kanyakumari District became part of Tamil Nadu. Kochi (earlier Cochin), Malabar and Palakkad (earlier Palghat) became parts of Kerala. Thiruvananthapuram became the capital of Kerala. In the newly formed district of Kanyakumari, many Malayalam-speaking people were apprehensive about becoming alienated in the new scheme of things. But was it practical to suddenly sell off all of one's land and go to Kerala? My father had no such confusion, since government employees had the freedom to choose service in either Kerala or Tamil Nadu. He decided to opt for Kerala.

The time had come for us to leave Thirunandikkara for good.

3

Finding My Rhythm

My family, comprising my father, mother and sisters, migrated to Thiruvananthapuram after the creation of Kerala, but many of the people who continued to stay there suffered. A majority of the Malayalis perhaps saw what could be in the offing and shifted to Kerala at the time of the formation of the state itself. Most of them settled down near the border.

My sister and I continued to live in Thirunandikkara until I finished Class 7. Ratnamma was then in Class 5. Father had already joined the Kerala State PWD service. He took us to the house he had rented in Thiruvananthapuram, at Sasthamangalam, 5 km to the north of Shree Padmanabha Swamy Temple.

The shift to the capital city opened up many new experiences for us. Both of us had many friends in our respective old schools, and even the thought of leaving them was deeply saddening. On top of that was the pain of leaving our grandparents. We had been dwelling under the shadow of their love, and they represented the whole world to me. But there was no other way. Afterwards, we were able to spend time with our grandparents only during school vacations.

Later in life, I was not able to visit Thirunandikkara often due to my busy schedule. I instituted two scholarships in the local school in the name of my grandfather. When I was the director of the Vikram Sarabhai Space Centre (VSSC), I once went to present the awards. On the way, I also visited the school at Thiruvattar. The teachers and students received me with great affection. Many of my old classmates came to see me, and we had a very happy time reliving our memories.

FIRE IN THE CUP: EDUCATION AND EXPERIMENTS

The top-ranking school in Thiruvananthapuram in those days was the Government Model School at Thycaud. But at a distance of 4 km, it was not easy for me to traverse with the meagre transport facilities. Hence, I was enrolled in Raja Kesavadas N.S.S. High School near our house. The school had many teachers passionate about moulding the character of the students and encouraging inherent talents. Rama Kurup from Omallur was the headmaster. A Gandhian who had taken part in the Indian independence struggle, he led an ascetic life. He influenced me greatly: I admired his sincere and hardworking nature, calm attitude towards everything and analytical approach to problem-solving. He was a strict vegetarian and used to do yoga daily. His aim was to train his students to become model citizens of the country. We were encouraged to practise yoga to help increase our concentration. Though I went for a few yoga lessons, I could not continue practicising it. But it convinced me that only concentrated efforts can bear fruits in life. Later in life, Rama Kurup once asked to meet me and I went to his house in Omallur. I recall that I was the ISRO chairman at that time. 'Oh Madhavankutty, you have reached such a high position! I always knew that you would,' he told me and blessed me by putting his frail hands on my head. He passed away a few years later.

Another dearly loved teacher was Nagappan Nair Sir, who taught us mathematics. Seeing my interest in the subject, he would explain many concepts even outside the syllabus to me. I was given the freedom to approach him to have my doubts cleared, and I went to him as much as I could. I was deeply interested in physics experiments, especially those related to electricity. I still remember the occasion when I had successfully passed electricity through saline water immediately after the class on electrolysis. I had torch cells and wires in my collection. I had filled a glass cup with salt water and conducted my experiment. I had been excited to see the yellow froth floating on top. My friends had been having a close look at it when, suddenly, a flame burst out of the cup. We did not know at that time that even a drop of sweat falling on nascent sodium can set it on fire!

My best friends in high school were Balan and Ashokan. Balan had great interest in extra-curricular activities. He used to subscribe to popular magazines that dealt with mechanical engineering and aerospace topics, and we both studied them carefully. Then we would try to build whatever we had read about. Ashokan had a passion for motor vehicles. Not many vehicles were seen in the streets in those days. One had to book ahead and wait for months to buy a car or bike. Ashokan used to experiment with old two-wheelers, making changes in whatever way he could.

In our youthful enthusiasm, we wanted to rewrite traditional customs and practices, and experiment with modern technology. That common goal bound us together. As our years in high school progressed, we drew closer.

In Class 10, Malayalam and social studies were the two subjects I had slight misgivings about, but I was confident about everything else. I tried to devote more time studying them to secure good marks. When the results were declared, I had passed, but I had scored just enough to secure first class. Still, I was the school topper—not a small achievement! Unlike today, marks were not given lavishly back then. The state topper had scored just 71 per cent! I was invited to many houses to be felicitated on my success and spent several days happily enjoying the festivities. My parents were overjoyed and proud—a good foundation had been laid for my future.

By that time, Kunjamma had had four daughters—my little sisters Vasantha, Manjula, Girija and Lekshmi. Ratnamma and the four younger girls were very close.

I was mostly a loner. Even during the holidays, I was not keen on playing with friends but rather spent time in libraries or in my room, engrossed in one experiment or the other. My father used to give me money to buy popular science magazines and electronic parts. Based on the magazines and my textbooks, I would make things like electromagnets and conduct experiments, invariably working till after midnight. Everyone knew that I didn't like to be disturbed, and I would be left alone. Since there was a door in my room that connected it to the outdoors, my comings and goings did not disturb the others.

While in high school, I happened to read about a system that would enable us to listen to radio programmes without needing electricity! Back then, only a few rich people owned radios, which were made with vacuum tubes. Building such a radio was very difficult and expensive. So I decided to make one using just one diode, as had I read about in the magazine *Wireless World*. But alas, I could not get the diode and a capacitor to tune it. I searched through many magazines and finally found a way out. I took a couple of thin aluminium foils from cigarette packets, put some soft paper between them, rolled up, and then cut them to get the required capacitance. I then connected wires to the foil ends, and my capacitor was ready! The next problem was the diode. I used something called *anjanakkallu* (phosphorus arsenide crystal) available at Ayurveda medical stores to make it! If you cut out a piece of this crystal and search, you can find a spot that functions as the p-n junction of a semiconductor. The antenna was a long wire connected across two coconut palm trees in the yard. A telephone headset was converted into a makeshift receiver. Without a soldering iron, the parts were joined together using lead heated by the flame of a candle. When I switched it on for the first time, programmes on the Thiruvananthapuram station of All India Radio were heard very clearly. My family, friends and neighbours considered that radio as nothing less than a wonder! Sometime later, when semiconductor diodes and transistors became available, I made radio receivers using them and even sold a few to my friends!

Communication facilities back then were very poor both inside and outside India. Amateur radios, also known as ham radios, were used to send messages during natural disasters. I used to know Parameswaran Pillai, who was an executive engineer at the Kerala State Electricity Board and a famous amateur radio operator ('Ham'). There was a military junk store at Poojappura from where one could get non-classified things, which were no longer needed by the military, at a reduced price. I managed to get all the necessary parts, such as vacuum tubes and resistors, and made a ham transmitter and receiver. I could then successfully send and receive messages with other ham enthusiasts.

During the holidays after our Class 10 exams, I took up making and flying a model airplane with Balan and Ashokan. We made the design very carefully. The next task was to get hold of the different subsystems needed. We put together our pocket money and started buying the parts.

One day, a balloon fell on the roof of Ashokan's house. The weather department in Thiruvananthapuram used to send radio-sounding balloons to the sky every week. The balloons were filled with hydrogen and fitted with instruments to measure atmospheric parameters like wind direction, temperature, humidity, pressure, etc. The balloons would also contain the necessary instruments for sending the measured data to the receiving station, along with a radio transmitter and battery. After reaching a particular altitude, the balloons would burst and drop to the ground. Luckily, it was one such balloon that we had come across!

The package attached to the balloon gave us several items necessary to make the remote controller of our airplane. We used balsa wood and wax paper to make the wings, fuselage and other parts. An alcohol-fuelled two-stroke engine was used to turn the propeller, which we got from an enthusiast from the United Kingdom (UK), whose contact was obtained from the magazine *Popular Mechanic*. Imagine our relief when the propeller started to turn! Once the airplane got sufficient speed and lift, it soared up. It flew to a few hundred metres and circled. It had mechanisms to receive the signals sent from a radio transmitter held in our hands to control the rudder and aileron. Everything performed very well. Our project was a huge success! Everyone who witnessed the flight congratulated the three of us. What a big boost that was to our confidence! We even formed a club named Sasthamangalam Aero Modellers. I do consider those efforts in realizing a radio-controlled model aircraft involving multiple technologies as the stepping stone to bigger projects and successes later in my life.

That was 60 years ago! Today, building a model aircraft is child's play since all components are available off the shelf in supermarkets.

Our next project was a water scooter. It was Balan's idea. It was a very serious commercial project for us. The scooter was to move by the action of a water jet created by sucking in water and expunging it through a nozzle at the rear. Indeed, a very modern technology under the circumstances! We cut open an old motorcycle, extracted the engine and coupled it with a centrifugal pump. The body of the scooter was to be built using fiberglass—a composite material absolutely new in the country, not only very expensive but difficult to get as well. Balan was adamant about somehow making the scooter and so we pooled together whatever money we had. Once our model was ready, we drove it through the backwaters of Veli. Filled with confidence, we wanted to make it a commercial enterprise and decided to approach a bank for capital. We presented a profitable business plan to the manager. He liked our plan and agreed to give us a loan, but where was the property to put as security? We were sure that the elders would laugh at us if we asked them for help. After all, we were just kids, weren't we? So our grand plan was destined to be confined to paper. But we continued to engage with different experiments.

We were regular visitors to the three main libraries in Thiruvananthapuram then—the British Library, Public Library and the US Information Service Library. The British Library was a favourite haunt for us. Books and international magazines related to technology were available there. Magazines like *Popular Mechanic* and *Popular Electronics* were very useful. When the USA and Britain closed down their respective libraries, perhaps due to the spread of the Internet, the book lovers of Thiruvananthapuram were deeply saddened.

Years later, Balan went on to work in Europe and later in the USA. Currently, I believe that he stays in an ashram in Munnar. Ashokan never lost his passion for vehicles and ran a good automobile workshop. Sadly, he is no more.

'CHIEF TECHNICIAN'

My other friends were Kesavan Kutty, Nandakumar, Michael and Rahman, among others. Friends used to call me Maathappan and, sometimes, with increased affection, Maathoos. We would often leave our homes in the evenings and head to the museum. Other friends like Mohandas, Gangadharan and Madhavankutty (Maati) also used to come for our discussions under the trees in the museum premises. Literature, psychology, philosophy—these were the main areas. The topics would come from our readings. I had collections of old *Mathrubhumi* and *Kalakaumudi* weeklies at my house. Short stories and humorous novels of Vadakkke Koottala Narayanankutty Nair, popularly known as V.K.N. (1932–2004), attracted me the most. I bought all his books. Sometimes our discussions would go on till 9.00 p.m. I would then get a sound scolding from my father for reaching home so late. If it became too severe, Kunjamma would barge in to mediate. She was an extremely caring person.

If not at my house, it would be at Ashokan's house that we met. We were always welcome there. In fact, people used to like me going to their houses as I was the 'chief technician' of the group. I would repair any malfunctioning electric or electronic equipment in the house. Even today, repairing household equipment is a hobby.

I was also deeply interested in cars. The popular brands in those days were Standard, Morris and Opel. Whenever I would be inside a car, my eyes would remain fixed on the driver. Changing gears according to speed, operating the clutch, accelerator and break using the feet—everything would be closely examined! Gradually, my desire to drive a car took root. I was confident that I would be able to drive. However, it was quite some time before I got the opportunity.

After joining ISRO, when I had some money in hand, I bought a Standard 10 car. It was the realization of a long-cherished dream. I drove it for some years and then bought a Fiat—a premium brand. What a high status the Fiat cars commandeered in those days! I subsequently changed cars several times. I have always loved driving. Alas, traffic jams and issues of security succeed in keeping me away from that pleasure now!

4

The Making of an Engineer

My college life started at the Intermediate College in Thiruvananthapuram—the college is now called Government Arts College. A one-year course, known as pre-degree, was a prelude to undergraduate courses. It is now extended to two years and has been made part of the higher secondary schools.

I had enrolled in the science group, which had maths, physics and chemistry. We also had to study two languages. English was one and that was not a problem. But choosing Malayalam was a strict no-no, and I thought Hindi may not fetch good marks. Then I received expert advice—take French! As a new language, one would have to learn only the basics, and it would be easy to score good marks!

French is a language with fine literature representing a great culture. Our lecturer Madhavin made learning it a pleasure. By the time the classes ended, I acquired proficiency in reading even classic novels like *Les Miserables* in French!

The decision to learn French was godsend. Many years later, France was the one country I had to travel to the most for official purposes. My 'second language' came in quite handy during those trips. Once I was part of an official delegation for a one-month training programme in France, where all the classes were in French. Scientists from other countries had to take French lessons prior to joining the course! I happily acted as an interpreter for them at local shops and restaurants. Even today, I can read and understand the language, though speaking is a little difficult due to lack of practice.

Studying my favourite science subjects made my pre-university days very enjoyable. I also got the opportunity to do experiments in physics and chemistry in a well-equipped laboratory. It was quite a thrilling experience.

Turning points in life often occur out of chance rather than by choice. My encounter with Radha was one such. I fell in love with this beautiful young girl at first sight. It was a taboo for boys and girls to meet outside of family circles in those days. We were studying in different colleges but used to take the same bus. She was very pious and used to visit the Subramanya Swamy Temple near my house. I, too, started visiting the temple with the sole intention of having a glimpse of her. In due course, I became an ardent devotee of Lord Muruka. Normally, she would come to the temple with her mother and sister. But on the rare occasions when she came alone, we would exchange a few words. What started in front of Lord Muruka continues to this day.

GETTING INTO ENGINEERING

Once I completed my pre-university course, my family started discussing what I must pursue next. I had no doubt that I wanted to go for engineering. My parents did not relish the idea of sending their only son to a far-away institution. Hence, the option was to select one of the three engineering colleges in Kerala, and I applied with great hope. However, my name did not figure in the selected list, possibly due to a recently introduced practice of reservation of seats on a district basis. As a fall-back option, I joined the undergraduate degree course in physics at the University College (UC), Thiruvananthapuram. Radha joined the chemistry course in Government Women's College.

The UC, established in 1866, was the oldest college in Travancore. I was proud to be a student of that renowned institution. The centenary celebrations of the college were inaugurated by the then president of India, Dr Sarvepalli Radhakrishnan.

Life was quite interesting and enjoyable as a student. We had to learn chemistry and mathematics in addition to physics. Languages included English and, of course, French. The UC had many eminent teachers, especially in the language departments. Students had the freedom to audit lectures in other departments, and I took advantage of that to attend classes in English literature, psychology and philosophy. However, physics and mathematics remained my passion. I still remember the informative classes by Professor Hariharan, which exposed me to the world of quantum physics and mysteries of the universe. The practical classes in electronics were also interesting.

The campus was beautiful and exciting in many aspects. There were lush-green lawns in front of the buildings. The old mango trees provided us with cool shade in addition to sweet mangoes in the season. There was an isolated corner frequented by lovers; several of them later ended up in happy marriages.

That was also a time when I could establish a large circle of friends as well as a few close friendships. P. Radhakrishnan, who was later selected to become an astronaut to fly in the Space Shuttle and who retired as the deputy director of the Liquid Propulsion Systems Centre (LPSC), was my bench mate. T.P. Sreenivasan and G. Krishnan were close friends, though they were students of English literature. I am indebted to them for cultivating in me a love for reading Shakespeare, Russell and Eliot. Krishnan triggered a passion for the humorous writings of P.G. Wodehouse, who wrote like V.K.N. Krishnan, and later became an Indian Administrative Service (IAS) officer in the Odisha (earlier known as Orissa) cadre and retired as the chief secretary of Jharkhand. Sreenivasan entered the Indian Foreign Service (IFS) and served as the ambassador in many countries. We met after a long time in Vienna, where he was the ambassador. I was the chairman of ISRO then. We worked together in the United Nations Committee on the Peaceful Uses of Outer Space (UN COPUOS). His style of work and life in palatial buildings impressed me very much. I had the privilege of having dinner at his place. His wife Lekha is a famous dancer and social worker and played the perfect hostess. So impressed was I that as soon as I returned, I advised my younger son to choose the IFS if he wanted to have a challenging and enjoyable life but, alas, he never opted for it!

One year passed quickly. I obtained a foundation in physics. When the results were announced, I found myself scoring a first class, thanks, of course, to getting splendid marks in French. Most of the vacation time was spent in the public library reading literature and perusing six-month-old editions of the journal *Science*, as it took three to four months for the journals to arrive from abroad.

Though mentally prepared to continue with my physics course, I was still sad about losing the chance to pursue engineering. So, I decided to apply afresh the next year, and this time, luck was in my favour. A single-rank list was prepared covering the entire state, and I found a respectable place in it. Most people had chosen electrical, civil and mechanical branches, in that order of priority. I opted for electrical engineering and joined as a fresher for the first five-year integrated course at College of Engineering, Trivandrum (CET). The year was 1961.

The college had been operating out of the old campus, which houses the office of the postmaster general today. Soon, we were asked to report at the new campus at Kulathoor, which was 9 km away. A modern building with corridors still smelling of fresh paint awaited us in the vast campus.

Though we had expected ragging, our reception was quite different. A dozen seniors came with rose buds and laddus and took us to the main office to complete the admission formalities.[1] Later, we came to know that elections for the college council were forthcoming. A tall, handsome man came forward and requested me to not only to vote for him but also help in canvassing for votes among the juniors. He was none other than late Dr D. Babu Paul, who impressed me with his leadership qualities and the ability to interact and share ideas with people. Later, he joined the IAS and provided exemplary service to the nation. I did not have much contact with him during his years in the government but later had the opportunity to interact in several public forums. He would invariably introduce me as his younger brother who had helped him to become the chairman of the college union! He passed away in 2017, leaving evergreen memories in the minds of the people of Kerala.

In the engineering college, we had to learn various subjects from the old British syllabus, including topics from civil and mechanical engineering, in the first two years. Subjects related to the selected major figured from the third year. Topics like telecommunications,

---

[1]Laddus are spherical sweet from the Indian subcontinent made of various ingredients and sugar syrup or jaggery.

power generators and electrical machines were taught in the last year. The fee was ₹15 per year. I could get a scholarship second year onwards and was even able to save some money, which was invariably spent in buying electronic items to make gadgets.

Our principal, Professor P.C. Chacko, was a strict disciplinarian. Professor Balakrishna Menon was the head of the electrical engineering department. Professor Venkataraman, who taught electronics, had a great influence on me. As electronics was my favourite subject, I used to frequently approach him with many doubts. He would always find time to talk to me and was happy when I asked him questions on topics outside of our college syllabus. He would recommend books from the library. Dr K.P. Parameswaran Pillai, a lecturer in the electrical department, also helped to expand the frontiers of my knowledge.

My best friends in college were my classmates Sankaranarayanan and John, as well as Soman Pillai from the mechanical department. We were inseparable. We would only need a little time to cover the syllabus topics. We used to get much more information by reading books outside the syllabus. We would spend the bulk of our time outside the classroom, either in the library or engaged in discussions in the campus on innovations or advances in technology.

I was not interested in taking part in any sports or art events in the college. On such days, we friends would make a beeline to the Sreekumar Theatre in the city to watch English movies. However, I do remember one particular college-day celebration when I set eyes on a spacecraft for the first time. It was nearly dusk, and as I stood gazing at the star-lit sky, suddenly some strange object like a big star was seen moving slowly from horizon to horizon. Our teachers told us later that it was Echo, the passive communication spacecraft recently launched by the USA—a metalized balloon satellite that could reflect back electromagnetic waves from the Earth for conducting communication experiments and for studying the ionosphere. It was shining in the sky due to the twilight.

Our batch had its first study tour in the second year. We were forced to confine our trip to places inside Kerala because of the Indo-China War. Even so, that trip became memorable to me as it was my first ever trip outside Thiruvananthapuram.

Classes became even more interesting in the third year. My friends and I built a robot for one of the events in the college. It cannot, of course, be compared to today's robots. Indeed, the making was risky, since robotics was not even heard of in those days. The main parts included a light-sensitive transistor and a small motor. We designed it in the guise of the Air India mascot Maharaja. Our friends from the mechanical engineering department crafted the outer structure using asbestos. We got a tailor to make the royal attire and headgear. When everything was put together, the robot looked really majestic! It could bow to visitors and greet them when they passed the gate. The hearty appreciation that we got from the teachers and the guests made us really happy.

In the third year, I also got a chance to make a radio. Transistor—the three-legged colossus—had just entered the market. I was envious of the transistor radios brought from abroad by my friends and was determined to make one on my own. I got hold of a circuit for construction, which was published in *The Wireless World*, but many parts were not available. A major dealer in radios then was Quilon Radio Service. I somehow obtained a Philips loudspeaker and other parts from them. The radio set I assembled looked quite professional and it cost me ₹200, while those from abroad cost around ₹1,500! I was very proud of the sound, which was at least ten times better than the sound of ordinary transistor radios. Everyone at home loved it, including my father. I acquired a radio license from the post office with a lot of difficulty in order to comply with the rules. I recall the small books with stamps of many denominations corresponding to the license fees. My small radio set could receive Chennai (earlier Madras) stations as well as the *Voice of America* radio programme. That radio continued to be with me for about 20 years!

FIRST ENCOUNTER WITH TERLS

A rocket-launching station had recently been established in Thiruvananthapuram, in the village of Thumba, near the sea. The centre had been named Thumba Equatorial Rocket Launching Station or TERLS. It was a topic of discussion and coveted destination for many of us in the college. We read in the newspapers that a rocket was going to be launched from TERLS on 21 November 1963. The rocket was imported, but the idea of a space-bound rocket flying off from the soil of India for the first time was so exciting! Our teachers informed us about the exact time of launch and led us to the top of the college building. We waited in the twilight hours with our eyes fixed on the sky.

At last, it was 6.25 p.m., the scheduled launch time, just after sunset on that winter day. As we watched anxiously, Nike Apache shot up in the sky like an arrow, splattering orange fire dust. Then it turned and disappeared among the clouds. It was quite dark by then. After several minutes, there was a glittering light in the western horizon and a loud hissing sound. A yellowish-orange vapour cloud spread up in the sky, like a pillar at first; a snake-like structure then emerged from it, formed by the electrojet currents.[2] Photographs taken simultaneously from Kottayam, Kodaikanal and Kanyakumari helped in identifying the path of the vapour cloud. The goal of the experiment was to analyse the pictures and study upper atmospheric winds and electrojets at an altitude of 20–120 km. The newspapers reported the next day that the wonderful sight was visible to the naked eye in many parts of South India. Thousands had witnessed that sight—the sky was clear and was not contaminated by pollution as much as it is today.

I had read about the launch in detail in a magazine at the British Library. What had set the ball rolling was an international meeting held in Paris in 1960. It was the meeting of Committee on Space Research or COSPAR, which had been set up in the wake of the first ever satellite, Sputnik, launched by the Soviet Union on 4 October 1957. The success of the satellite had enthralled Prime Minister Jawaharlal Nehru, who loved science. He tabled a motion called Scientific Policy Resolution in Indian Parliament in 1958, paving the way for an Indian space programme.

The next milestone came three years later, in August 1961. The Department of Atomic Energy (DAE) was tasked with doing

[2]Above the Earth's magnetic equator, at an altitude of 80–150 km, there is a belt of electrically charged particles. This flow of electrons from the west to east is called equatorial electrojet (EEJ).

space research for peaceful purposes. Dr Homi J. Bhabha, the famous atomic scientist and father of the Indian atomic research programme, was the secretary to the department. His appointment was a deviation from the normal custom of putting senior officers from the IAS as heads of crucial departments. Dr Bhabha used the opportunity very productively indeed. Along with J.R.D. Tata, he established the Tata Institute of Fundamental Research (TIFR) in 1945 to carry out research in cosmic rays and nuclear physics.

The Indian National Committee on Space Research (INCOSPAR) was formed under its banner in 1962 for formulating an Indian space programme. The Committee had many goals—to bring about international cooperation to fulfil Indian interests in space research, to use the research for peaceful purposes and to work hand-in-hand with the COSPAR. Dr Bhabha included many experts in the committee. The chairmanship was entrusted to a stalwart—none other than Dr Vikram Sarabhai, then a scientist at the Physical Research Laboratory (PRL) in Ahmedabad, and other luminaries like Professor M.G.K. Menon of the TIFR; Atmospheric Scientist Professor P.R. Pisharoty; Dr M.K. Vainu Bappu of Astrophysical Laboratory; P.R. Krishna Rao, the director general of observatories, Indian Meteorological Department; Professor E.V. Chitnis and Professor K.R. Ramanathan of the PRL; A.S. Rao of the Atomic Energy Establishment, Trombay (AEET); Professor S. Mitra of Indian Statistical Department; and P.J. Rodgers of Overseas Communication Services were members—all eminent scholars in their respective disciplines.

Dr Bhabha had earlier sent Dr Sarabhai to attend a COSPAR meeting in Paris in 1960. The latter already had contact with many international experts and made the best use of the chance. He called for international cooperation for the study of equatorial electrojets (EEJs) as well as the laws of interaction with the upper atmospheres. The international assembly supported his endeavour. He then developed close relations with Professor Jacques Blamont, patron of the French space research organization. Professor Blamont had great influence in the French administration. The main interface between him and Dr Sarabhai was Dr Praful D. Bhavsar, who was later entrusted with the first rocket launch from TERLS. Later, I, too, built good relations with Professor Blamont.

When the COSPAR had another meeting after two years, in 1962, the main topic of discussion was atmospheric studies at areas near the Earth's magnetic equator. As the representative from a country with such areas, Dr Sarabhai made use of that opportunity very well. The committee decided to immediately form an international network of centres for conducting sounding rocket launches to study the ionosphere. The UN COPUOS offered sponsorship.

Dr Sarabhai consolidated his moves fast. India had to start from zero. Rocket technology then belonged to the US-led Western countries or the communist countries led by the then Soviet Union. It was a time when the Cold War was at its peak. But Dr Sarabhai's ingenuity overcame even that. He obtained a Nike Apache rocket and a telemetry station from the USA and a Minsk computer, the best in the world then, along with a small helicopter from the Soviet Union. The telemetry station was to acquire data from the rocket after launch. It was not difficult to get a radar as well as the sodium vapour payload needed for the rocket from France. We were about to witness the initiation of the Indian space programme with these international inputs!

H.G.S. Murthy was the first director of TERLS. An expert mechanical engineer, he had earlier been with the ammunition production centre of the Department of Defence, where Dr Sarabhai noticed his abilities and invited him to join TERLS. He was sent to NASA for a short training on rocket launching. The training sessions were elementary and covered only the basic principles of sounding rockets and preparations for launch. No strategically important information or details of the technology of rocket systems were shared with people outside the USA.

My first visit to Thumba was to invite Director Murthy for a lecture at our college. After getting down from the bus at Kulathoor, we had to cross a water canal on the way by boat, followed by a long walk of about 2 km on the sand. Anybody would be wonderstruck looking at the vast stretches with no roads or buildings around, where the country's space programme was taking root! Everything had to be built from scratch! The office of the director was near the seashore, in a building which used to be a small primary school. I got permission from the chief security officer, K.R.C. Nair, and met Director Murthy. He accepted our invitation, came to the college and made an excellent speech about the importance of Thumba and how technology can lead a nation and its people on the road to progress. I never imagined then that, soon, I too would step inside TERLS as an engineer.

THE JOB HUNT

The five years of my engineering education flew by. We were introduced to computers, which were just appearing on the scene. Another highlight for me was my seminar papers on lasers and atomic power—both topics were quite advanced at that time.

At last, it was March 1966—time for the final exams. As always, I immersed myself in studies during the week before the exams and could write all the papers quite satisfactorily. The short vacation after the exams was spent with my friends, going around libraries and sitting in the museum grounds. Sometimes, everyone would come to my house and gather around my radio, listening to music.

I sent out a few job applications to organizations like the Railway Engineering Services, Bhilai Steel Plant and Bhabha Atomic Research Centre (BARC). Since we students were obliged to work for the state government due to a bond we had signed, there was no anxiety about getting jobs. But I had my eyes set on the endless opportunities awaiting me in the world outside and wanted to leave Thiruvananthapuram.

Our exam results were declared at the end of June. I passed, scoring first class. My friend John, who had always competed in studies with me, was the topper. Many years later, when I went to the Karunya Engineering College in Coimbatore for a programme, I met John, who was then a professor there after completing his term at the Central Engineering Services.

As soon as the results were published, I was handed an order appointing me as a lecturer in the same college. I was hardly interested, but there was the ₹5,000 bond that I had signed to think about. So I joined with a heavy heart and was entrusted with the boring job of managing the laboratory. After somehow enduring it for three weeks, when a call letter came for an interview at the BARC in Mumbai (earlier known as Bombay), it was like the proverbial light at the end of the tunnel!

It was going to be my first trip outside Kerala, not counting the regular Thirunandikkara trips to my ancestral house. I was thrilled and not at all intimidated about going to an unknown place. I recall that I did not even reserve a train ticket. My classmate N.R. Unnikrishnan Kartha was also called for the interview. So, both of us just put a few things in a bag and started off. Later, he too joined TERLS with me, and we have been neighbours in Sasthamangalam since then.

There was no direct train between Thiruvananthapuram and Mumbai in those days. Only the Thiruvananthapuram–Chennai line through Sengottai was available, or one could catch a train from Kochi. We went to Kochi by bus, but it was not as simple as the five-hour journey today. There was no bridge connecting Alappuzha (earlier known as Alleppey) and Ernakulam at Aroor, so we had to get down from the bus and hop on to a rowing boat, which took us to the Edakochi Boat Jetty. Then we again got into another bus till Thoppumpady bus stop, from where we went up the bridge and reached the railway station at the Cochin Harbour to catch the Bombay Express.

Since we had no reservation, we got into a jam-packed general compartment. We had heard that the porters may help us get a seat. But the 'seat' they found for us was on the upper luggage rack! We spent the entire journey there. With no Konkan rail line at that time, the train went via Chennai, which was quite a roundabout way. At last, we reached Mumbai after two days, just in time for the interview.

India's first atomic energy research centre, the BARC, was located at Trombay near Mumbai. It had been set up by the DAE, which had made a head start under Dr Bhabha just a few months after Enrico Fermi had discovered the theory of chain reactions. The USA was then yet to test the first nuclear bomb. I was interviewing to join an institute set up there to mould young scientists for the atomic programme. The interview was not difficult, and I was quite hopeful.

When I reached home, I found the appointment order from the BARC waiting for me! What a pleasant surprise! I took the telegram to our college principal, Professor Chacko. I had to join by August, so I requested him to relieve me from the college before that. But he did not agree, since I was still under the bond to serve the state government. My argument was that the BARC was under the central government and that I was not leaving to join a private-sector company. I did not press my point but just submitted my resignation letter by registered post and left for Mumbai. A risky decision, of course. Sometime later, I tried to get my pending salary for the service in the engineering college. The attempt failed, since no record of my service could be traced in the college. Thank God, there was no follow up on the bond either! Sometimes, red-tapism comes to one's rescue!

5

Initial Milestones

I joined the tenth batch of the BARC training school. The school was functioning from a rented building in Marine Drive in Mumbai. Many brilliant engineering and science graduates from different parts of the country were in that batch. Dr Anil Kakodkar, who later became the chairman of the Atomic Energy Commission (AEC), was in the seventh batch and was my senior.

The principal of the school was Dr K.K. Damodaran, who hailed from Kollam in Kerala. He had joined the BARC in 1950 after completing a master's degree in physics and was a strict disciplinarian. All the subjects were taught by scientists from the BARC, which gave a practical touch to the lessons. Dr Raja Ramanna, who was then a senior scientist, was the officer responsible for our training.

Dr Bhabha had passed away a year earlier, but his enlightening spirit was still palpable in every grain of sand at the BARC. It is beyond doubt that Dr Bhabha was one of the greatest sons of India. He was born on 30 October 1909 in Mumbai to a rich Parsi family related to Dorabji Tata. I wonder whether his parents knew how apt his name 'Jehangir', meaning 'conqueror of the world', would turn out to be. Dr Bhabha was a wizard at mathematics and, after graduation, attended the University of Cambridge in England. That was a time of great groundbreaking inventions in the field of atomic energy. Dr Bhabha got the priceless opportunity to interact with experts in the field as well as to conduct research in the Cavendish Laboratory with James Chadwick, the great scientist who had discovered the charge-less neutron particle in the atomic nucleus.

Dr Bhabha himself proved to be no less accomplished in research. His thesis, which dealt with the scattering of electrons and positrons, was much discussed in scientific circles. The phenomenon was christened 'Bhabha scattering', and Dr Bhabha received the rare honour of the Isaac Newton Studentship. After coming back to India, he highlighted to Prime Minister Nehru the need for prioritizing atomic energy research in the country. Those efforts led to the establishment of the AEC, with Dr Bhabha as its first chairman. Before that, he had joined the Tata Group to establish the TIFR and had accepted the post of professor of physics there. In later years, he attracted many eminent scholars like Dr Vikram Sarabhai to the institute. Afterwards, he went on to sow the seeds for space research activities in India. As a member of the UN committee for atomic research, he was on a flight to Vienna for a meeting when he died in an air crash on 24 January 1966, shocking the entire nation. In his memory, the AEET was rechristened on 22 January 1967 as the Bhabha Atomic Research Centre or the BARC.

TRAINING AT THE BARC

The atmosphere at the BARC training school was very different from all my previous educational institutions. Till then, I had felt the syllabus to be very light, but at the BARC, the opposite was true. The topics were more elaborate and detailed compared to the MTech courses of today. The subjects were also new. We had to take courses in nuclear physics, nuclear chemistry, thermodynamics, control systems, nuclear engineering, nuclear power plants and material science, among others. The sheer knowledge and enthusiasm of our instructors invigorated me. They were all young scientists of international standing and many of them were products of the training school itself. Earlier at my colleges, I used to look forward to the fun of bunking classes, whereas at the BARC, I found myself eagerly waiting for them!

The students were also of a high calibre. The high stipend of ₹300 per month served to attract good scholars to the institute. The engineering giant Larsen & Toubro was offering a meagre ₹250 as salary to freshers at that time! Along with this, the library and laboratories offered excellent materials and facilities. The school had contacts with many universities abroad, which facilitated access to good books. After the training, students could opt to do a PhD at one of those universities. My senior Dr Kakodkar made use of such an opportunity and finished his PhD from a university abroad. We were also provided with study notes.

Though the course was tough, I enjoyed it, and we used to have a few interludes of fun in between. The visits of Dr Ramanna were really memorable. His was an electrifying personality. He was the perfect combination of an artist and a scientist, and was capable of rendering Beethoven's symphonies on the piano. Along with advice, he would give us the pleasure of his piano-playing. When he sat in front of the piano, we would remember the great scientists Albert Einstein and Max Planck. Einstein, it seems, was at first not much enamoured with Planck's quantum theory. But whenever they met, both would immediately take out their violins from the cases, and any scientific discussion had to wait till they finished a duet!

Dr Ramanna hailed from Karnataka and was a much-loved disciple of Dr Bhabha. Born in 1925 in Tumkur, Mysore Presidency, he learnt classical music along with his scientific studies, earning a BSc in physics concurrently with a BA in music! Later, he got his MSc in physics as well as in music theory! He then went to England on a Commonwealth scholarship and did his PhD in nuclear physics in 1954. After studies, he came back to India, became the successor of Dr Bhabha and led the Indian atomic energy research for nearly four decades. He was indeed the main brain behind all our atomic energy experiments, including the bomb trials.

Our hostel building, at the edge of Bandra beach, was a little far from the training centre. It was an old military barrack unit and had stone walls with asbestos roofs. Each unit had two modules and was furnished with cots and other amenities. Two people could sleep in a module, but for all other necessities, we had to depend on the common facilities outside. Kartha occupied the second cot in my module. He had the habit of reading aloud while studying. A great boon to me, as I would simply lie on my cot listening to his reading, which would help with my own revision!

I never even looked once in the direction of the badminton or tennis courts in the hostel campus. Every day, we used to go from the hostel to the Bandra station by bus and then by train to the

Marine Drive station. One could get a first-class train ticket for one month for just ₹20 and have comfortable rides. Our hostel warden Narayanaswamy was very strict and insisted that we all should be inside by 8.00 p.m., when the gates would be closed. But there were many things outside to attract us! Standing near the wire mesh surrounding the hostel premises, we would fondly gaze at the beautiful Bandra beach studded with rocks, stretches of sand and the crowds.

The hostel mess was on the top of a hill in the campus. It was a beautiful bungalow, built according to Dr Bhabha's ideas. One had to formally dress in full-sleeved shirts with ties and strictly observe British table manners in the dining room. Since the food was excellent, we would somehow comply with the rules. I have always been rather careless about the way I dress. Formal dressing has never interested me. Imagine how much I must have exerted myself in those days! However, it is also true that those customs benefited me greatly in my later official life.

RADHA

While our studies and training were progressing well, something was brewing in my family which troubled me greatly—marriage proposals for me! Engineers were then in great demand as grooms. I had started getting proposals even while I was in college. There was no impediment to my marriage, since my sister Ratnamma's marriage had already taken place. She even had a daughter by then. My father was quite pleased with one particular proposal that came from Thakkalai, a place on the way to Thirunandikkara from Thiruvananthapuram. He wrote to me asking for my opinion, setting off alarm bells in my mind. Those were the days when the elders could decide upon a marriage even in the absence of the groom! I realized I could not delay any longer and wrote a detailed letter to my father's elder brother Sreedharan Nair about my love affair with Radha.

My letter sparked off a series of events in Thiruvananthapuram. My family informed Radha's father about the matter. I think her father was convinced that we were in love and did not put forth any opposition. I was about to join one of the premier organizations of the country. So he must have been happy about the idea. He called me one day and asked many questions, quite naturally, like any father concerned about the future of his daughter would. We talked for some time, and I think he liked me. It was decided that the wedding would be conducted soon.

Radha had by then completed her BSc in chemistry from the Government College for Women, Thiruvananthapuram, and was working as a chemist at the Fertilisers and Chemicals Travancore Limited (FACT) in Eloor, Kochi. She was the eldest child in her family. Her brother Rajeevan became an executive engineer at the Kerala Water Authority in Thiruvananthapuram. Her sister Dr Rama was the principal of the Government Medical College in Thiruvananthapuram, and later, the director of the Directorate of Medical Education, Kerala. Her youngest sibling, Dr Sreekumar, worked as a surgeon in state government service and continues to practise privately after retirement. Even today, I depend mainly on Sreekumar for medical consultations. His vast experience always leads to practical solutions.

Our marriage was fixed for 24 May 1967. I applied for leave and was granted barely two weeks. In any case, it was not wise to miss too many classes, as it would become difficult to catch up later. I reached Thiruvananthapuram a few days before the wedding to invite my friends in person and do some essential shopping. The wedding was arranged at Radha's ancestral house in Machat. Her grandmother insisted that the first wedding in the third generation of the family should take place at the *tharavadu* (ancestral house). Usually, marriages in Trichur and Palakkad are conducted at the Guruvayoor Temple. That practice is followed even now, but nobody wanted to oppose grandma's wishes.

The auspicious time for the *thalikettu* ceremony (tying of the thali) was in the morning. So, we started the day before in a bus from Thiruvananthapuram, visiting many temples on the way, and finally reached Guruvayoor when it was time for the puja at dusk. The temple was not as crowded then as it is today. We all had darshan very peacefully. The beautiful and serene deity is believed to grant the heartfelt wishes of lovers. Marriage is one of the most important turning points of life—a wrong turn can make life full of misery. I believe that if one does not succeed in family life, all other successes become futile. I surrendered mine and Radha's future life at the feet of Lord Shri Krishna.

It was midnight by the time we reached Trichur. All the children had fallen asleep. Radha's family had arranged for our stay. We slept for some time and then got ready early the next morning to reach the family house in Machad. I was not disturbed by doubts or misgivings. Instead, my heart was full of hope. I entered the *pandal* with prayers and tied the mangalsutra on my beloved's neck.[1] There was *kurava,* and Radha and I garlanded each other.[2] I presented her with the *pudava* (ceremonial saree). Thus, we became husband and wife in front of all our elders and relatives.

In Trichur, the custom was that the bride and groom stayed at the bride's house on the wedding day. Hence, all my relatives left after the sadya but my father, mother and my youngest sister Lekshmi stayed with us at Radha's house. Thus, I was able to get acquainted with all the relatives on that day. It would have been difficult for me to go back to Radha's house within my short leave period. Radha's siblings and the other children in the family began to call me 'Machettan'. The title for elder brother, which is 'ettan' in Travancore, becomes changed to 'chetan' in Malabar. So, 'Madhavettan' became 'Machettan'. The next morning, we started our journey back to Thiruvananthapuram by car. Radha was not perturbed in the least—after all, she was going to a familiar place, and that too with someone whom she had known for a long time.

The sun had already set when we reached Thiruvananthapuram. Cars were not as fast then as they are today. All my relatives and friends were eagerly waiting to welcome us at Sasthamangalam. There was a small pandal near the house and a sadya was laid. Kunjamma welcomed her daughter-in-law by handing over an auspicious lighted lamp. My friends waited in a long queue to express their happiness and warm wishes. I did not know how the time flew!

---

[1]A pandal is a decorated temporary structure where the wedding ceremonies are conducted.

[2]Kurava is an auspicious and rhythmic sound made by women using their tongue and cheek.

The next few days were busy with visits to relatives' houses. My holidays were coming to an end. Radha also had only a few days of her leave left. Those were the glory days of FACT and all the chemists were very busy! I left Radha in Kochi and took a train back to the BARC.

Once back at the BARC, I threw a party for my friends.

ANOTHER ENCOUNTER WITH TERLS

Only a few months were left to complete the course, and we had one examination every month. At the end of the training, there was a placement interview as a prelude to appointing us to our respective departments.

The topics were interesting and the study load was not much. I used to go to the labs with great passion. The modular lab in Trombay was about a kilometre long! The labs were equipped with the necessary facilities and very serious research was being conducted there. In those days, India had only one atomic reactor, built with Canadian support. Uranium was the fuel in use. Research related to the use of plutonium as fuel was in progress. Much later, India switched mostly to plutonium.

A new atomic reactor was to be set up in Kota, Rajasthan. I was mentally prepared to opt for nuclear engineering for my posting in order to go there. I had the feeling that I would be very closely involved with the moulding of modern India's future if I could work in that area.

A sudden turn of events completely changed the course of my life.

On the day before our placement interview, a visitor came to the BARC: R. Aravamudan, head of the ground support division of TERLS. He came as the representative of TERLS to the placement interview. It was in the mess during dinner the previous evening that I met him. He briefed us about Dr Sarabhai's vision, India's goals in space and the activities at Thumba. He also mentioned that they needed a few engineers. It sounded very exciting because it was about a new and emerging technology. I remembered the model planes that I had made and flown during my student days. The possibilities seemed sky high. Added to that was my affinity for my birthplace. So I told him that I would be happy to join TERLS.

The next day was the placement interview, with a board chaired by Dr Brahm Prakash, head of the Department of Metallurgy. Aravamudan was also on the board. Earlier, when asked, I had indicated the atomic power plant as my choice. Now, I informed the board that I wished to join TERLS. 'Why this change of mind?' Dr Brahm Prakash asked curiously. 'Sir,' I explained, 'First of all, space is a new area. There will naturally be big challenges. I like to take up challenges. I also like to engage with things which are out of the ordinary.'

Aravamudan was listening to me intently. The passion and confidence in my voice must have struck that great scientist. Thumba Equatorial Rocket Launching Station was under the administrative control of the DAE at that time. Hence, there was no hurdle, and I was posted to TERLS. Dr A.P.J. Abdul Kalam was at TERLS at that time. I did not have any inkling that I was going to be included in his team.

Many people, having trained at the BARC, went on to hold important positions in Thumba. M.R. Kurup, who used to lead the rocket engineering division at the BARC, was one of them. That project had the technical support of France, which was then leading rocket technology. Kurup had been sent to France to learn about Centaure rockets being manufactured at Sud Aviation. When he returned, he was sent to establish the first rocket fuel plant in Thumba. He continued his services in Thumba till the development of the SLV-3 rocket. When the first director of the launch centre in Sriharikota retired, that post was taken up by none other than him, a native of Ambalapuzha in Kerala.

6

Catapulting to a New Orbit

I was really excited about the outcome of my placement interview. The turn of events later that afternoon took me by surprise. Just as the results were out, a teleprinter message arrived from Thumba appointing C.R. Rangarajan, N.R.U.K. Kartha and me as entry-level 'SC'-grade scientists at TERLS with a starting monthly salary of ₹400—the highest for a fresher in government service back then! We were also asked to report immediately. The order was signed by H.G.S. Murthy, the director of TERLS. Our travel documents arrived soon after, arranged by the DAE, for us to go to Kochi via Pune by train the very next day! I was reminded of my short stint at the Kerala government service at the CET. Even after three weeks of joining, they had not confirmed my posting order. Such are the wonders of red-tapism. I was happy to note that the DAE at that time, and the Department of Space (DOS) later, proved to be free of this evil.

We had never dreamt of such swift action. The farewell party of our batch at the BARC had been held the previous week. Even till the previous day, I had my eyes set on joining the atomic power station in Kota and was mentally prepared to work in nuclear engineering, following the footsteps of people like Dr Bhabha. Everything had changed in a day! My journey was to be not into the microscopic world of atoms but towards the infinite realms of outer space. I was catapulted into an entirely new orbit in my life.

The dream of getting into the driver's seat of the Indian space programme one day was definitely not on my mind at that time. In hindsight, I see that providence had planned great things for me: opportunities to closely interact with doyens like Dr Vikram Sarabhai, Professor Satish Dhawan and Dr A.P.J. Abdul Kalam;

stewardship of mammoth projects like the PSLV and Chandrayaan-1; and so on. Once again, my belief in benign accidents changing the course of one's life was confirmed.

The three of us started our trip the next day. Kartha and I were together in a first-class coupe. There were private attendants to look after the conveniences of first-class passengers, a legacy from the days of the British Raj. The contrast with our first trip to Mumbai, which was spent on the luggage berth, courtesy a porter, was striking. Life is like that—the highs and lows happen unexpectedly. Those who understand this and are able to accept both with equanimity are able to live peacefully.

At Pune, we changed trains to finally reach Cochin Harbour Terminus two-and-a-half days later, where we caught a bus to Thiruvananthapuram. There was another surprise for us at the Thampanoor bus station—a jeep from TERLS was waiting to receive us!

It was 10.00 a.m., and we had to start work in the afternoon. With little time to spare, the jeep sped to Sasthamangalam. At home, the atmosphere was quite festive. I had sent telegrams to my father and Radha. My parents embraced me with great happiness and pride. The son, who they thought was going to settle down somewhere in North India, was now going to be at home with them! The only institution doing research in space technology in those days was in Thumba. I took a bath, quickly had some food and started straight for Thumba.

The jeep went past Vellayambalam, left behind my alma mater, the engineering college at Kulathoor, and went straight to the seashore. Kartha was sitting with me and we shared our hopes about the future. The jeep stopped in front of a small water canal. We had to climb into a country boat to reach the other shore, where we found a tent manned by security personnel. We showed them the order from the director and they let us in. The director's office was 2 km away and we had to walk all the way on kuccha roads.

Director Murthy received us with warm handshakes and asked us to meet Administrative Officer Rajan V. George. The latter took our appointment orders and kept a register open in front of us. We affixed our signatures, thereby becoming part of the great institution. It was 4 August 1967, just four years since TERLS had started functioning in Thumba.

SETTING UP THUMBA

The love for Kerala and the search for a suitable place near the magnetic equator of the Earth had brought Dr Sarabhai to Thumba. The scientists of the INCOSPAR were searching for such a location in India. The line connecting the magnetic poles of the Earth is inclined at an angle of 8 degrees with the Earth's axis and, hence, to that extent, the plane of the magnetic equator is inclined to the geographic equator at 8 degrees too. Above this magnetic equator, at an altitude of 80–150 km, there is a belt of electrically charged particles around the Earth, and the flow of electrons from the west to east is EEJ, a phenomenon of great interest to scientists. Since balloons cannot reach beyond 30 km in the sky, small rockets are launched to cut across the electrojet to study its characteristics. Such rockets that carry instruments collecting data from the upper atmosphere are called sounding rockets and need to be launched from places near the magnetic equator.

Noted Malayali meteorologist Professor Pisharoty, along with Professor Chitnis, had scanned different places in Kerala for a suitable location. They soon found two possibilities—Vellanaathuruthu in Kollam District and Thumba in Thiruvananthapuram. The first was closer to the magnetic equator and more suitable for the purpose. Thumba is half a degree away to the south, and, in addition, there were some religious and social challenges to be addressed. But the name 'Vellanaathuruthu' posed an issue. Professor Pisharoty had translated 'Vellana' into English for Dr Sarabhai, explaining that the word meant 'white elephant', a phrase indicating an edifice of no use. Dr Sarabhai, being the proponent of professionalism, did not want his premier space venture to carry such a name. Additionally, Thumba was closer to the capital city of Thiruvananthapuram, where logistics and more connectivity were available. He took the decision to establish the launching station in Thumba.

Many challenges were awaiting him there. A beachside site of at least 2 sq. km was required. More than 500 families lived within that area in Thumba, most of them fishing folk. There was also a church belonging to the Thiruvananthapuram diocese (today called the Latin Archdiocese of Trivandrum) and a bishop's house. There was a cemetery as well.

In the early 1900s, Bishop Abillus of the diocese had rebuilt the Mary Magdalena Mariam Church in Thumba. He also built a few houses at different places, including one in Thumba, to help with administration of his vast diocese. When the Portuguese rule in Kerala came to an end, the Kochi diocese split into many, and Thiruvananthapuram gained a separate diocese. When the first Belgium-born bishop of this diocese was about to retire, he appointed Peter Pereira, a Malayali, as assistant bishop. Pereira chose to live in the old 'camp house' of the Kochi bishop.[1] Later, he became the bishop and moved to the official residence.

The local people had many misgivings about the new institution—that they may lose the facilities for catching and selling fish, there may be delays in allotting them houses or plots of land for rehabilitation and they may lose their place of worship along with their cemetery. Dr Sarabhai realized that land acquisition in Thumba may cause major religious and employment-related issues. Efforts were concurrently made to find a suitable location nearby and provide the facilities required to rehabilitate the people. This was undertaken with the help of the chief engineer of central PWD, who provided the necessary resources to build houses for rehabilitation on a war footing.

After ensuring this, Dr Sarabhai met Bishop Pereira in person, along with K. Madhavan Nair, then district collector of Thiruvananthapuram, and others, to convince him of the need to hand over the church and residential premises to the government. He found the bishop to be very progressive.

Bishop Pereira quickly understood the geographical uniqueness of Thumba for atmospheric studies as well as the importance of

[1]A camp house is the place where a person stays when on a visit to a place other than his/her HQ. It is usually used in connection with formal or work-related visits.

the proposed institution. He asked the officials to come back after the following Sunday. When the people came to the church on Sunday, in the middle of the service, the Bishop made an emotional appeal to them. He requested them to relinquish their church for the cause of scientific development in India and assured them that the government would provide alternative facilities. The people raised their hands together and acquiesced.

Collector Nair swung into action. The revenue officers took measure of the land and the compensation money was distributed promptly. The construction of houses for rehabilitation and a church progressed swiftly. Concurrently, officials of the DAE initiated construction of the new buildings required for TERLS as, till the formation of ISRO, space research activities were functioning under the AEC.

As soon as the land was acquired, TERLS activities were shifted to Thumba and a few pukka buildings there were converted to office spaces. The school building was to function as the director's office and another house was identified as the site office for the construction activities. Dr Sarabhai was impressed by the beauty of a virgin hillock to the south of Thumba and gave directions for that to be acquired for space research activities as well. That was nothing other than Veli Hills, which later became the Centre for Space Science and Technology (later renamed as the VSSC).

SPACE RESEARCH: A CLEAR VISION

Six months after I joined TERLS, there was a major event on 2 February 1968: the dedication of TERLS to the UN by Prime Minister Indira Gandhi.

The twentieth session of the UN General Assembly on 21 December 1965 had approved the sponsorship of TERLS. An international advisory committee was formed consisting of Professor J.E. Blamont and M. Binier from France; Dr John W. Townsend Junior and Arnold Wolfe Frutkin from the USA; and E.G. Shidkovsky and S.M. Poloskov from the Soviet Union. Dr Sarabhai was the chairman. Professor K.R. Ramanathan was also a member. I had the opportunity to interact closely with many of these people later. A few of them have now passed away. I was in contact with Professor Blamont of the Centre National d'Études Spatiales (CNES) until his demise in 2020.

Dr Sarabhai, undoubtedly the soul of the organization, began the proceedings with a detailed speech describing all the milestones in seeding Indian efforts towards space research. A Centaure rocket was launched from Thumba on that day. Though I was busy because of that launch, the highlights of Dr Sarabhai's speech are still etched in my mind. He started with reminiscences about the great contributions made by Pandit Nehru and Dr Bhabha towards the development of science and technology in India. Then he dwelt upon the criticisms raised in India against efforts in atomic energy and space. Since we continue to hear those arguments even today, the following words of Dr Sarabhai on the topic are still relevant:

> There are some who question the relevance of space activities for a developing nation. To us there is no ambiguity of purpose. We do not have the fantasy of competing with the economically advanced nations in explorations of the Moon or the planets or manned space flights. But we are convinced that if we are to play a meaningful role nationally and in the comity of nations, then we must be second to none in the application of advanced technology to solve the real problems of man and society in our country. And we should note that the application of sophisticated technologies and methods of analysis to our problems is not to be confused with embarking on grandiose schemes, whose primary impact is for show rather than for progress measured in hard economic and societal terms.[2]

Dr Sarabhai went on to make clear the aims and aspiration of Indian space research, highlighting its practical applications.

With the ceremony, TERLS became a part of the global alliance for space research, the UN Office for Outer Space Affairs. It was nothing short of a leap into the limitless vistas of science and technology for India. I am happy that I, too, could play a small

---

[2]Rao, P.V. Manoranjan and P. Radhakrishnan, *A Brief History of Rocketry in ISRO*, Orient Blackswan, 2012, p. 39.

yet significant role in that endeavour, along with the doyens in the field. As I look back today at my early experiences, a sense of deep satisfaction fills my heart.

7

Building Foundations

Thumba Equatorial Rocket Launching Station had four divisions: the rocket assembly division headed by D. Eswaradas; ground support division headed by R. Aravamudan; rocket engineering division under Dr Kalam; and a fourth division named electronic systems division headed by B. Ramakrishna Rao. All four of the division heads had been selected by Dr Vikram Sarabhai. They were then given roles in the newly formed INCOSPAR. He arranged for them to obtain training at NASA in the USA. In the early days, the four agencies—NASA, USA; CNES, France; Inter Meteorological Department, Soviet Union; and British Space Agency (BSA), Britain—helped Indian space research under a joint cooperation programme of the UN. India also had strong links with Japan. Later, the BSA's help dwindled, perhaps since Britain began to lag behind the others in the space programme.

Among the four who were sent to NASA for training, Dr Kalam could get only two weeks there. He had to return to India to prepare for the first rocket launch from Thumba. One can say that at NASA, Dr Kalam got initiated into the realm of rockets, nothing more. The training was conducted at the Langley Research Center in Virginia, Goddard Space Flight Center in Maryland and the flight test facility in Wallops Island, where NASA's sounding rocket centre was situated. He got exposed to the preparation of various small rockets and the procedures for their safe launches. That was all. In his autobiography, *Wings of Fire*, Dr Kalam describes a picture on an office wall at NASA. It was a depiction of one of Tipu Sultan's battles with the British, with rockets zipping all over the battlefield. The fact that India was the first to use rockets, albeit as weapons, was a matter of pride for him.

DR KALAM'S TEAM

We did not have much to do on our first day at TERLS except familiarize ourselves with the organizational set-up. We went to the library in an old school building vacated by the local community. There were a few pukka buildings in the campus. The new buildings were still at various stages of construction. The staff strength was only about 150. The fleet of vehicles consisted of one jeep, a Standard van for the director and a few bicycles. The staff used the cycles to shuttle between the workshop, office, library and mess, which were all at some distance from one another. One often had to go walking in the hot sun from one facility to the other.

As we were scanning through the collections in the library, the procedures related to our work allotment were progressing. Kartha got posted first. He was placed in the rocket assembly division headed by Eswaradas. Rangarajan and I now found ourselves placed on a balance. Rangarajan was a gold medallist at the BARC and, hence, both Aravamudan and Dr Kalam had their eyes on him. I came to know later that both of them had fought in front of Director Murthy for him. Aravamudan was heading a division dealing with ground stations, including telemetry, radar and their operations. Finally, the director intervened and decided to place Rangarajan in the ground support division headed by Aravamudan and me in the rocket engineering division under Dr Kalam. My interest and practical experience in electronics seem to have led Director Murthy to that decision, as these were needed in the electronics integration section, which had been newly formed in the rocket engineering division. The division's responsibilities included the design as well as mechanical and electronic integration of rocket systems, which demanded multidisciplinary engineering skills. This early experience was to lay a strong foundation for my future activities.

The next day—my second day in office—I reached Thumba by 8.00 a.m. I only realized that I had been posted in the rocket engineering division when I signed in the office register. No other details were provided—just the directions for reaching the bishop's house, where Dr Kalam had his office. I got on a bicycle. The church was visible from a distance. Near it was a small tile-roofed building—the erstwhile bishop's house. All I knew was that Dr Kalam from Tamil Nadu, who was a protégé of Dr Sarabhai, was in charge of the division. I found no one on the veranda. I stepped inside the house, and in the room to the right, found a person sitting near a small table with his feet perched on a chair. He was of short stature with curly hair, dressed in pants and a slack shirt with a pair of ordinary chappals on his feet. He looked solemn.

'Sir, I am Madhavan Nair,' I introduced myself.

'Yes, yes. I know,' He replied and received me as if I were an old acquaintance. I could make out from his subsequent words that he had already read my biodata. But not many pleasantries were exchanged; he just enquired about how I had reached there. This was followed by a short description of the activities of the division.

'A new section has to be started. A new laboratory has to be set up for payload integration,' he continued. During his talk, many new terms rolled out, like instrumentation, telemetry, radar, silver-zinc battery, etc. I could not even make out the meaning of many of the words. I think he, too, realized that.

'Thankappan Nair,' Dr Kalam addressed a young man sitting nearby, 'Give him a notebook.' Thankappan Nair, who hailed from Thiruvananthapuram, was Dr Kalam's stenographer cum personal assistant. He took a 200-page notebook out of his table drawer and handed it to me. Dr Kalam then directed me to write down what he was saying and once again started to rattle off many terms. Most were totally unfamiliar. He was talking continuously, and I was busy scribbling. By the time he stopped, nearly three pages were full. He then asked me to study and be well versed in all those topics by the end of the month. Was I flabbergasted! I thought it would easily take at least six months to even have a preliminary understanding of them. There was no Google like today to bring information to your fingerprints. One had only the library for help. Alternatively, one could ask knowledgeable people. I made use of both the avenues.

Dr Kalam then introduced me to the other division heads. An internal telephone network linked the division offices, workshops, library and the director's office. It was also possible to make local calls. But for long-distance calls, instead of today's STD, one had to call the exchange, book a trunk call and wait. However, Thumba, even then, had 'dedicated lines' and facilities to make 'lightning calls' to the DAE in Mumbai and Delhi during emergencies. A high-frequency (HF) wireless connection and teleprinter were available in place of the computers and printers of today.

Drawing confidence from Dr Kalam's introductions, I started visiting the other divisions one by one. I would typically spend around two hours at one place, discussing the division's activities with the head of the division, interacting with the team members and going around the workshops. I had never seen most of the instruments in the laboratories before, either in my college or in the BARC during my training. Many had been provided by the USA or France as per the UN agreement. Dr Sarabhai aimed to make these in India concurrently, while pursuing the immediate activities with the imported equipment.

After visiting the divisions, I would head to the library. Every word in my notebook stared at me as if challenging me. I had to search through many books and journals, read and study some new designs as well. There was not much time at hand. As it was my very first assignment, I was determined to do well and tried to absorb everything like a sponge. I asked questions and read until I finally felt confident.

It was then that I understood the true goal of my boss. He wanted me to be proficient in modern technology and use it for achieving perfection in my job. Dr Kalam was a gifted taskmaster and team leader. Slowly, a *guru–shishya* (teacher–student) relationship began to develop between us. It strengthened when he received more support on electronic subsystems from me than from anybody else. In the course of a few years, it became a strong bond and remained so until his death.

We used to have long discussions about several matters, but never personal matters. However, if any team member had a personal or family emergency, Dr Kalam would be the first to pitch in to solve it. Most of us had such experiences. I can never forget what happened when my elder son Dileepan was just a year old. It was the end of 1969 or the beginning of 1970. I was in the lab busy with some project work. A phone call came from home to Dr Kalam's office saying that my son was ill. He had been having fits and had to be taken to the hospital immediately. Later in the evening, Dr Kalam told me, 'Madhavan, Dileep was not well. We have done whatever was needed. Now he is okay.' I realized that Dr Kalam had not informed me as soon as the message came! Feeling distraught and a little piqued, I rushed to the hospital. My son was indeed better.

Afterwards, I came to know the care with which Dr Kalam had handled the situation. As soon as he got the message, he sent the administrative officer to my house and made all necessary arrangements to take Dileepan to the hospital. He also called the hospital superintendent and ensured prompt attention. Dr Kalam then visited the hospital, saw my son and reassured Radha. When I came to know all this, whatever little resentment I had in my mind simply vanished.

Dr Kalam understood the demands of family life even though he himself was a bachelor. We see this when we read a poem written by him later, after the successful experimental flight of the Agni missile. In the poem, he asks who crafted the Agni success and states that it is in fact the wives and mothers of the team members. Dr Kalam was 10 years older than me, and for me, he was nothing less than an elder brother.

In contrast to many other scientists, Dr Kalam had been educated and trained in India and not in institutions abroad. But his hard work, focus on goals and exemplary management qualities put him a step ahead of the others. He was a real workaholic. He used to avoid the topic of his marriage. Several suggestions would come from his family and friends, but he would somehow find his way out of those discussions. Once, the matter reached the stage of meeting a girl and her family. Unfortunately, Dr Kalam's sister-in-law, who was to accompany him, became unwell, and the meeting had to be postponed. The next time it was scheduled, it coincided with one of the launch events, and Kalam opted to stay and work. The matter could not be taken up again as Dr Kalam simply refused to go for any such meetings. He was very reticent in his personal and family matters and never spoke to us about such things. He may have shared a little with his close friends Aravamudan and M.R. Kurup. My wife and kids used to be annoyed at me whenever I reached home very late from the office. 'Kalam Sir does not have to worry about family. But that is not your case. You also could have married your work rather than me.' This was my wife's constant complaint.

One day, Dr Kalam's elder brother came to Thiruvananthapuram to meet him. Once he arrived in the office jeep, Dr Kalam took him to the mess for lunch and promptly sent him back. He then insisted on paying the charges for the jeep and the lunch. That was the kind of person he was! There was no change in him even when he became the president of India.

Dr Kalam used to set very tight schedules for activity completion. He would empower his colleagues to undertake their responsibilities and help them to complete the tasks on time. This invariably enabled them to advance well in their careers too. I had to meet him every day at least a couple of times. I became the person to assist in any electronics-related matters. I used to try to finish my tasks as best as I could. When my outputs began to be better than others, Dr Kalam and my personal relationship became stronger. He began to take greater interest in my affairs. In those days, many teams of scientists used to visit Thumba from abroad, and Dr Kalam would normally conduct discussions with them. He would invariably take me along. This proved to be a great boon to me, as it gave me opportunities to cultivate international contacts and get exposure to the latest technologies. I would interact with the other teams at TERLS during lunchtime. That also definitely helped to expand my horizons of knowledge.

My wife Radha used to be a career-oriented person. Immediately after graduation, she joined the prestigious FACT at Kochi, about 220 km away. Later, in October 1969, Radha was selected as a scientific assistant in the Space Science and Technology Centre (SSTC). She had already resigned from her job at FACT. She joined the battery division at the SSTC, where silver-zinc and nickel-cadmium batteries were being developed under the leadership of Dr M.K. Mukherji. She served ISRO until 2003 as a scientist in the energy systems area.

DR SARABHAI'S GOALS

When I joined TERLS, efforts had just begun to develop the indigenous sounding rocket series, Rohini, as part of a three-part vision by Dr Sarabhai. The first goal was to undertake regular launches of rockets imported from abroad, like the Centaure and M-100. After the inaugural launch of the US-made Nike Apache, most of the launches conducted used the French Centaure rocket. Between 1965 and 1988, a total of 81 such rockets were launched from TERLS. A second type was the M-100 rockets from the Soviet Union. A number of these rockets were also launched from Thumba during 1970–93.

In those early days, the main tool for observing the atmosphere was hydrogen-filled balloons. A small package of instruments called radiosonde attached to such a balloon would measure various parameters and transmit them to the ground. The ground tracking system also collected data on wind velocities in the upper atmospheres. The data would be transmitted during the ascent phase. It would take about 30 minutes to reach an altitude of 20 to 25 km. By that time, the balloon would burst. Our meteorology department makes use of a similar system even today.

This method had no means to collect data beyond 30 km. That was when rockets came to the rescue. Rockets could measure various parameters of the rare atmosphere up to 100 km as well as the ionosphere and the EEJ phenomenon beyond it. The set of instruments along with a transmitter, called 'payload', would be attached to the front of the rocket. The data would be collected for the 10–15 minutes of the rocket's flight.

The M-100 rockets were capable of taking a 70-kg payload up to a height of 85 km. It had a special feature of deploying the instruments using a parachute system when at peak altitude. This slowed the descent, thereby extending the observation time to more than 45 minutes. Experiments using this rocket were conducted from TERLS every week for three years continuously. A lot of information about the atmosphere associated with the monsoon and climate changes was collected. The Centaure rockets were capable of taking a 30-kg payload to an altitude up to 150 km. Experiments conducted using Centaure rockets covered aspects like electron density and EEJ above the magnetic equator as well as X-ray and gamma ray radiations from stellar constellations.

The second goal of Dr Sarabhai's mission was the indigenization of the Centaure rocket. Other than the first 10, all the rockets were made in India under license from the French agency Sud Aviation. At first, the rocket cases were fabricated at the BARC and used fuel sourced from a French collaborator. Later, the production was shifted to Thumba. Dr Sarabhai created two divisions in Thumba for this—Rocket Propellant Plant (RPP) for making the solid propellant fuel and Rocket Fabrication Facility (RFF) for building the rocket. He sent two scientists from the BARC, Dr S. Srinivasan and Bhargava, to France to get training in the facilities needed for fabricating rockets. Buildings and other facilities were simultaneously being set up at Thumba. It was again M.R. Kurup who led these efforts. The main components of the rocket fuel were ammonium perchlorate and polyvinyl chloride (PVC). The fuel-making facility at the RPP was augmented in stages to acquire the capability for building propellants for motors of diameters from 300 mm up to 1 m, which later helped in realizing the first satellite launcher, SLV-3. The RFF was also augmented similarly. It was my friend Kartha, along with Eswaradas, who played major roles in these efforts. Later in his career, Kartha went on to make complex mechanical systems required for launch vehicles.

Creating competing teams with expertise in different aspects of rocket technology and building a swadeshi rocket was the third goal of Dr Sarabhai. Each team had the freedom to make its own version of a sounding rocket. What Dr Sarabhai aimed at through this healthy competition was to identify team leaders for his future endeavour to build an SLV. The pioneers included Dr Kalam, Director Murthy, Dr V.R. Gowarikar, Dr A.E. Muthunayagam, V. Sudhakar, Dr S.C. Gupta, M.R. Kurup, Dr Y.J. Rao, B. Ramakrishna Rao, R. Aravamudan, P.P. Kale, D. Eswaradas, Dr D.S. Rane, etc.

MEETING THE FATHER OF THE INDIAN SPACE PROGRAMME

The Rohini Sounding Rocket Programme, named after Dr Sarabhai's favourite *nakshatra* (astrological star) Rohini, matured into its final form in 1975. The first Indian rocket, RH-75, had been built and launched on 20 November 1967, just three months after I joined TERLS. By today's standards, the RH-75 was a toy rocket. Its diameter was the diameter of the biggest aluminium alloy tube readily available in the market—75 mm. The fuel was sourced from a factory in Tamil Nadu. It could only carry a payload of about 7 kg. After that, the next Rohini sounding rocket with a diameter of 125 mm was made. Use of a propellant composition containing aluminium and magnesium powder realized at the RPP made it possible to improve the propulsion efficiency. Finally, the Rohini-560 rocket was built—a two-stage rocket consisting of a 560-mm diameter booster and a 300-mm diameter sustainer. It had the capability to take a 90-kg payload to a height of 360 km and was launched on 27 January 1973 from Sriharikota, ISRO's new launch site on the east coast of India. Today, RH-200, RH-300 MK-II and RH-560 MK-II sounding rockets in the Rohini series are being made in Thumba and are used for weather studies and scientific research.

During that period, a warm brotherhood was nurtured among the scientists and supporting staff in Thumba. No one used to try one-upmanship. Everybody had just one hero—Dr Sarabhai. Everyone wanted to excel in front of him. Whenever he came visiting, everyone would try to show him the innovative products they had developed.

It so happened that Dr Sarabhai visited Thumba in the very month I joined. Everybody was in a festive mood that day. Teams had been working day and night to complete their products in time to show them to him. Indeed, these are among the finer aspects of ISRO culture even today.

I met Dr Sarabhai for the first time in the makeshift guest house established in a building vacated by the fishermen, where we were invited for lunch. We waited for some time for his arrival. I was expecting a man in Western attire with a serious and haughty look on his face. Instead, I found a man draped in a simple white kurta–pyjama with a pair of beach *chappal*s on his feet. He looked around 50 and had a charming expression. He greeted everyone heartily. He called out to the cook, 'Where is Chellappan?' Chellappan came running. Dr Sarabhai asked what was on the menu. Chellappan knew his favourite dishes and used to prepare them well too. 'Rice, *sambar*, *avial*, *olan* and *kalan* are ready, Sir,' said Chellappan. The dishes were brought to the table, and Dr Sarabhai relished every bite. It was obvious that he loved Kerala cuisine.

I felt as if I had been transported to another world. The Father of the Indian space programme and disciple of the one and only Sir C.V. Raman, who had won a Nobel Prize for his discovery of the Raman Effect, was sitting in front of me, eating simple Kerala food with gusto and chatting with scientists and the cook alike! I spent most of the time listening to his lively conversation rather than eating.

Dr Kalam introduced me to him and said that I had been selected from the BARC training school. Dr Sarabhai did not search for my credentials further, since only the best used to be selected to the BARC. He patted my shoulder and said, 'Welcome, young man, to the world of space, which is full of challenges. Keep your eyes and ears open and strive to excel.'

At every turn of my life, I have remembered these words.

Dr Vikram Ambalal Sarabhai was born on 12 August 1919 into a family of businessmen in Ahmedabad. Rabindranath Tagore gave a referral letter to the University of Oxford for him. After getting a master's degree in physics, he concentrated in research on cosmic rays. He also undertook advanced research in photo-fission under Sir C.V. Raman. Even during his student days in England, he tried to connect with people who had made their mark in the areas of science and technology. These connections became very useful later during the development of INCOSPAR and TERLS.

When India became independent, Dr Sarabhai obtained the support of his friend and mentor Pandit Nehru and sowed the seeds for many academic institutions in India. When the Soviet Union created history by launching the Sputnik satellite, Dr Sarabhai turned his attention to space research.

Apart from his contribution to his family businesses, Dr Sarabhai worked as a member of various national and international organizations, including the International Council of Scientific Unions and the International Atomic Energy Agency, to cite a couple. He had an extraordinary capability to build wide, international networks. It is not a simple thing that during the Cold War, he managed to bring both the Soviet Union and the USA together in support of Indian space research! He was determined that the fruits of space research must reach the ordinary citizens of India.

Dr Sarabhai maintained very close relations with Kerala, which had started through the famous dancer Mrinalini Swaminathan, whom he had met in Mumbai as a student and married in 1942. They had two children—Karthikeyan, a social scientist, and Mallika, a dancer. Mrinalini helped advance her husband's interests in the fields of literature and arts through an institution called Darpan, which they had established together. I am amazed at how Dr Sarabhai could be engrossed in artistic pursuits while concurrently crafting success stories in business and science. He was a man who counted painting, photography and observing butterflies among his hobbies!

After lunch that day, Dr Sarabhai talked to all of us gathered in the library hall. 'We are in the process of acquiring expertise in sounding rockets,' he said. 'Now we must also think about how to go to the next step of satellite launches and put a small artificial satellite of our own in an orbit around the Earth, like the Russians and the Americans.'

The question kindled great excitement among us young scientists. I could see waves of thought on the faces around me. Suggestions came from all around—a few perhaps a little silly, but Dr Sarabhai listened to all patiently, with a smile on his face. One of his blue-eyed boys came out with a bright idea: 'Sir, now we have Rohini rockets of 560, 300 and 100 mm in our hands. If we integrate them one over the other, we would be able to launch a small satellite.' Although theoretically feasible, such a rocket would be able to carry only a few kilograms as a satellite to orbit. Nothing useful can be achieved with such a small payload. Dr Sarabhai cited the example of the

Scout rocket in the USA, which was capable of carrying a 40-kg satellite. Scout, too, was realized with four solid rockets developed as part of their missile system.

Realizing the need for focussed activities in rocket technology, Dr Sarabhai consolidated all the development activities under one roof and formed the SSTC. It started functioning inside the Mary Magdalena Mariam Church obtained from the local bishop. The SSTC was started with a few expert scientists from India and abroad. Dr V.R. Gowarikar, Dr Y.J. Rao, Dr S.C. Gupta, Dr D.S. Rane, Dr M.K. Mukherji and Dr A.E. Muthunayagam from abroad as well as Dr Kalam, Director Murthy, Aravamudan, Eswaradas and Kurup from Indian institutions were among those pioneers. Later, the SSTC grew, became the mother of other ISRO institutions and evolved into the present-day VSSC.

BIGGER RESPONSIBILITIES: MY FIRST LAUNCH

A new beach-side building was completed for TERLS, intended to house the director's office and a control centre for launch operations. A part of the building was earmarked for the new payload integration activities. Dr Kalam gave me the responsibility of setting up that laboratory. As soon as the construction was over, I occupied that place before anyone else could stake their claim!

A month into my job, I was assigned an important responsibility. An X-ray astronomy payload had to be prepared to integrate into the next Nike Apache rocket. The X-ray astronomy experiment was being attempted in India for the first time. The payload was being prepared at the PRL in Ahmedabad. Dr Kalam insisted that I should join that team. Professor U.R. Rao was the project scientist. He was one of the first disciples of Dr Sarabhai and had been trained at NASA. Professor Oda, who was part of the Japanese space programme, was the collaborator. I joined them as an assistant.

It was the first opportunity for me to make a telemetry system. The job had to be completed in six weeks. Many subsystems had to be imported from different countries. The detector, signal conditioning modules and telemetry had to be seamlessly integrated.

Some countries had shifted to the new metric system of measurement, with centimetres and kilograms, while others continued to follow the old British system, using inches, feet and pounds. The units for electricity, pressure, magnetic field, etc., were also different. We had to take these differences into account while integrating the different systems. Additionally, we also had to solve interface issues. The output of one subsystem might not match with the input of the next system. Such differences had to be ascertained exactly and rectified, so that the system as a whole would work. There could be differences in electrical interfaces and interference problems too! The system's compatibility with the ground station also had to be checked. Finally, we had to conduct a vibration test on the integrated payload to ascertain that the system could tolerate the vibrations and accelerations it would undergo during the flight. We completed all the tests successfully. K.V. Venkatachary, who had joined the ground support system, was with me in these efforts.

The payload was then brought to Thumba and was integrated with the rocket. Finally, it was time for the launch. I was feeling excited and tensed at the same time. It was the first opportunity for me to show my mettle on the job.

The rocket was put on a hydraulic lift connected to a truck in order to hoist it up and into the position for launch.

Dr Kalam had narrated how a similar system had malfunctioned during the very first launch from Thumba. That day, when that first Nike Apache was put on the system and was hoisted up, somehow, the mechanism did not work as expected. The rocket had kept sliding off. In spite of the best efforts, the system could not be rectified. Finally, the well-proven Indian method had been used by which a few people lifted the rocket manually and put it on the rails! Looking back, it had indeed been a highly risky operation! The launch had then taken place successfully, right on the dot.

Now our rocket was on the launch pad with my payload and was ready for launch. The 3-feet-long and 10-inch-diameter X-ray payload had been integrated perfectly with the rocket. The countdown started: 'Ten, nine, eight, seven ... zero.' The rocket lit up with a roar and scintillating light. The next second, it zoomed up into the sky. Now we had to wait to scan the signals using the radar system. Only after getting the data could we conclude that the launch had been a success. Dr Rao and Professor Oda were waiting breathlessly. I was very perturbed, worried whether any mistake had been committed by me, a newcomer. A little later, the signals started arriving. There were smiles of relief on all the faces. Alas, they were not to last long!

After the signals, the scientific data was expected to arrive, but it did not. Our wait ended in disappointment. We could not understand the problem. Grief-stricken, Professor Oda started to cry. Dr Rao was looking dumbfounded. Dr Kalam rushed into the room and consoled everybody. We realized that our mission had failed.

Immediately everybody's attention turned towards a detailed analysis of the failure. All the experts sat together and verified the systems but no shortcoming could be found anywhere. Since no specific defect was detected and the correct time for observing the specific star was to end in a few weeks, the decision was taken to launch the second payload, which had also been kept ready. Within two weeks, the next launch was conducted. But the result was the same.

Now the discussions really heated up. We needed to find out the exact reason for the failures. There was no question of the TERLS scientists conceding defeat. All the minds worked in tandem. Many hypotheses were put forward and analysed. Finally, the issue was located in the Japanese power control relay, which could not withstand the shock during the rocket's firing. Though the mission had not succeeded, there was a sigh of relief about the fact that all the Indian systems had performed normally.

To verify our hypothesis of the relay failure, a shock test was needed. But only vibration tests could be conducted at the Thumba facility. It was Sudhakar who made a practical suggestion to overcome the limitation. A capable engineer who, like me, had been trained at the BARC, he was three years my senior and Dr Kalam's right-hand man. The story of how Sudhakar had once risked his life to save Dr Kalam is narrated by Dr Kalam in his autobiography.

We carried out the shock test in the makeshift facility developed by Sudhakar and a US-made control relay was tested. It could withstand 100 times the gravitational pull of the Earth. However, the Japanese relay could withstand only up to 60 times! Once the exact problem was identified and corrected, the next launch became a complete success.

All mission successes hitherto achieved in the Indian space programme can be attributed to a simple philosophy: learning from failures and using those lessons to ensure further successes. Failure gets criticized by the outside world, but internally, it is taken as a challenge and converted into a stepping stone to success. The causes are carefully analysed, systematic corrective actions are undertaken and necessary changes are implemented to march ahead ever stronger. This could be seen as an expensive learning process. It is indeed so, but ultimately, India is conducting satellite launches more reliably and at lower costs than all other nations, thanks to this methodology.

'ONE SMALL STEP FOR MAN...'

The time spent on that payload gave me varied experiences. On many occasions, I had to work non-stop for up to three days. We would finish work only very late at night, and all the shops nearby would be closed. There would be nothing to eat. Dr Kalam would go out in search of something for us on such occasions. He knew a small tea-shop owner near the railway gate at Kulathoor. Sometimes, the shop would be closed when Dr Kalam reached. He would then go straight to the shopkeeper's house, wake him up, get some biscuits or buns and bring them to the office. He would also make some black tea for us.

On one such night, we were working on integrating a Russian-made radio frequency mass spectrometer in the payload. After eating a couple of biscuits each and drinking some water, we took a short break on the beach. I sat on the beach and tuned the small radio I had with me to catch the news broadcast on the *Voice of America*. After some time, we heard the newsreader make an announcement, 'Neil Armstrong has landed on the surface of the Moon. Let us listen to his words.' All of us, including Dr Kalam, waited in pin-drop silence. Then we heard those famous words in the voice of Neil Armstrong: 'One small step for man, one giant leap for mankind.'

Years later, in the Chandrayaan-1 mission, we had made arrangements to take photographs of the marks left by the lunar module, Eagle, when it had landed on the Moon. Our spacecraft captured the Eagle's marks along with many other vehicles'.

Recently, when I was giving a talk at a school, a student asked me, 'Sir, is it true that man has landed on the Moon?'

'Yes, it is true,' I said emphatically. 'I have listened to the live broadcast on the *Voice of America* on the occasion of the first man landing on the Moon and heard the historic words of Armstrong directly. Not only that, our own Chandrayaan-1 has photographed the marks left by their vehicle on the Moon.'

That night, while sitting on the Thumba beach, Dr C.R. Sathya, Sudhakar, Dr Kalam and I discussed an Indian mission to the Moon. In our youthful enthusiasm, we concluded that it was quite possible for us also to achieve, if political will, as demonstrated by President Kennedy, was available. However, Dr Sarabhai's vision had no place for Moon missions. He declared that we did not have the intention to go to the Moon or other planets, like the rich nations. Space technology was only to be used to enrich the quality of life of the poor in India. I am proud that we did fulfil all his dreams in due course.

The next year, when the position of the stars became favourable, we conducted two more successful X-ray astronomy experiments using Nike Apache rockets. This time, we used Indian-made relays. Both Dr Sarabhai and Dr Kalam were determined to make use of locally made devices as far as possible. That vision enthused and inspired us. That spirit of indigenization still continues at ISRO.

My participation in the X-ray payload project proved highly beneficial. Interactions with Dr Rao gave me an American perspective, while my closeness with Professor Oda gave the feeling of being trained in Japan. Following the thoughts of a genius like Sudhakar helped me sharpen my own problem-solving skills. Later, he left ISRO and took up the responsibility to establish the first aerospace manufacturing unit under the Kerala government—KELTEC. He hailed from Cherthala and used to live in PTP Nagar, Thiruvananthapuram. We lost him recently—one of my best friends ever.

Dr Rao reached the helm of ISRO later as its chairman. He had amazing scientific and technical knowledge as well as practical wisdom. He was passionate about many subjects, ranging from the constellations across the universe to exploration of the surface of the Earth and the depths of oceans. He took up the challenge of developing several cutting-edge technologies at ISRO, both for launch vehicles and satellites. It was during his chairmanship that I was given the stewardship of the PSLV project. He would always hold my hand while solving complex technical problems and was also very helpful in finding practical solutions. We became very close. He passed away on 24 July 2017 in Bengaluru. I had met him just two weeks earlier. In spite of his ailments, we talked about many ideas on the future of ISRO even then, which turned out to be his last days.

8

A Mammoth Task

When I joined Thumba in 1967, there was only TERLS—the sounding rocket-launching station recognized by the UN, enabling the international scientific community to carry out upper atmospheric and ionospheric studies in the equatorial region. A year later, with the farsighted vision of Dr Sarabhai, a number of organizational changes were implemented. The first was the reconstitution of the INCOSPAR as an advisory body under the Indian National Science Academy. The next was the most important one—the formation of ISRO, under the AEC, to lead the Indian space programme. Dr Sarabhai took charge as the first chairman of ISRO in 1969.

By then, sounding rockets were regularly being launched from Thumba. A new centre called the SSTC was created at the old church building and started research and development (R&D) work in different areas like propellant fuels, control systems, materials, fabrication technologies, etc. Design and development of a sounding rocket to replace the imported Nike Apache and Centaure rockets was progressing well. But Dr Sarabhai was impatient. Instead of small steps, he demanded leapfrogging to catch up with the developed countries. That was how the idea of developing India's own SLV was nucleated.

A launch vehicle, as conceived then, meant putting together three or four rocket motors, which were fired one after the other, to carry a spacecraft, which is its payload, to a height of about 400 km and impart a velocity of about 7.5 km/s to it to keep it orbiting around the Earth. As a humble beginning, Dr Sarabhai suggested NASA's small launcher Scout as a model. The project became the SSTC's main responsibility and was called the SLV Project. The goal was to place a satellite of around 30 kg into a near-circular orbit with a radius of 400 km. Dr Sarabhai set a target to complete the project by the middle of 1974, giving India self-reliance in satellite launch capability. He even defined a 'decadal programme' for 1970–80, incorporating the SLV and several other projects involving satellite services in communication and Earth observation.

SRIHARIKOTA AND THE LAUNCH VEHICLE

The infrastructure in Thumba had safety concerns for launching big rockets. It was impossible to adhere to the safe distance criteria required for handling large quantities of propellants. Moreover, an easterly launch gives the benefit of the Earth's rotational velocity while launching satellites. Hence, Dr Sarabhai started searching for a location with a large land area on the eastern coast of India, as close to the equator as possible. After considering several sites in Odisha, Andhra Pradesh and Tamil Nadu, he zeroed in on Sriharikota in the Nelloor District of Andhra Pradesh. About 100 km from Chennai airport, Sriharikota is a semi-elliptical land mass surrounded by water bodies and with a long coastline of the Bay of Bengal, about 50-km long and 8-km wide. The total area is about 44,000 acres. The place was very sparsely populated. The few people living there were from tribal communities that depended on forest produce and fishing for their livelihood.

The inhabitants were suitably rehabilitated and assured jobs at the new launch centre. Finally, the Sriharikota Range (SHAR) Satellite Launching Station came into being. This spaceport of India has now been rechristened as Satish Dhawan Space Centre (SDSC-SHAR) after the pioneer of Indian space programme and the second chairman of ISRO, Professor Satish Dhawan.

Before starting work on the SLV, extensive brainstorming was done with all members of the SSTC on the vehicle configuration and technology options, like whether to use three or four stages, whether to utilize solid or liquid fuels, how to cluster the boosters, etc. Nearly 10 possible configurations were studied, and the third one was finally selected. Naturally, the rocket was named SLV-3. The finalized vehicle configuration had four stages, all working with solid fuels.

Soon, a number of teams were constituted to evolve the detailed engineering designs. Dr V.R. Gowarikar, M.R. Kurup, Dr A.E. Muthunayagam and Dr Kalam were made responsible for stages one to four, respectively. The 'heat shield' that protects the satellite was entrusted to Dr M.K. Mukherji, and the vehicle's navigation, guidance and control were assigned to Dr S.C. Gupta. Dr C.L. Amba Rao was identified for realizing a launcher and the telemetry and tracking systems were given to B. Ramakrishna Rao and R. Aravamudan, respectively. Dr U.R. Rao was responsible for realizing the satellite that was to be launched. The overall design coordination was made the responsibility of Dr Y.J. Rao.

I became part of this team, perhaps, partly by chance and partly through a selection process. If deviations occurred during the flight of a launch vehicle, it had to be destroyed. The rocket, thus, has to contain a destruct system responsive to telecommands from the ground. The rocket engineering division under Dr Kalam was to develop these explosive systems. So, he wanted the telecommand system to be with him as well. Dr U.R. Rao, who was heading the satellite systems division of the SSTC, had assigned the work to a senior engineer in his division. Certain imported components were required for realizing a proto model. The designers were waiting for these to arrive, which was delaying the development. An idea flashed in my mind: Why not use the technique from my old aero-modelling experience? I went to the old military junk store and obtained the valves required to make a transmitter. In those days, a private company in Delhi named Continental Device India Pvt Ltd had started making transistors in India. I got a few transistors from them and quickly developed a receiver and decoder.

Dr Sarabhai was in Thumba as part of his monthly visits. As usual, all of us were eager to show him something new. I had the opportunity to demonstrate the remote-controlled ejection of a rocket nose cone kept at a distance of about 100 m, using the telecommand system I had developed. It took Dr Sarabhai completely by surprise, and he was highly pleased with the development. 'Well done, my boy, well done,' he patted me on the shoulder and congratulated me. Praise from none other than the doyen of the Indian space programme! My confidence got a real boost. In the review meeting held that night, the decision was made: I was to be appointed as project leader for the telecommand system development!

Years later, Dr Kalam wrote in his autobiography: 'Prof. Sarabhai did not have to think much in selecting this young engineer for the task in place of another experienced scientist. Madhavan Nair not only satisfied his expectations but even surpassed them.'[1]

During a later visit, Dr Sarabhai took a review of the design projects of the SLV. Starting from the first stage, the team leaders made presentations—nothing less than sales speeches—of the first three stages. When it came to the fourth stage, instead of making the presentation himself, Dr Kalam asked his team members to speak on the design of their individual subsystems, which together made up the full fourth stage. As they were explaining the details, Dr Kalam just sat silently with a smile on his face.

This new method upset one of the senior scientists. 'Dr Kalam, what is it that you have done?' he asked. Dr Kalam just smiled.

Things became clearer that night during dinner with Dr Sarabhai. Dr Kalam was, in fact, exposing his style of management to Dr Sarabhai. Deviating from traditional ideas of hierarchical management, he was embracing novel methods of participative management, giving due credit to each team member. He had entrusted specific persons with each subsystem of the rocket and had given them the required directions. Each of them had been enthused to show their mettle by bringing their ideas to the table. Dr Kalam had then integrated all those ideas into the final design of the fourth stage of the rocket. He wanted to ensure that every designer got his due recognition during the review. Dr Sarabhai greatly appreciated this style of management.

This was also the primary reason why Dr Kalam was identified as the project director for India's first launch vehicle. This management style was later extended to the entire SLV-3 project.

[1]Kalam, A.P.J. Abdul, *Wings of Fire,* Universities Press, 1999, p. 61.

TRAGEDY AND TRANSITION

The preliminary design report of SLV-3 was ready by October 1971. The detailed project report and the management plan were prepared next. All the paperwork was completed within the next two months. The engineers were eagerly waiting to start the metal cutting. It was then that a shocking event took place. Dr Vikram Sarabhai, the architect of Indian space programme, suddenly left us forever!

Whenever he came to Thiruvananthapuram, Dr Sarabhai would stay in the Halcyon Castle in Kovalam, a heritage hotel. That night, he had retired to bed at midnight after a day of long discussions and reviews at the SSTC. His last discussion was supposed to have been with Dr Kalam. Dr Sarabhai's private secretary, K.V. Warrier, told Dr Kalam to meet Dr Sarabhai the next morning on the way to the airport, as he had planned to go back to Delhi by the morning flight on 30 December 1971. But that meeting never took place. When Dr Sarabhai did not get up in the morning, people tried to wake him, but the soul of that great genius had already departed from the body.

Dr Sarabhai's sudden demise at such a young age shocked the entire nation. The country was only beginning to recover from the great loss of Dr Bhabha, who had died in a tragic plane accident. Yet another untimely death!

However, I think Dr Sarabhai's spirit has not left Thumba till today. Even those of us who were very young then are still inspired by his invisible presence. He was a model for us young scientists. Unlike Dr Kalam, who was wedded to his work, here was a person who did justice to both his work and family! It was indeed his daughter Mallika's phone call asking him to be with the family on New Year's Eve that had made Dr Sarabhai change his plans and decide to leave on 30 December. Alas, that family reunion never happened.

The nation honoured the memory of that great man by bestowing the Padma Vibhushan on him posthumously.

Though Dr Sarabhai's demise upset everybody at ISRO, it did not hinder them from carrying forward his vision. He had introduced to ISRO another charismatic leader who could become his torchbearer—

Professor Satish Dhawan. Born in Srinagar in 1920 and a graduate in aeronautical engineering from the famous California Institute of Technology, or Caltech, USA, Professor Dhawan conducted research under the great Dr Hans Leipmann and had doctorates in both physics and mathematics. After returning to India, Professor Dhawan became the director of the prestigious Indian Institute of Science (IISc) in Bengaluru. He had many close contacts in the USA, and Dr Sarabhai used to often ask for his help. The government did not have to labour much to find a successor for Dr Sarabhai.

Professor M.G.K. Menon, who was the director of the TIFR, had been appointed as the interim chairman of ISRO after Dr Sarabhai's demise. A few months later, Professor Dhawan received a message from Prime Minister Indira Gandhi to meet her urgently. He was on sabbatical from Caltech at the time.

'We intend to appoint you as the next chairman of ISRO,' the prime minister, who also held the charge of the DOS, told him. 'I hope you will take up this challenge.' Though Professor Dhawan had some reservations about leaving his academic career, after careful consideration, he expressed his willingness to accept the offer on one condition—that he must be allowed to concurrently pursue academic work and hold the post of director of IISc, Bengaluru.[2]

Prime Minister Indira Gandhi agreed. Thus, on 1 June 1971, he took charge as the chairman of ISRO. He continued to stay in Bengaluru during his tenure. This was the reason why the ISRO HQ was set up later in Bengaluru.

Professor Dhawan quickly got into the stream of activities. With his academic bent of mind, he focussed on scientific explanations going hand in hand with experimentations. He also had the vision to create the basic infrastructure for space research in the country.

As a first step, the different departments in Thumba—SSTC, TERLS, RPP, RFF, etc.—were brought under a single umbrella and named Vikram Sarabhai Space Centre, making Dr Sarabhai's name immortal. This historic action took place on 10 July 1972. Dr Brahm Prakash, a renowned metallurgist from the BARC who had taken

---

[2]Manoranjan Rao, P.V. and P. Radhakrishnan, *A Brief History of Rocketry in ISRO*, Orient Blackswan, 2012, p.85.

charge as the director of the SSTC, was made the first director of the VSSC. The skies of Indian space research were once again studded with sparkling stars.

THE 'SARABHAI CULTURE'

Both Professor Dhawan and Dr Brahm Prakash gave developing SLV-3 the highest priority. The earlier individual development projects for the major subsystems were dissolved, and a single SLV-3 Project was constituted. Soon, the project proposal was submitted to the government. It was approved in November 1973. A total of ₹15.6 crore was sanctioned, with ₹3.29 crore available in foreign exchange. Later, this was increased to ₹20.49 crore and ₹6.09 crore, respectively. This was a miniscule amount compared to international standards. However, it was still ridiculed as a national waste of money. Obviously, such critics had no idea about the financial gains and social applications facilitated by the technology, systems and instruments resulting from successful ISRO missions.

A search was then on for a project leader capable of integrating the multidisciplinary activities. After extensive discussions and interviews with senior colleagues, Professor Dhawan and Dr Brahm Prakash converged on Dr Kalam. Professor Dhawan had been Dr Kalam's examiner when he was a student at the Madras Institute of Technology. Dr Brahm Prakash had seen the hovercraft made by Dr Kalam during his first job at the Aeronautical Development Establishment in Bengaluru. Neither doubted Dr Kalam's capabilities, which had been demonstrated during the design projects. Dr Sarabhai himself had chosen him for integrating the system projects as well as to bring out a unified project report for the SLV-3 development.

In ISRO, personal influence or seniority never factored into such selections, with only performance and commitment being considered. It is merit that qualifies anyone to take up leadership positions. Whoever demonstrates capability receives recognition. This was the model demonstrated by Dr Sarabhai. That was how a relatively junior Dr Kalam got appointed as the SLV-3 project director. Such actions have rarely led to internal conflicts or bad feelings at ISRO. Many a time, the leader of a group would be junior and drawing a lower salary than the members!

The 'Sarabhai culture' was a unique one, based on participatory management. Through a transparent system of reviews, all team members, irrespective of grades, participated in decision-making. Youngsters like me were often invited to even the most important meetings. Junior employees like technicians and scientific assistants would be called for technical review meetings. Their ideas have proved to be very useful on several occasions.

To cite an example, an innovative idea from a technician working with M.K. Abdul Majeed solved the collision problem of sensitive instruments within the payload of a sounding rocket when the protective nose cone is separated from the spinning rocket. Majeed was a member of our rocket engineering division and became a very good friend of mine. Subsequently, he took up the challenge of developing aerospace mechanisms for SLV-3 as well as mechanisms for separating heat shields in bigger rockets like the PSLV and Geosynchronous SLV (GSLV). He was the pioneer who introduced the system of configuration control and quality auditing in the Indian space programme.

Around this time, I was being considered for a promotion. Promotions were based on continuous evaluation of performance at regular intervals, the criterion being demonstrated excellence in the work. Those who obtained the best service records could aspire to reach the highest post within the span of just 20 years.

I still recollect my first such evaluation. Dr Sarabhai had conducted the interview. It had been just before dinner time. I had prepared well for all the technical details of my work and achievements of three years. He had put me at ease by giving some warm remarks with a broad smile. But the first question had really taken me by surprise: 'What are your future plans?' Usually, the discussion would be about activities completed, but here the question was about the future! I had explained that many more things can be achieved using computers, data analysis and advanced instrumentation systems. The interview had lasted nearly 15 minutes. My reading of journals and contacts with scientists from abroad had come in handy while facing the questions. Dr Sarabhai concluded the interview with 'Keep up your good performance!' The next day,

I had got the message that I had been promoted.

Dr Kalam was busy assembling his core project team consisting of hand-picked people like Dr Srinivasan, Professor N. Sundararajan, D. Sasikumar, Dr M.S.R. Dev, E. Janardhana, E.V.S. Namboodiri, V.P. Sandlas, P.S. Veeraraghavan and M.K. Abdul Majeed. He inducted me into the core team in charge of overseeing navigation, guidance and control systems and the development of checkout systems. My tasks were indeed very challenging, since these complex activities were being pursued for the first time in the country.

As mentioned earlier, Dr Kalam was the author of a new management style that defied the traditional hierarchical distribution of authority and responsibility. It was based on a matrix-like relationship between the different development groups and the core project. The SSTC had formed specialist groups for developing basic technologies like propellants, avionics, control, etc., each group being headed by group directors having relevant specializations. When the development responsibility of a specific SLV-3 subsystem was given to a specialist belonging to a group, they reported to the group director but were accountable to the project director as well. The project director was responsible for defining systems, ensuring interfaces and integrating subsystems as well as leading the overall mission.

Quite often, conflicting ideas and perspectives cropped up between the development teams and the core project. But Dr Kalam's special management acumen successfully got the best out of such situations. The teams would meet regularly. Anyone could bring up problems and seek a solution. No question could be left unanswered. One could argue but was expected to not be stubborn. Anybody could suggest solutions for any problem in such group meetings, and the final decisions were made based on the suggestions' technical merit.

Dr Kalam took the bold step of cutting across the barriers of specialized groups to identify team leaders for the various subsystems. After extensive discussions with the senior colleagues heading various technology groups at the SSTC, persons to lead the development in particular domains were identified. This included Dr V.N. Krishnamurthy for rocket fuels, V.V. Babu for pyrotechnics, Dr C.R. Sathya for composite materials, Sridharan

Dhas for control systems, N. Vedachalam for inertial systems, Dr V.P. Kulkarni for electronics, Dr K. Sudhakara Rao for autopilot, etc. Certain vital functions were directly controlled by the project team. E.V.S. Namboodiri was in charge of rocket development and D. Sasikumar of the fabrication of metallic hardware. The overall design and structural designs were handled by Dr S. Srinivasan and mission analysis by Professor Sundararajan. Dr M.S.R. Dev was responsible for mechanical integration and V.P. Sandlas was in charge of electrical integration. I had the additional responsibility of developing a computer-based checkout and launch control system.

METICULOUS REVIEW AND ANALYSIS

With practically no experience or expertise, developing an SLV for the first time in the country was a mammoth task. New technologies involving huge risks were being attempted. For example, composite materials were being used for the motor case. Today, composite materials made with glass or carbon fibres and plastic resins are very common. But back then, the technology was under the process of being developed, even at the global level. Dr Sathya, who was entrusted with the development, had only the textbook in front of him! There were no machines or ovens for product realization. He set up the basic facilities himself and, through a series of experiments and evaluation, successfully developed the upper-stage motor cases for SLV-3 through sheer perseverance and hard work. Later, this technology was transferred to the industry, which is reaping the benefits even today.

Initially, the offices and laboratories in Thumba were operating from the old buildings left by the fishermen. The Mary Magdalena Mariam Church became the cradle of Indian space technology development, housing the first avionics and control system laboratories. The altar was always left untouched, permitting devotees to worship once in a while. Today, the building houses a space museum and has become a place of worship for space enthusiasts.

Almost two years after taking birth at the church, the SSTC got its own three-storeyed building on the Veli Hills, and all the laboratories and scientists moved there.

The project teams had to suffer neglect even in those early days. The SLV-3 project was operating out of a few rooms in the guest house on the Veli Hills. A few temporary sheds covered with asbestos sheets were built quickly on the seashore of Thumba, where India's first launch vehicle was designed and developed. Some of us were upset with the development teams enjoying air-conditioned rooms on the Veli Hills, while we, in the project team, toiled in the hot and humid sheds. This was brought to Dr Kalam's notice. He reminded us that Jesus Christ was born in a hay-roofed hut. 'The luxury of AC rooms is not needed for innovative work. Sacrifices and good work will succeed and glory will come to us.' The words turned out to be true.

Systematic reviews, monitoring of progress and real-time decision-making are the key to project success. Project review meetings (PRMs) were scheduled every Monday, starting after lunch and going on until late into the night. The makeshift canteen in the campus would close by the evening. Consequently, the engineers behind the then largest rocket of the most populous democracy in the world used to work on empty stomachs on several nights. Many times, the project director would suddenly vanish from the meeting and return with small bites like *vada* or *pazham pori* (fried snacks made of gram flour and ripe bananas, respectively) from the tea shop outside the campus. He would then make some black tea to go with that. On most Mondays, it would be midnight when I reached home, much to Radha's displeasure.

Project engineers worked along with development teams to make progress in the complex technologies. Dr Kalam also brought in a new concept of 'programme management'. Dr A. Sivathanu Pillai, R. Ayyappadasan Pillai, D. Narayana Moorthi—these *thrimurti*s (triumvirate) of the SLV-3 project core team were given the responsibility of thc 'programme office'. They would collect details from the project teams and prepare charts showing various schedules leading to the final event. The Programme Evaluation and Review Technique (PERT) and Critical Path Method were the main tools used, and the schedule charts were prepared on drawing boards. There were no computers or PowerPoint presentations then. The programme office updated the project director on the progress of

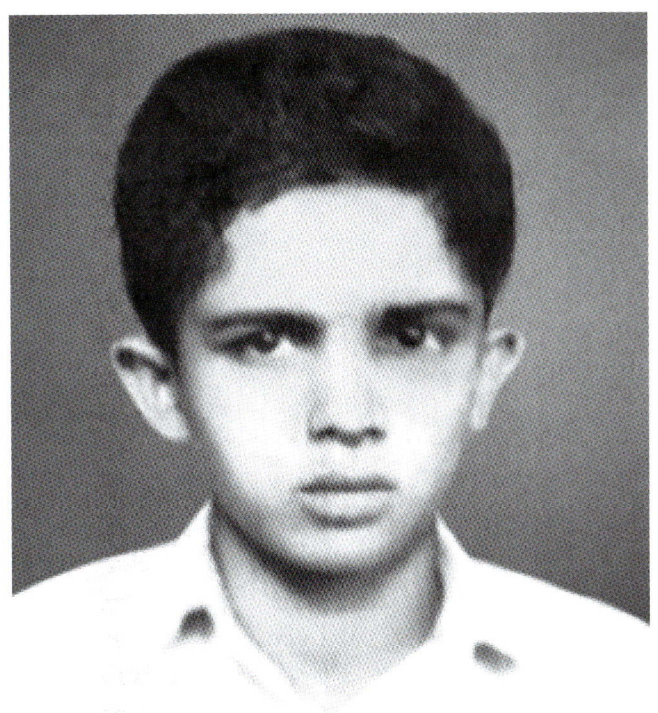

During my school days

Origins of an organization: The Mary Magdalena church building and the bishop's house at Thumba during the 1960s

Early efforts: Nike Apache rocket being made ready for launch at Thumba Equatorial Rocket Launching Station (TERLS) in 1963

Courtesy: ISRO Archives

Hard at work: Dr A.P.J. Abdul Kalam (right) and R. Aravamudan (left) intently trying to set right a rocket timer sitting in front of the church at TERLS in 1964

Courtesy: ISRO Archives (by Henri Cartier-Bresson)

Prime Minister Indira Gandhi speaking while dedicating TERLS to the UN in 1968. Dr Vikram Sarabhai is second from left, with Rev. Peter Pereira on the left of the Prime Minister.
Courtesy: ISRO Archives

Early days at TERLS: Testing a sounding rocket payload, c. 1969
Courtesy: ISRO Archives

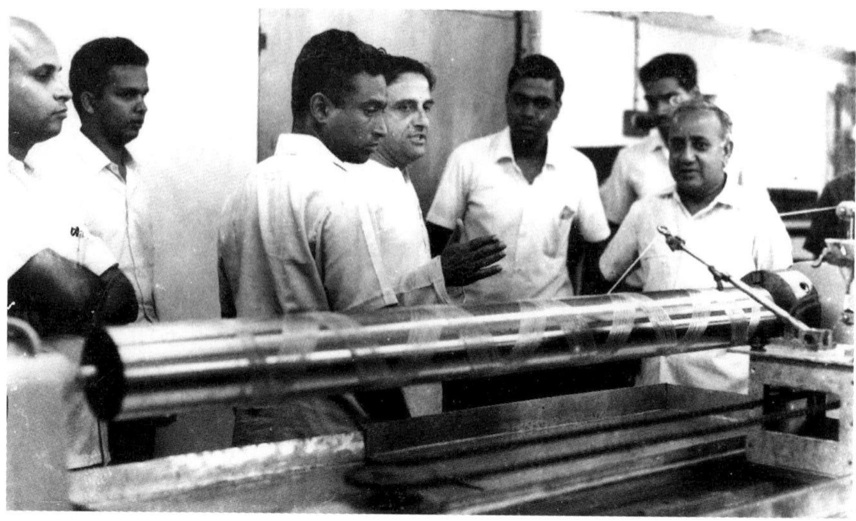

From left: Dr S.C. Gupta, I, Dr Kalam, Dr Sarabhai, Dr C.R. Sathya and H.G.S. Murthy at work at TERLS in the 1960s
Courtesy: ISRO Archives

With Professor Satish Dhawan (extreme left) and my colleague M.K. Abdul Majeed (extreme right) in the 1970s at the integration lab at the Space Science and Technology Centre (SSTC)
Courtesy: ISRO Archives

Brainstorming with the greats: A review meeting in mid-1970s at the SSTC with Professor Dhawan (standing), Dr Brahm Prakash (at the desk), Dr Kalam (seated, extreme right) and others. I am seated at the back, at the top left of the photograph.

Courtesy: ISRO Archives

Progress through discussions: At a technical project review meeting of Satellite Launch Vehicle-3 (SLV-3) chaired by Dr Kalam in the 1970s at the Vikram Sarabhai Space Centre (VSSC). Also seen are N. Sundararjan (second from left), Dr S. Srinivasan (fourth from the left) and D. Sasikumar (third from the right).

Courtesy: ISRO Archives

Walking alongside a rocket: SLV-3 being taken to the launch pad at Sriharikota before its first launch in 1979. Dr Kalam (left) is walking with Professor Dhawan (right).
Courtesy: ISRO Archives

Lift-off: SLV-3 taking off at the Sriharikota Range (SHAR) in 1981
Courtesy: ISRO Archives

The SLV-3 team with the chairman of ISRO after the successful launch in 1981. Seated from the left are Dr A.E. Muthunayagam, Dr S.C. Gupta, Dr V.R. Gowarikar, Dr Kalam, Professor Dhawan, Dr Brahm Prakash, M.R. Kurup, D. Eswaradas and R. Aravamudan. I am in the second row, standing behind Dr Brahm Prakash
Courtesy: ISRO Archives

Problem-solving on our feet: During the development of Polar Satellite Launch Vehicle (PSLV) at the Sriharikota launch complex in the early 1980s. Dr S. Srinivasan is on the left, with Professor U.R. Rao in the centre and K. Narayana beside him.
Courtesy: ISRO Archives

With some colleagues and seniors: At the SHAR in front of PSLV-D1 in 1993, with Professor Yash Pal (fourth from left), Professor U.R. Rao (fifth from left) and others.
Courtesy: ISRO Archives

Looking up at the sky: With Professor U.R. Rao in Sriharikota for the first launch of the PSLV in 1993
Courtesy: ISRO Archives

work and any critical issues. This mechanism helped find timely solutions for many issues and foresee potential problems. It led to good control of the schedule, budget and resource utilization. All three of these managers reached high levels later in their careers. Dr Sivathanu Pillai became the initiator of Indian cruise missiles. Narayana Moorthi retired as director of ISRO's launch vehicle programme. Ayyappadasan Pillai became the deputy director of the VSSC. Undoubtedly, it was the foundational experience gained during the SLV-3 days that enabled them to move upward.

When the SLV-3 project was initiated, many of the team members did not have even a basic understanding of rocket technologies. Most had joined ISRO directly after undergraduate engineering courses. Mistakes or even failures are common when developing new technologies. Hence, a new initiative called 'design reviews' was started. Teams were formed with people having the necessary technical knowledge from ISRO as well as experts from academic and industrial institutions from outside the organization. These design review teams were chaired by senior ISRO engineers and thoroughly reviewed all technical designs. The review committees scrutinized the entire development details, including designs, drawings, selection of materials, development plans, test results and the analysis of any failures.

The services rendered by some of the senior scientists chairing the review teams were exemplary. M.R. Kurup conducted excellent reviews of control systems, though his expertise was in the area of solid and liquid rockets. Dr S. Ramnath, brother of Nobel laureate Professor S. Chandrasekhar, merits special mention. Though physics was his subject, all the electronic systems of SLV-3 were reviewed under his leadership. Dr Rane was a computer specialist who made exemplary contributions in the area of checkout systems and software.

Once the reviews of individual systems were concluded, Dr S.C. Gupta and R. Aravamudan efficiently handled reviews of the launch vehicle as a whole. It is imperative that all the systems—the rocket, the satellite and the launch facilities—together are subjected to meticulous reviews before any launch. Col N. Pant, director of Space Applications Centre (SAC) in Ahmedabad, was responsible for building India's first satellite communication system with a 30-m antenna and ground systems at Arvi near Pune. He chaired the mission reviews of not only the SLV-3 mission but, later, the PSLV and GSLV as well.

The process of sharpening design ideas through a transparent review system and participatory problem-solving sets ISRO apart from other institutions. That is one of the secrets of ISRO's success.

SOME PERSONAL MATTERS

In those days, I was unable to spend much time looking after family matters. Initially, we stayed with my parents in an old rented house. The almost-300-sq.-m plot where my present house is located was bought in 1970 at the cost of ₹15,000. The owner had suggested we buy a little more land at the back, but we did not have the money. Today, I regret not buying that extra land, as it would have allowed me to pursue my passion for gardening after retirement.

We planned to build a house on the plot. My father and father-in-law took the responsibility of overseeing the construction since I could not spare the time. It helped that my father was an engineer himself. The house-warming ceremony was in 1975. The house was extended by another floor in 1979. This time, I designed and supervised the construction. When all the work was completed, I was left with just ₹10 in my pocket. The plight of a poor government scientist!

My second son Jayakrishnan was born on 11 July 1975. I could not spend much time at home when my children were growing up. My wife Radha took charge of everything. Effectively, she worked two shifts, first at the SSTC and then at home. But for her cooperation and commitment, I could not have succeeded in my career.

Dr Kalam visited our house for the first time in 2001. He was then a professor at Anna University, Chennai. Radha wondered what to serve him along with tea; I remembered that Kurup and Dr Kalam were very close friends in Thumba and that the latter used to visit the former often. Thus, Kurup's wife would know about Dr Kalam's favourite food items. When Radha asked her for his preferences, she suggested *idiappam*, *pulissery* and *boli.*[3] Radha made these items, and Dr Kalam relished every bit of the meal. My older son Dileepan was not at home on that occasion. Only my younger son Jayakrishnan, who was then pursuing his bachelor's degree in psychology, was present. 'It is a good subject. You must specialize in it. There is an expert in psychology at the Defence Research and Development Organisation (DRDO). I will introduce you,' Dr Kalam told him. That was Dr Panneerselvam, a senior scientist. He later visited us as per Dr Kalam's suggestion to persuade Jayakrishnan to pursue a career in psychology, but Jayakrishnan's interests had, by then, shifted to management!

In those SLV-3 days, my only outing, other than to the office, was an evening jaunt with the kids on Sundays. My youngest sister would join us, as well as my other sisters' children. We would go either to the museum or the beach at Shanghumugham—the only areas for entertainment in the city in those days. Sometimes, we would visit a movie theatre.

At least once a year, we went to Guruvayoor for Lord Krishna's darshan. We would spend a couple of days at Radha's ancestral house in Machad near Trichur. It was a solid 10-hour drive. I have always been passionate about driving, but purchasing a car was a luxury in those days. I had to shell out ₹17,000 (equivalent of nearly 18 months' salary), raised through loans, for a second-hand car. There used to be a long wait of three years to buy a new one. People who worked in developed countries could buy a car with just three months' salary! This showed the state of our economy at that time and the plight of poor, salaried government employees. I used to do most of the repairs on my cars myself. My younger son Jayakrishnan shares this passion—he started driving when he was studying in Class 10. He used to experiment with all kinds of two and four wheelers.

Let me continue the story of SLV-3 development in the next chapter.

---

[3]These are typical delicacies of Kerala. Idiyappam is steamed rice noodles; pulissery is spiced buttermilk cooked with vegetables and a coconut mixture; and boli is a dosa-shaped sweet prepared with dal and sugar/jaggery.

9

Making Progress

My work for the SLV-3 project was very challenging. As mentioned earlier, I had been trying to develop a computerized fully automated checkout system.

A technical tie-up with France proved to be very helpful. I visited French Guiana at the northern coast of South America through an engineering exchange programme. The major launch facilities of Europe were established in Kourou, a French colony. I had, then, made my way to France, which was my second trip to the country. The first had been in 1969 for a one-month training on the basics of space technology. Since the French rarely speak any language other than their own, everyone has to learn French before visiting. My French classes from college came to be of much use, but I took some time to get used to the spoken language, which sounded like poetry!

I had stayed on the University of Paris campus on my first visit. The hostel had been very good and the classes informative. But on my last day, when I had to go the warden's room to settle the hostel bills, I had simply barged into the room as per our practice in India. I had received a good scolding—I had violated the etiquette of knocking before entering the room! In India, nobody teaches such manners to students in schools or colleges. Experience has always been my teacher.

My exposure to Diamont BP4, the first-generation satellite launcher in Kourou, was very useful. The engineers Janardhana and Balachandran accompanied me. There was no technology embargo in those days, and the French engineers were free to explain the finer aspects of rockets and launch systems to us. We absorbed all the details and, after returning, passed these on to our development teams. Those inputs helped me greatly while developing checkout systems. What I had seen in France was a semi-automatic system based on an older technology using a sequencer, different panel metres and strip-chart recorders for data display. Instead, based on the functional details that I could get, I tried to develop a computerized, fully automated checkout system for SLV-3.

THE FIRST COMPUTERS AND THE RACE AGAINST TIME

Only a few computers existed in the country back then. The first computer in Thumba was a Russian-made Minx computer. It filled a room but could do only very basic calculations. Punched tapes were used to enter data. Then, the SSTC got an IBM machine that was a hundred times more powerful. The programmes had to be written in FORTRAN or COBOL languages and input through punched cards. Nearly 5,000 punched cards had to be prepared manually on a teletype device for feeding the trajectory programme of SLV-3 into the computer. A single error in any card would derail the whole programme! The BARC and TIFR had a few computers, and the latter also had an indigenous machine made by the Electronics Corporation of India Limited (ECIL) under the guidance of the BARC. It was in this context that we took the decision to use a digital computer for the automatic checkout system.

The computers had to be imported from abroad through cumbersome procedures. In spite of interventions by Professor M.G.K. Menon, who was the chairman of the Electronics Commission, it took one year for us to get the necessary permissions and for the computer to arrive. It was a PDP-11 computer from the USA, obtained at the cost of ₹15 lakh. Quite expensive! It needed as much space as three steel cupboards. It is interesting to recall that the performance of this computer was only one-thousandth that of a personal computer today!

The computer was installed in Thumba, and then there were technical issues to be resolved. All our instruments were analogue. How could we create an interface between the analogue instruments and the digital computer? But there were capable engineers like Veeraraghavan, John P. Zachariah, T.R. Chidambaram and G. Raveendranath in my team to solve the issue. Dr R. Vikraman Nair, an expert in software, also joined in.

When the French experts came to Thumba for an interim review and saw what we were attempting, they were shocked. 'This is not feasible in such a short time!' they admonished us. 'Only two years are left for the launch! It is impossible to develop all the hardware and software within that time.'

They were surely used to normal eight-hour work schedules. We took it up as a challenge and toiled 24x7. We put our heads together, learnt things by ourselves and did what was necessary. The hardware and software for the checkout system were developed well ahead of the launch schedule.

Dr Kalam always encouraged the development of new technologies. Our initial design concept was to use an analogue autopilot with mechanical gyros and sequencers for guiding the vehicle. The project team took the bold decision to use digital timers and programmed electronic control, replacing the old mechanical design evolved for the V2 rockets. We had a tough time selling this novel concept to the development teams. Dr Kalam gave us the freedom to develop both systems concurrently. He conducted extensive reviews of the performance of both systems. In the end, the advanced architecture using modern electronics that we proposed was accepted. Chidambaram, a bright engineer who had joined the project, was made responsible for that development.

Active control was not used in the sounding rockets launched from TERLS. The rocket would be given a spin in order to stabilize it during the flight. For SLV-3, we needed active control. Sridharan Dhas made a control system for changing the direction of thrust by injecting a fluid in the nozzle of the first-stage rocket. During the design review of the system, many people raised doubts. All these doubts were answered through the flight of an RH-560 rocket, in which the system was demonstrated. Two successful launches were conducted. In the process, we learnt many things about rocket control. Fin-tip control using hydraulic actuators was also demonstrated by the flights. Through these flights, the basic concept for control of the first stage of SLV-3 was proven. The upper stages used small liquid rockets for their attitude control. The liquid propulsion group at the VSSC was entrusted with the responsibility of developing the necessary systems.

During the development of SLV-3, delays occurred in realizing two stages out of the total four. Hence, an interim launch of a two-stage rocket was suggested before attempting the launch of the full SLV-3. The idea was to flight-test the second and fourth stages in six months as an interim milestone. It was discussed in a PRM and was on the verge of being approved. Then came a question from Majeed: 'All the aerodynamic tests and mission designs will have to be made afresh. This could lead to a total derailment of the main objective. What will we lose by not doing this?'

It was indeed a thought-provoking question. The team members in the project core team and the SSTC were virtually split into two groups and had heated arguments about the pros and cons. Finally, the proposal was abandoned. If we had gone ahead with that two-stage rocket, we would have easily lost a couple of years! Once again, our full attention was on the four-stage SLV-3.

I can never forget some accidents that had occurred. Once, there was an explosion caused by the leakage of concentrated nitric acid—the oxidizer for the second-stage control system—while it was being readied for a ground test. It had spilled out in a spray and six people working nearby suffered burns. I was there near the spot and informed Dr Kalam. He came running, made arrangements to take the injured to the Government Medical College Hospital in Thiruvananthapuram and managed to reach the hospital before them. He met the hospital superintendent and apprised him of the unique nature of the acid burns. By the time the injured reached, all the doctors and nurses were ready. Since there were no free beds, the people had to lie on the floor until the next day, when they were moved to rooms. Sivaramakrishnan Nair, who was the chief designer of small liquid engine control systems, had the worst burns. Dr Kalam stood near him until he regained consciousness. It was clear that he had not slept at all that night.

A SERIES OF CHALLENGES

The SLV-3 design consisted of 250 subassemblies and 44 subsystems. The total number of parts numbered more than 10 lakh! The estimated manpower requirement was at least 275 scientists and technicians, but the government recruited only 50 people. We had to adopt the philosophy of 'beg, borrow and steal' to make up for the deficiency! In addition to all the departments at ISRO, more than 300 external industries were roped in. Any shortfall was overcome by Dr Kalam's management skill and the expert guidance of leaders like Dr Brahm Prakash and Professor Satish Dhawan. The experience that we had while being on the project was both exciting and enriching, and all the 50 people in the project core team reached great heights later in their careers.

Developing the big rocket motors required for SLV-3 was a huge task, as we had only the experience with small motors that used less than 1 ton of propellant. It took almost five years to develop all the stage motors and complete the static tests. The first stage was the largest one, with 10 tons of propellant.

The maiden ground test of the first-stage rocket of SLV-3 was a thrilling event. All the systems were assembled at the static test facility at the SHAR. The secondary-injection thrust vector control system was also being tested along with the motor. When 10 tons of the propellant was burnt in just 50 seconds, everyone jumped with joy. We were greatly excited with the successful first attempt! Along with the first-stage motor, the 3-ton second-stage, 1.6-ton third-stage and 650-kg fourth-stage motors were also made ready.

The third and fourth stages posed a number of issues. The outer covering for the lower-stage motors was realized with high-strength steel, while that of the upper stages was made of a fibreglass composite. The technology required for that was also a big challenge. The motor case had to be made into a cylindrical body with both ends closed, but with cut-outs for the assembly of nozzle and ignitor.

Concurrent to these new developments, a pulse-code modulation system for telemetry, C-band transponder system for tracking, telecommand receivers and decoders, as well as sequencing and power modules were developed by the electronic systems division at the SSTC. We realized the control system needed to control the rocket as well as the navigation system and autopilot required to steer it through a predesigned trajectory. The autopilot required for attitude control of the vehicle was designed by the control and guidance division and was implemented using analogue amplifiers and filters. Since SLV-3 had only an open-loop guidance scheme, the attitude information was stored in an electric unit and was implemented as per a ground-computed sequence. The fourth stage was to be stabilized by spinning it, which was done using small solid rocket thrusters.

In addition to developmental tests, the control systems, along with storage tanks, pressurized gas bottles, control valves and electronics, were integrated in the respective inter-stages and were put through qualification tests.

The equipment bay (EB) housing the major avionics modules was located between the third and fourth stages and powered by silver-zinc batteries made at the VSSC using technology from the Central Electrochemical Research Institute, Karaikudi. The telemetry, tracking and command modules were integrated in it along with the inertial measurement unit, where an imported system was initially used.

Developing the required launch facilities at the SHAR was initiated under the leadership of Dr Y.J. Rao. He set up the launch installations, control centre and the tracking system. The launch facility had been commissioned earlier in 1971 by launching an RH-125 sounding rocket. Another facility called the Solid Propellant Space Booster Plant with the capability to produce 500 tons of propellant was also set up at the SHAR by M.C. Uttam to cater to the big rockets. Similarly, a static test facility to test big rocket motors was also set up.

A DISCOUNT INSTEAD OF A BRIBE

The AEC can be termed as the mother of ISRO. When the AEC came into existence, there was an understanding between Dr Bhabha and Prime Minister Nehru that full authority for implementing the atomic energy programme would rest with the AEC and its chairman. A similar organizational structure was adopted for the DOS also, with a technocrat holding the posts of secretary to the DOS and chairman of the Space Commission simultaneously, and reporting to the prime minister. The full powers of the government related to space activities rests with the Space Commission. An IAS officer was appointed in the dual role of additional secretary and financial advisor to carry out the orders of the government. A representative of the finance ministry was also included in the commission. An internal auditor oversaw the daily financial dealings in the department. This model is unique to the DAE and DOS, and that is the main reason why these agencies are able to perform well.

Earlier, the INCOSPAR and TERLS were part of the DAE. When ISRO was formed, they were moved under the PRL, a society registered for science research. The personnel and assets became part of that society. Funding for the PRL was provided as a grant-in-aid by the DAE. The rules and regulations of the PRL became applicable to ISRO as well. The annual budget of the PRL was less than ₹2 crore. As activities expanded with more people and facilities as well as increased funding, this model was no longer feasible, so ISRO was brought directly under the government. All the employees were given the option to continue with service norms as per the old autonomous body (PRL) or to opt for central government service rules.

Many feared that the change would lead to the hitherto autonomous organization getting entangled in the proverbial red-tapism of government administration. To address these apprehensions and aid the transformation, a committee was formed, consisting of the heads of different groups of ISRO and higher officials of the DOS. T.N. Seshan, who was the joint secretary to the DOS at that time and who later became Cabinet secretary and chief election commissioner, was named as the convener of the committee. He took the lead and convinced everyone that a full government set-up would ensure continuity of service and protection of the employees. His farsightedness, efficiency, honesty and quick problem-solving skills earned everybody's respect. The administrative manual prepared under his leadership is still the bible for ISRO. It specifies not only how to manage big contracts and efficiently control the budget but also establishes rules to ensure employee well-being.

Seshan shone in the role of the additional secretary to the DOS for several years. An officer with utmost integrity, he never caused any issues for us. I recall us going on a few foreign trips together.

Dealing with foreign suppliers was never an easy job. On such missions, we used to face a number of problems. Seshan used to solve the issues with expertise and fine negotiation skills.

Most foreign companies had the impression that no sale happened in India without paying a commission to agents, who in turn grease the palms of officials. 'What percent is your commission? How should we pay it?' a foreigner salesman had once asked us bluntly. Though Seshan had seethed internally, he had replied calmly, 'There is no such thing in ISRO. You can give us that much reduction in your price.' During that mission, Seshan had saved more than 10 per cent, amounting to a gain of nearly half-a-crore rupees for the exchequer!

I learnt many lessons from Seshan. His table was always clean. I once asked him, 'Sir, how come your table is always so clean?'

'Oh, it is very simple,' he explained with a smile. 'If it is a file on which a decision can be made, then I take it immediately. If a decision cannot be taken, then I send it back with a few questions. If it is junk, I put it in the wastebasket.' An excellent philosophy held by a bold bureaucrat!

Towards the end of the SLV-3 project, we were running out of the sanctioned budget. Seshan was prompt in giving the solution. 'Take money from the project's budget only for the core team expenses. Meet all other expenses, including salary, from the SSTC budget. We will approach the government for formal approvals after your successful flight.' That practical advice ensured continued progress, and we received additional funding after the completion of the project.

After retiring from service, Seshan settled down in Chennai. I used to consult him regularly until his demise. He was the chairman of the Sneham Trust based in Muthalamada, Palakkad, which undertakes many social service projects. I recall that the trust honoured me once with an award. Seshan was ailing and at his house in Chennai at that time. He congratulated me over phone from his bed. Sadly, he is no more.

Two interesting audit-related issues came up during the SLV-3 period. Four inertial measurement units had been procured from France at ₹30 lakh each. As per government rules, anything costing more than ₹10 lakh was classified as a 'capital item' and, hence, must be physically verified. One out of the four items purchased was used for ground tests. The rest had been used in the three SLV-3 rockets. When the auditor came, he asked for the units to be shown to him. How could we, when the units had gone with the rocket! Thankfully, the issue could be solved with an explanatory note.

On another occasion, the Comptroller and Auditor General (CAG) team responsible for the DOS sent Dr Kalam a 10-page questionnaire about SLV-3. It was not possible to prepare a reply without examining the relevant files over 10 years! When the audit director came to Thumba in connection with this issue, Dr Kalam sought his advice. 'How should I prepare a reply for this long list?' Directives about preparing the answer were given to the purchase and accounts divisions. While they were at it, the SLV-3 launch took place and was successful. The audit director visited again, and he was shown video recordings of the launch as well as the data obtained. All his doubts simply evaporated. 'Please tear up the questionnaire,' he said. He was convinced that the money had been well spent and he went back.

TRAGEDY AND NEARING THE FINISH LINE

The years nearing the completion of the SLV-3 programme were very painful for Dr Kalam. The deaths of three very dear family members shook him. First was his sister's husband Ahmed Jamaludeen, who had played a crucial role in enabling Dr Kalam to continue his education. A close friend, he was the only person who was literate in English in the entire island of their native Rameswaram in his childhood. How could Dr Kalam ever come to terms with that untimely death? But after returning from the funeral, he once again immersed himself in work. Not long afterwards, his father Jainulabdeen Marakayar also breathed his last, after more than 100 meaningful years in this world. It was from his *bappa* that he inherited his deep-rooted spirituality. Dr Kalam's mother passed away soon after as well. On hearing about her death, he rushed home in a passenger bus for her last rites. He contained all these sorrows within himself and headed the SLV-3 project.

Dr Kalam deepened his innate spirituality with constant reading and prayers. He was well versed in all major religions, both Indian and foreign. I have not seen many like him who are able to talk about the Quran, Bible, Thirukkural and Bhagavad Gita with the same depth. A devout Muslim, he would perform namaaz daily, fast during Ramadan and read the Quran. He engaged with temples and churches with the same intensity. One could witness a rare mingling of many great Indian values in him.

Before every rocket launch, the project director and a few others used to visit the Tirupati Temple and make an offering of a small model of the rocket. It is a ritual followed even today. I had the opportunity to go to Tirupati with Dr Kalam once. The chief priest was surprised to see a Muslim scientist coming for darshan. He received Dr Kalam cordially and took him to the guest house. There, they talked about many things. In due course, their discussion reached the topic of Hindu philosophy. It turned out that the pujari had a doctorate in it! Still, he was deeply impressed with Dr Kalam's knowledge on Hindu philosophy.

Rocket systems used for the flight are made after completing qualification tests. They are then subjected to 'acceptance tests'. The cleared rocket systems for SLV-3 were directly sent to the launch complex at the SHAR, but all other modules were integrated in the respective inter-stages at a specially created facility at Thumba before being transported to the SHAR.

The rocket motors and subassemblies were received at the newly built integration hall at the SHAR by the beginning of 1979. The final integration was carried out on a trailer that was nearly 25-m long and equipped with support and alignment fixtures. The subsystems were integrated one after the other. Finally, the Rohini satellite developed by the ISRO Satellite Centre (ISAC) was placed at the 'head-end' of the rocket. The heat shield, made in two halves using a phenolic honeycomb structure, was assembled around the satellite.

The rocket, thus integrated at the vehicle assembly hall at the SHAR, was brought to the launch pad after the necessary preparations. The integrated vehicle was connected to the automated checkout system located in a blast-proof bunker-like room called the 'block-house' with a sheath of wires called the 'umbilical cord'.

Extensive tests were conducted using the checkout system. Finally, the performance of all subsystems was also verified with simulated countdown sequences.

The rocket was ready for launch.

It was a nearly seven-year-long dedicated and continuous hard work by several hundred people that led to the realization of the extremely complex technologies needed to realize the SLV-3 rocket—that, too, without the assistance of any foreign country!

10

The Sour and the Sweet

The maiden flight of SLV-3 was scheduled for 10 August 1979. Prime Minister Morarji Desai had announced the schedule in Parliament. It seemed as if not only India but the whole world was watching us intently! The launch pad, radar and telemetry systems were all ready. The four-stage SLV-3, nearly 23 m in length and 17 tons in weight, along with the 40-kg Rohini satellite, was ready on the launch pad after finishing all the final tests. Such a heavy rocket had never been launched from India before.

Four hours before the scheduled launch time, the rocket was lifted to a vertical position using the mechanism on the launch tower. The software programs running on the checkout-system computers in the block-house were continuously monitoring and checking the health of the different systems of the rocket. After ensuring that everything was working normally, the authorization for the launch was given.

The last 10 minutes of operations prior to the launch were fully under the automatic control of the checkout computer. The countdown to the launch was progressing. Everything went on normally for the first six minutes. Suddenly, the computer found something amiss and the countdown was stopped. On such occasions, the countdown resumes only after the problem is fixed.

To identify the issue, a small team comprising Sridharan Dhas and Professor Sundararajan, with me as the convener, carefully examined the data generated by the checkout computers. The status of the different operations until that point of time was printed out and given to us. What we found was that the pressure in the gas storage tank in the second stage had fallen below the lower limit and triggered the countdown hold. We thought that the drop in pressure could be due to a small leakage in the gas circuit. Based on a quick analysis of the leftover gas and the mission requirements, our assessment was that even if that leakage continued consistently, enough gas would remain for the mission. On this reasoning, we decided to overrule the computer and the countdown was restarted. The launch took place by issuing the ignition command to the first-stage rocket motor exactly at 7.58 a.m. and was witnessed by many top officials, including Professor Dhawan and Dr Brahm Prakash. The SLV-3 rocket shot up into the sky with a thunderous roar and a blinding light.

We waited, breathlessly looking at the computer screens in the block-house and control centre. The first stage of the rocket performed very well. The empty rocket case got detached, and the second stage was ignited. Immediately thereafter, the rocket tumbled instead of keeping a steady course forward! Finally, after 317 seconds into the launch, SLV-3 fell deep into the Bay of Bengal, 560 km away—our hearts sank along with the rocket.

We were overcome with sorrow and disappointment. Journalists from all over India and abroad had been waiting outside the control room. That day, we witnessed the greatness and real mettle of Professor Dhawan as the chairman. He met the media and calmly informed them that the mission was a failure. To a query regarding who was responsible for the failure, he replied calmly, 'The whole responsibility is mine.' He did not point fingers at anybody. It was a demonstration of the noble culture cultivated in ISRO by Dr Sarabhai and Professor Dhawan, which continues till date.

FAILURE-ANALYSIS MODE

A failure-analysis committee was immediately constituted, with Dr S.C. Gupta as the chairman. The events prior to the launch needed to be meticulously studied and large volumes of data from the flight analysed. However, only the CCTV pictures and the trajectory plots from the range safety control room were available for immediate analysis. The detailed instrumentation data from the flight was being processed at the ground stations and was expected only by the end of the day. Hence, detailed discussions about the failure were postponed to the next day. When the team met briefly, Professor Dhawan and Dr Brahm Prakash consoled us and gave us directions about further actions. They did not criticize anybody and instead helped us regain our lost spirits.

A very elaborate instrumentation system had been incorporated to acquire data from the launch vehicle and transmit it to ground receivers through the telemetry system. The data gets recorded on magnetic tapes during the flight; later, it is decoded and recorded on long strips of paper. The performance of each subsystem had to be verified by studying strip-chart records, which were many kilometres long! It was a great achievement that the system designers could painstakingly analyse so much data and pinpoint the exact reason for the failure. Today, in contrast, we have powerful computers to carry out this work in real time.

Each subsystem-analysis team presented their findings to the failure-analysis committee. The first stage of the rocket had worked perfectly, following the pre-planned path, and had reached the intended altitude and velocity at burnout. Then the second stage had ignited, but the direction could not be stabilized. The rocket had twisted and turned like a gymnast before falling into the sea. Before impacting the seabed, the third and fourth stages had also ignited. The telemetered data confirmed normal burning of these rocket motors as well. In spite of all the rocket motors performing normally, the satellite had not been able to reach the orbit due to control failure during the second-stage flight.

The day after the launch, I was on my way back home, since I had been away for more than a month. When I was already halfway to Chennai, a messenger from Dr Kalam intercepted me and wanted me to return to the SHAR. On reaching there, we went straight to the launch pad. The sight there revealed the reason for the failure. The entire area was flooded with a yellowish, pungent-smelling fluid. It was N_2O_4, the oxidizer for the second-stage control system!

Detailed failure analysis later revealed that it was not the gas that had leaked but the pressurized oxidizer. The pressure drop was caused by the draining of the oxidizer rather than the perceived gas leakage! The computer had warned us correctly, but we had proceeded based on a wrong assumption and the mission had failed!

In spite of the avoidable mistakes, Dr Kalam did not blame any of us for the failure. Instead, he urged us to identify the reason for the oxidizer leak and to find a solution to avoid it in future.

Detailed examinations as well as simulated experiments revealed that the real problem had been caused by an electromagnetic control valve in the second stage. The design team confirmed that the valve had been qualified through a series of ground tests, so it had no reason to fail. The valve was controlled by an electromagnetic plunger. The plunger was found to have been stuck in an open position when a test command was given prior to the launch. The reason was a large metallic particle, which had passed through the filter fitted for intercepting such particles. This led to the entire quantity of the oxidizer stored for the second stage to be drained before the launch, which manifested as a drop in the gas pressure. In hindsight, a very simple problem—a mismatch of solenoid gap and filter sizing—had caused the mission failure. It was indeed a very painful realization.

After modifying the design and completing the fabrication, a thorough cleaning operation was conducted to ensure that no particles were present. No similar failures occurred in later flights of SLV-3. One must thank the extensive documentation and quality control for that.

In the high-level review meeting conducted after the failure analysis, Dr Kalam took full responsibility for the failure on behalf of the project team. But nobody, including Professor Dhawan, censured him or took any action against him. Instead, they all provided encouragement and support for the next mission. A great model of leadership was being demonstrated before us, and it definitely proved useful when we had to take up similar responsibilities later in life.

Due to the huge expense involved, coloured camera images of the launch pad were available only in the range safety room during the SLV-3 launches. When the recordings were later played back, we could clearly see the yellow fumes of N_2O_4 leaking from the control package just after the test command. If only we had a colour CCTV at the block-house, we would have noticed the leak right then and saved the mission! We would not have lost the opportunity to craft a successful first launch.

Dr Kalam made me participate in all the failure-analysis meetings. Perhaps he had noticed a keen problem-solving acumen in me. If I had any, it was definitely thanks to my training at the BARC and the logical thinking instilled in me by my mathematics teacher Nagappan Nair at school. Any methodology would invariably enter my mind in a mathematical form. Nagappan Sir used to explain algebra, geometry and trigonometry using practical examples. Most kids are afraid of trigonometry, but not anyone who ever sat in Nagappan Sir's classes. I wish our country had more such teachers!

THE SECOND LAUNCH OF SLV-3

The second launch of SLV-3 was on 18 July 1980. We were constantly being criticized by the media during the preparations for that launch. We had internalized the lessons learnt from the previous failure and taken all possible precautions.

I reached the SHAR six weeks before the launch. We had to repair some parts of the checkout system that had been affected by lightning. All the failed parts were fixed properly.

At the scheduled time, the rocket was pulled up to the vertical position. Just before the launch, when we gave the command to release the external umbilical cables connected to the rocket, we found that the actuator concerned was not functioning. By that time, safety precautions were in place and nobody was permitted to go near the rocket. What could be done? There was no time to think. Then, P. Bapaiah, a technician at the SHAR, boldly climbed atop the launcher and removed the umbilical using his bare hands! It was a very brave thing to do! But if it had not been done, crores of rupees and the hard work of thousands of people would have been wasted in the next few moments.

The countdown resumed. At T-0, the first-stage ignition command was given by the checkout, and the rocket blasted off at exactly the designated time, with a new Rohini satellite weighing 40 kg ensconced inside. First, second, third, fourth—all the stages worked as intended. When the rocket reached the planned altitude, it acquired the required orbital velocity. The Rohini satellite was separated and was pushed into the orbit.

An Indian satellite had been placed into the designated orbit by an Indian rocket for the first time! The SHAR and the entire ISRO erupted in an upsurge of joy. We lifted Dr Kalam up on our shoulders. This time, it was not Professor Dhawan who went before the media to announce the historic success. Instead, he sent Dr Kalam! Professor Dhawan was an exemplary model of a leader who would take the responsibility for a failure but would give the credit of success to those in his team!

The success of SLV-3 was celebrated across all ISRO centres. Thumba wore a festive look. There was a tea party for all employees. It was this success that made the country take notice of Dr Kalam. Prime Minister Indira Gandhi and leaders of all political parties congratulated him.

Two years later, on 26 January 1982, the nation honoured Dr Kalam by conferring the Padma Shri on him. Professor Dhawan was awarded the higher recognition, Padma Bhushan.

I am afraid that many people in Thumba envied Dr Kalam for this great honour. Life was not smooth for him afterwards. The VSSC Centre Management Council (VCMC), with five senior scientists, had been constituted to take policy-related and other major decisions. We used to call the team '*pancha* (five) pandavas'. They came up with the bright idea of offering Dr Kalam the post of group director for aerodynamics and structures and making him a member of the VCMC. He had been denied this membership while he was handling ISRO's largest project at the time. It seemed a brilliant idea, but in reality, it was a move intended to clip Dr Kalam's wings. But he, true to his nature, took it as a challenge. He virtually transformed the team in his group by enthusing them to do advanced research and software development.

However, Professor Dhawan sensed a general discomfort and created a launch vehicle directorate at the ISRO HQ. He established Dr Kalam as its programme director. Dr A. Sivathanu Pillai also moved to the HQ along with him. Together, they drew up a road map for Indian launch vehicles.

That was the time when a high-level committee expressed concerns about the state of affairs of the DRDO. Dr Raja Ramanna, then the scientific advisor to the Minister of Defence, wanted Dr Kalam to head that organization. It became a reality only after some time, due to certain procedural problems. By then, R. Venkataraman was the defence minister. He had great faith in Dr Kalam. The paperwork was speeded up and, in February 1982, Dr Kalam was appointed as the director of the Defence Research & Development Laboratory, Hyderabad.

Our SLV-3 team was overjoyed that Dr Kalam was to assume the high responsibility to lead the R&D for Defence. There was also the potential for indirect technology transfer of rockets for the country's missile programme. We were sure that Dr Kalam's legacy in ISRO would stay forever in our minds. Hence, we were not sad about him leaving us.

Years later, when I was going through something similar, Dr Kalam recalled Thumba and said, 'When we leave a place, we should not carry with us the weight of all the good or bad memories of that place.' He was silent for a moment, then continued, 'Jealousy and back-biting exist everywhere. If we try to oppose that, we will only fail. So just ignore all that and move forward.' I have always kept this message in my mind.

During the eventful months before Dr Kalam left ISRO, Professor Sundararajan and I, along with Dr Kalam, prepared a plan for an application for the defence forces. The idea was to make a ballistic missile of 1,500 km attack radius, using the first and second stages of SLV-3. But Professor Dhawan did not approve the plan. 'ISRO's goal is to develop space technology for peaceful purposes. Hence, we should not indulge in the defence area,' he said. But after reaching the DRDO, Dr Kalam used the same plan and made the Agni missile. If only ISRO had attempted it, five years could have been saved!

11

Augmented Learnings

On 10 January 1978, while the development of SLV-3 was in full swing, we received an instruction from Dr Brahm Prakash regarding ISRO's next project. The task envisaged launching an operational satellite into an orbit 400 km above the Earth, capitalizing on the systems already developed and proved for SLV-3. The rocket described was to be between SLV-3 and the PSLV in terms of capability and was named Augmented SLV (ASLV). While SLV-3 had only a limited payload capability of 40 kg, the payload requirement for the ASLV was 150 kg, as the target of the ASLV was to launch a satellite of about 150 kg. Such satellites were required for the scientific community to conduct experiments on X-rays as well as on electric and magnetic fields. In addition, new technologies required for the future launch vehicle, the PSLV, were to be tested.

Studies had been initiated in 1977 towards the development of the more capable rocket, the PSLV, which was to be used in the future. As per Dr Brahm Prakash's orders, a committee headed by Dr S. Srinivasan started work on it. The goal was to take a 600-kg satellite to an orbit at an altitude of 550 km around the poles and, thus, overcome dependence on the Soviet Union for launching heavy satellites. The in-between ASLV, in addition to giving more payload capability, would allow us to experiment and prove some of the critical technologies required for the PSLV at the earliest and with minimal cost. The PSLV was a giant project requiring an outlay of more than ₹300 crore. Any setback in such an expensive project would be costlier, attract more severe criticism and could even hold back ISRO's progress. On the other hand, the ASLV was to cost less than ₹20 crore.

ASLV: DEVELOPMENT AND LAUNCH

One new requirement was 'strap-on technology', by which two or more already developed rockets are strapped laterally onto the main rocket in order to increase the payload-carrying capacity. Two such strap-on rockets were to be used in the ASLV. Use of liquid propellants to generate more power and yaw-manoeuvring technology for precise control of the rocket were some of the other new areas, along with closed-loop guidance and use of a thermal shield. The core of the ASLV was essentially SLV-3. To provide the required take-off thrust and enhanced payload capability, two motors derived from the first stage of SLV-3 were strapped onto the core to form the 'zeroth' stage. With only two strap-ons, the configuration was not symmetrical, which resulted in several aerodynamic and control problems that had to be solved.

Several new systems were to be developed, including an inertial navigation system, a digital autopilot and command system and a new mission computer and software. The telemetry system had to work in the S-band and not in the older P-band. Hence, new ground stations had to be set up not only in Sriharikota and Thumba but also in the Car Nicobar island to accurately observe the path of the rocket and collect data during the flight.

The body of the ASLV was 24-m long. To build it, a new infrastructure called a mobile service tower (MST)—a giant steel tower on wheels—was necessary. The construction of the tower progressed in Sriharikota while other developmental activities went on concurrently in Thumba. I was heading the electronics group, developing the on-board computer and telemetry system.

The project management technique for the ASLV was quite different from that used for SLV-3. The practice of central command and control by the core project team instilled by Dr Kalam was abandoned. Instead, a loosely coupled system, where the development teams were given a lot of freedom and the project integrated all the activities, was adopted. Many heads of the subsystem development teams functioned more or less independently, with the core project team members being mere onlookers. Technical problems also caused delays.

Finally, the first launch of the rocket, named ASLV-D1, took place on 24 March 1987. Problems started just 50 seconds after the lift-off. Although the rocket had reached the predicted altitude and velocity, immediately after reaching it, the mission failed and the rocket fell into the Bay of Bengal.

The chairman of ISRO, Professor U.R. Rao, appointed a failure-analysis committee chaired by Aravamudan. I, too, was a member. Additionally, 17 subcommittees were formed. I recall that Aravamudan consulted Dr Kalam. In-depth studies and analyses were carried out. The causes for the failure slowly began to unfold.

The two strap-on motors (zeroth stage) had functioned as intended. However, the first-stage motor (AS1) did not ignite. This was the cause of the failure. An electro-mechanical safety device, indigenously made for the first time, controlled the ignition. The device had to be armed just before the launch to make it operational. During the failure analysis, we observed that the required current had passed through the squib. So, the doubt remained as to whether the arming operation had taken place properly or some disturbance during the flight had caused the non-ignition. Finally, it became clear that the particular device had not been adequately inspected and tested before the launch.

FAILURE AND EVENTUAL SUCCESS

Based on the recommendations of the Aravamudan Committee, necessary corrective actions were undertaken. The electrical circuits were revisited based on some doubts and end-to-end redundancies were incorporated. Finally, after one year, preparations were made for another launch. The rocket, called ASLV-D2, was launched on 13 July 1988 at 2.48 p.m. The strap-on rockets on both sides ignited first. The vehicle lifted off and the zeroth stage functioned well. The first stage also ignited as scheduled, but soon, there was loss of control. Instead of going straight up, the rocket tumbled and fell! Again, the mission was a failure.

This time, Dr S.C. Gupta chaired the failure-analysis committee. In addition, Professor Rao created an expert review panel headed by Dr R. Narasimha, director of National Aerospace Laboratory. Both committees submitted their reports. Many reasons were cited, but the basic problem highlighted was an inadequacy in the design of the autopilot software. In spite of adequate control force being available, it was not fully commanded. Errors in attitude had built up very fast too, during a no-control zone in the flight due to the asymmetrical aerodynamic configuration. Conversions from analogue to digital had not been understood fully. The simulation studies conducted had been insufficient. It was also a project-management failure. It came to light that before the launch, many review committees had highlighted the need for changes in the software, but the stubbornness of the software designer had prevented any such modifications. That had led to the mission failure.

We had to wait for three long years to solve all the issues and get ready for the next launch. Because of a small increase in the rocket's mass, the weight of the payload had to be reduced. Instead of 150 kg, a smaller SROSS-C satellite weighing 105 kg was carried. On 20 May 1992, ASLV-D3 blasted off from Sriharikota. This time, all the stages and systems performed successfully. Within 10 minutes, the announcement that the whole nation had been waiting for was made. The mission was a huge success and the satellite had reached its orbit! A sigh of relief passed through ISRO. We felt sufficiently confident and ready to proceed with more vigour for the PSLV development.

After two years, a fourth rocket called ASLV-D4 was also successfully launched. The ASLV programme was then concluded, since there were not many takers for 100-kg-class satellites. Many valuable lessons had been learnt from the first two failed launches. All these insights were valuable inputs for the PSLVs.

Dr M.S.R. Dev, the project director of the ASLV, was an aerodynamic engineer who was earlier in charge of the mechanical integration of SLV-3. He had the extraordinary capacity to keep his colleagues motivated even after two consecutive mission failures. He finally emerged triumphant with back-to-back mission successes. After that, he decided to leave ISRO and started offering management consultancy services on his own. A good friend of mine, I found him to be a very contented man when we met recently.

12

The Genesis of the PSLV

The development of the PSLV was a giant leap forward for the Indian space programme. The rocket has carried out many successful missions, including Chandrayaan-1. It has also set several world records over the years and is still continuing its journey successfully. It is my great fortune to have played a significant role leading the ISRO team in realizing this vehicle.

The design work for the PSLV was initiated under Dr Srinivasan in 1977. Parallel to the development of launch vehicles of the time, design and development of satellites was also taking place under Professor Rao. The Aryabhata and Bhaskara satellites, developed by ISAC in Bengaluru and weighing about 500 kg, were launched using Russian rockets. Dr Srinivasan's design team was given the target of designing a vehicle capable of carrying 500 kg to a 550 km orbit.

The difficulty at that time was the non-availability of the basic technology for large rockets in India. The SLV-3 project had established our competence in solid rocket motors of 1-m-diameter class as well as the basic principles of controlling the flight path of rockets for orbiting satellites around the Earth. The main remaining challenges were developing large-sized rocket systems and mastering the crucial technology of closed-loop guidance and control of the rocket to achieve precise orbits for satellites.

The study project headed by Dr Srinivasan required a lot of hard work to finalize the configuration of the proposed rocket. The initial configuration was similar to the ASLV, using 2-m-class solid motors just to meet the 500-kg target, for which a new solid rocket with propellant loading of 80 tons was to be developed. But the Bhaskara launch had exposed the potential of remote sensing satellites, and the specification was changed to 650 kg into a polar, sun-synchronous orbit.

Several revisions were made in the five-year span of the study. Mid-course specification changes can lead to delays in any project. Finally, the design team took the bold decision to freeze the specification as 1,000 kg to 600-km polar orbit. Further studies then progressed to achieve this goal. Several reviews were conducted with experts from within ISRO and academics during that period.

LIQUID VS SOLID

In the beginning, based on the SLV-3 and ASLV development, there was strong faith in solid motors, which were considered extremely reliable. Hence, the initial configuration designed for the PSLV used solid motors for all the stages. However, liquid fuels are typically more efficient than solid, resulting in considerable savings in the mass and cost of the launch vehicle. Of course, cryogenic fuels are the most efficient of the three, but cryo technology is more complex by an order of magnitude than the liquid one.

Liquid propulsion activities were then at a nascent stage. A team led by Dr A.E. Muthunayagam and S. Nambinarayanan strongly believed even then that liquid rockets were the future. Our discussions were influenced by the advanced launch vehicles operational in the USA and Europe. Both the American Space Shuttle as well as Europe's Ariane rocket used a mix of solid boosters and liquid or cryogenic rockets.

The design group was divided into two—one supporting solid rockets and the other liquid propulsion systems. Both fielded their arguments strongly. Since solid motors had been used in the SLV-3, ISRO had rich experience in that area. Hence, the choice of solid fuel for the booster stage of the PSLV was obvious. S. Nambinarayanan and his team were quite familiar with the Viking engine used in the Ariane launch vehicle. They wanted an all-liquid rocket system. Finally, instead of putting all eggs in one basket, it was decided to design the first stage with a large solid motor and the second stage using a high-thrust liquid engine. Solid motors were to be used in the last two stages. The upper-stage configuration was similar to the perigee–apogee motor being developed as part of the American Space Shuttle programme, which kindled a hope that after developing our stage, we may be able to sell it later to the USA. To trim the velocity to achieve a precise orbit, a small liquid stage was required as the final rocket stage.

The final decision, thus, was to use a four-stage rocket configuration with a solid booster, liquid second stage and solid third and fourth stages, along with a velocity-trimming package. Further, to augment the thrust at lift-off, six first-stage SLV-3 rockets were to be strapped around the first-stage booster.

SETTING UP CAMP

Based on the project report submitted by the study team on the above configuration, the government, in 1982, accorded formal approval for the development of the PSLV at a cost of ₹315 crore over six years. Naturally, Dr Srinivasan was appointed as the project director. The PSLV project's office started from a few temporary sheds in the 70-acre complex, as was done during SLV-3. The luxurious buildings on the Veli Hills were still monopolized by the elite R&D community. However, work on the project started off well.

The core-stage hardware of the PSLV rocket was 2.8 m in diameter and several metres long. The large area needed for handling such structures was not available in the Thumba/Veli campus. More land was required. Dr Srinivasan literally staged a satyagraha at ISRO HQ to obtain the necessary approvals as well as budget for the land purchase.

Land acquisition has always been a problem in Kerala. While the search for at least 20 hectares of contiguous land was progressing, an offer came up unexpectedly. The head of the Kerala Police, P. Ananthasankara Aiyar, used to take daily morning walks with my colleague M.K. Abdul Majeed. On one walk, Majeed mentioned the need for additional land to Aiyar. Immediately Aiyer suggested a solution, saying, 'You need not go anywhere else. The police have a vast firing range in Valiamala. We can give you some space there.' Valiamala is near Nedumangad on the route to Ponmudi from Thiruvananthapuram. The Forest Department had given 20 out of

100 hectares to the Kerala Police for the shooting training centre, but the police were shifting out from there. The matter was taken up with the Kerala government under Chief Minister E.K. Nayanar, who gladly agreed to make not just 20 but the entire 200 hectares available for the PSLV project.

Once the land was allotted, work began rapidly. The place was lush with trees and vegetation. Venomous snakes, including a rare king cobra, were spotted while surveying the land! Within two years, all the basic facilities were built by the civil engineering division of the DOS, led by Chief Engineer R.D. John. The core team of the PSLV project, including Dr Srinivasan, moved to the offices there. However, the sheds in the 70-acre campus in the VSSC were still retained to maintain effective liaison with the VSSC.

While establishing the campus, both in Valiamala and Mahendragiri—which lies across the Kanyakumari and Tirunelveli districts in Tamil Nadu—only the minimum area required for the buildings was carefully cleared, and more than double the number of trees felled were planted. There was no unnecessary human intervention in these protected areas and, consequently, the campuses are now covered with lush vegetation and rare flora and fauna.

PROJECT MANAGEMENT

The project-management philosophy adopted for the PSLV was based on the experience of launch vehicle and satellite projects undertaken until then. The intention was to use the best from both the domains. However, perhaps it led to some initial confusion.

The basic matrix management philosophy implemented by Dr Kalam during the development of SLV-3 was adopted. Seeing the after-effects of major credit going to the core project team after missions, some changes were felt necessary in the organization structure, which aimed at giving more responsibility, authority and visibility to the development teams. Dr Srinivasan believed in total delegation of power and responsibility.

While the core team under Dr Srinivasan managed the overall programme, different system projects reporting to the PSLV project director were constituted for realizing the major subsystems like rocket motor, control systems, stage auxiliary systems, navigation system, guidance system, launch complex, test facilities, etc. The core project team was responsible for overall coordination. A management board chaired by Dr Srinivasan was constituted to oversee project implementation. Various systems had separate boards headed by deputy directors of the centres, who in turn nominated senior scientists from their entities as system project directors. Consequently, numerous centres of power developed.

The core team acted as a centralized nodal agency and defined the overall vehicle configuration, managed the interfaces and oversaw the development of systems. It also consolidated all the activities and directly controlled the final integration of the launch vehicle. The main players in the core team, to start with, were R.V. Perumal, P.R. Sadasiva, U.S. Singh, E. Janardhana, Dr K. Sudhakara Rao, P.S. Veeraraghavan and S. Ramakrishnan.

The system projects were given the freedom to make their own decisions on the identified subsystems within the allotted time and resources. During development, changes are required on many occasions. To harmonize such changes, the overall configuration control was vested with the core team. Care was taken to ensure that the core team did not infringe upon the freedom of the development teams and that crucial decisions were taken in a timely manner, avoiding red-tapism.

PROMOTION: DIRECTING THE PROJECT

After the SLV-3 project concluded, I was posted as the head of the electronics development division at the VSSC. That was indeed my favourite area. However, I could not see that assignment as a promotion. I felt that I was being pushed into a corner, perhaps because I was identified as one of Dr Kalam's favourite disciples. It was then that I received an office-order from the chairman of ISRO saying, 'You are appointed as the associate director of the PSLV project.' It also stated that I would have as much power as the project director. This new appointment was indeed a turning point in my career. By then, I had completed 17 years at ISRO.

After about two years as the head of the electronics division, I had moved into a ground-floor room of the multi-storeyed building in Veli. Nobody had stayed in that room for long. Professor U.R. Rao, who started the satellite systems division, was the first occupant of that room, but he moved out to set up the division in Bengaluru, which later evolved into ISAC (now U R Rao Satellite Centre [URSC]). I, too, ended up leaving the room within a few months—of course, to shoulder bigger responsibilities concerning the PSLV.

The 200-acre land in Valiamala had been developed and the new buildings and facilities completed by the time I joined the PSLV project in 1984. As the associate project director, I worked closely with Dr Srinivasan, the project director, to control the system projects more tightly with periodic reviews of technical and managerial issues.

I found several problems. Even though all the team members were putting in their best efforts for the common goal, issues among the teams needed to be resolved. As the project activities picked up momentum, technical and managerial conflicts occurred. A lot of the time and energy of the core team was wasted in resolving them. A few of the system projects started working independently, and this often led to personality clashes too.

I tried to bring harmony between all the system projects. I feared that the PSLV would have the same fate as the Europa, a collaborative launch mission among several countries of Europe, each working autonomously, with poor communication and lack of coordination between the different teams. The programme had failed, and if we continued to provide full autonomy to each team without tight control, I feared that we would too.

Hence, I tried to give the core team more control over tasks like configuration definition, mission design, interface control, technical reviews and quality management. The core team took the responsibility of integration, checkout systems and final launch operations too. Action was taken to define tasks without diluting the responsibility of the system projects and without hurting the specialists' ego.

Integrating and reviewing the work of the system projects and solving interface issues were extremely difficult. Maybe due to the high-stress situation, Dr Srinivasan developed cardiac problems. He was then elevated to the post of director of the newly constituted

Integrated Launch Vehicle Programme Office (LVPO), overseeing the activities of all the launch vehicle projects. He made substantial contributions to the SLV-3, ASLV, PSLV and GSLV, demonstrating his technical acumen, analytical design capability and problem-solving skills. Only he can be called the chief designer of both the PSLV and GSLV.

As a result of these shuffles in the management, the responsibility to lead the PSLV's development at its most crucial juncture fell on my shoulders. I was designated as the project director of the PSLV in 1988.

The practice of conducting core-team meetings every Monday to review the progress, identify problems and take corrective actions was continued. If any specific issue related to a system had to be discussed in detail, the corresponding experts from the system projects were also invited to the meeting. The apex project management body was the PSLV Project Management Board (PMB), chaired by the project director. The directors of system projects, the financial advisor and representatives from ISRO HQ were also members of the PMB. Each system project had a board that was earlier chaired by the chief of the corresponding entity—mostly deputy directors of the VSSC, Liquid Propulsion System Centre (LPSC) and SHAR. We changed it so that the system project directors could chair the respective boards, making them directly responsible and accountable to the core team. The system project directors were functionally reporting to the PSLV project director, while administratively reporting to the deputy directors of their respective entities.

While most of the technical reviews and resolutions were carried out by these boards, the major decisions were taken by the management council, chaired by the director of the lead centre, which in this case was the VSSC. Directors of other centres, additional secretary of the DOS and programme director of the LVPO at ISRO HQ were the members. Final decisions on all financial and technical issues as well as corrective actions were taken by this body. Thus, the system was non-hierarchical, with monitoring and control functions delegated at appropriate levels. It was a major contributor to the speedy implementation of the project.

The practice of consulting experts in relevant fields in case of any doubt was strengthened. I tried not to allow stubbornness in any of the team members, and encouraged all teams to report failures and openly discuss corrective actions. I wanted to be involved directly in every important activity, and, hence, I used to always be on the move from one work centre to another. The time spent in the office and on paperwork was very little.

Dr Srinivasan was a stickler for documentation. He would never allow any compromise in accuracy. While continuing these practices, I tried to promote free communication. Anybody could directly come to me at any time or contact me over the phone. All problems would be discussed with an open mind and solved amicably. I was ready to make small compromises if the ultimate goal was not affected. Some people always want an ideal solution for everything. That is not practical. Often, the next-best solution may have to be accepted. Of course, taking decisions without hurting anyone's sentiments was a real challenge.

I established a friendly working relationship with the nine development teams, giving due recognition to their achievements and joining hands to solve problems. These included the solid motor team led by Rajaram Nagappa, liquid propulsion led by Nambinarayanan, control systems under N. Sridharan Dhas, guidance system headed by Dr B.N. Suresh, inertial systems under N. Vedachalam, integration and checkout of the vehicle led by P.S. Veeraraghavan, aerospace mechanisms by M.K. Abdul Majeed and pyro systems under V.V. Babu. The various facilities in Sriharikota were overseen by the team of R. Jeyamani, K. Narayana, M.C. Uttam and K.V. Venkatachary.

When design teams work independently, each team tends to keep their activities, especially designs, confidential. This had created huge issues during the ASLV's development. Hence, for the PSLV, we insisted upon open reviews in every area. An expert scientist was made the chairman of each of the review committees. Experts from ISRO centres, academic institutions and national laboratories were the team members. These review teams played a crucial role, right from the initial stages of the design to the final launch.

In addition to handling the overall management, I really enjoyed my role as a member of the design-review teams for liquid stages and for avionics.

We tried to introduce new technologies wherever possible. The state of the technology after five years had to be visualized and new ideas adopted while recognizing the associated risks. In that way, when the launch took place after some years, all the systems would still be state-of-the-art. We depended mainly on the information from professional journals all over the world. However, the articles contained only broad outlines of the new technologies. While taking technical decisions, only 80 per cent of the evaluation is based on facts and figures. The remaining 20 per cent is intuitive, and that leads to innovations.

LIQUID PROPULSION SYSTEMS

Let me briefly recount the origin of liquid propulsion systems at ISRO. Many scientists had apprised Dr Sarabhai about the advantages of liquid engines even before the start of the SLV-3 project. The visionary in him recognized the importance of this technology. He initiated a study team under Dr Muthunayagam to develop liquid-fuelled rocket engines. Unfortunately, Dr Sarabhai did not live to see the culmination of those efforts.

The erstwhile liquid propulsion group of the SSTC was engaged in developing small liquid engines for the SLV-3 and ASLV. Dr Muthunayagam was heading this group and Nambinarayanan was his right-hand man. The latter had joined Dr Kalam at TERLS and had worked on small solid rockets. Dr Sarabhai noticed a spark in him and sent him for a one-year sabbatical to Princeton University in the USA. When he returned after a post-graduation in rocket propulsion, Dr Muthunayagam roped him into his group. Nambinarayanan then started the development of small liquid-fuel engines in the makeshift test facilities in Thumba. He strongly believed that the future of rocketry lay in liquid propulsion.

In 1974, an offer came from the then Société Européenne de Propulsion (SEP), France, expressing their willingness to cooperate in developing Viking engines. In a barter deal, the SEP wanted 10,000 pressure transducers to be manufactured in India, and, in return, skilled engineers from ISRO could participate in their Viking engine development. There would be no transfer of funds, and each party had to meet their own expenses. T.N. Seshan, then joint secretary to the DOS, saw this as a golden opportunity and convinced Professor Dhawan to approve the contract. Professor Dhawan agreed that India would develop and provide 7,000 transducers as per the French design, and ISRO engineers would be deputed to the SEP work centre in France for an equivalent of 100 man-years. This was how a team of our engineers led by Nambinarayanan got to work with French engineers in the SEP laboratories on the design and testing of liquid engines. Our engineers absorbed the details of the Viking engine, which was being developed for the French launch vehicle Ariane. They also learnt about the cryogenic engines used in Ariane through their personal contacts.

Seshan was an active partner in the overseas trips to the SEP. When an Indian version of the Viking engine was later developed, it was Seshan who suggested the name 'Vikas'. The name was coined from the letters in 'Vikram Sarabhai'. The cooperative work with France was concluded in 1978. Development of an indigenous engine was indeed a herculean task. Nambinarayanan was quite confident that a liquid engine of 60-ton thrust could soon be developed in India using the French know-how.

A new unit had been set up in Bengaluru for manufacturing transducers to meet the SEP's contractual obligation. Satellite thruster development was integrated with this unit. At the SSTC, a project was formed to develop large liquid engines. Later, in 1987, the project, liquid propulsion group and auxiliary propulsion system unit were merged, and a new centre, named the LPSC, dedicated to the development of liquid propulsion systems, was formed with its HQ in Valiamala. Sridharan Dhas, M.K.G. Nair, V. Gnana Gandhi, K. Kasiviswanathan, N. Sivaramakrishnan Nair, Dr Anantha Ram, E.V.S. Namboodiri, M. Annamalai, Dr K. Ramamurthy, N.K. Gupta, Muhammed Muslim, K. Sivaramakrishnan, C.G. Balan and S.C. Ghosh also played key roles at the LPSC.

SOME MID-COURSE CORRECTIONS

Certain mid-course corrections were needed during the PSLV project implementation. Such changes can sometimes derail the project, but if decided upon after due consideration, then they will undoubtedly lead to the project's success. The PSLV project has undergone several small and big changes, not only during the development phase but also in operational missions. Indeed, that has ensured its continued success and makes it gallop onwards even today.

A major change was required regarding the vehicle configuration: The final solid stage and liquid module were replaced with a single liquid stage, the fourth stage, to enhance performance and ensure accurate injection of satellites into the orbit. The necessary end conditions for the satellite to enter its precise orbit could be achieved only with liquid engines, which could be stopped and restarted according to mission requirements. Additionally, the fourth stage, being the last, had to correct any accumulated deviations from the previous stages. An engine with 1-ton thrust was the optimum requirement. To develop the engine afresh, a lot of money and time would be required, which had not been budgeted in the original proposal! Instead, we decided to modify the roll control thrust (RCT) motors used in the first stage to make a high-altitude engine with 700-kg thrust and use two of them for the fourth stage, thereby eliminating the need for new developments.

The plan, though simple on paper, presented many challenges. The RCT engines were designed to function only for about 110 seconds. The fourth stage had to work for 420 seconds! The thrust also had to be increased from 0.65 ton to 0.759 ton. At the same time, the weight of the engine could not exceed 20 kg! It meant that the efficiency of burning had to be increased from 90 per cent to 98 per cent. The engine had to work in a hard vacuum at an altitude of 500 km above the Earth, too. But the team led by C.G. Balan and Sivaramakrishnan Nair started development in 1983 and delivered the flight engine successfully.

Several options had to be considered for the technology to be adopted in many subsystems. Detailed technical reviews by specialist teams were carried out before finally converging on one.

One of the first such decisions was on the choice of the solid propellant fuel. Until then, the chemical carboxyl-terminated polybutadiene, a natural rubber-based polymer, was used for rockets developed at the VSSC. In its place, a synthetic rubber called hydroxyl-terminated polybutadiene (HTPB) was suggested. We did not know much about HTPB at that time. However, scientists like Dr V.N. Krishnamurthy and Dr K.V.C. Rao were ready to take up the challenge of the new development. Discussions on this issue lasted for nearly a year. The R&D was initiated to characterize the two and explore the feasibility of making HTPB indigenously. Ultimately, the decision was made to use the HTPB-based propellant, which was instrumental in building a strong edifice towards making world-class solid propellant rockets in the country.

Similar was the story of choosing the material for the first-stage motor case. The then director of the VSSC, Dr Brahm Prakash, also an expert metallurgist, decided to use maraging steel, which is five times stronger than ordinary steel, for the PSLV. Maraging steel is a dual-use material and can be used in atomic weapons as well. Therefore, the USA, Japan and Britain refused to supply it. The scientists at the VSSC, led by Dr M.K. Mukherji and Dr Brahm Prakash, collaborated with the public sector unit Mishra Dhatu Nigam (MIDHANI) and developed maraging steel indigenously. Indeed a feather in ISRO's cap! The same steel later found application in many of our missiles and nuclear weapons.

The first stage of the PSLV was a huge rocket with a 2.8-m diameter and used 129 tons of solid propellant. It was the third-largest solid motor in the world. Manufacturing such a large motor case using the high-strength maraging steel was a daunting task for the metallurgists and fabrication engineers. The total length of the solid motor was 20 m. There were several issues in manufacturing a single, 20-m-long shell and filling it with large quantities of propellant in one go. Hence, the motor was made in five segments. Each segment was then filled with propellant, and all of them were joined together. This was risky—the explosion of the American Space Shuttle Challenger immediately after lift-off was caused by a small glitch in the solid motor segment joint. The Challenger's experience made us incorporate mid-course design corrections in the PSLV's segment joints. The attention and care given to the segment manufacturing and joining has resulted in a motor that has been working flawlessly through all these years as part of the PSLV.

To augment the thrust of the first-stage motor, the 10-ton propellant rockets developed for SLV-3 were attached as strap-on motors. Later, the propellant loading in these motors was enhanced by stretching them, leading to the formation of the PSLV-XL rocket, which was used for launching the Chandrayaan-1 spacecraft.

When a rocket ascends, its orientation has to be precisely controlled in the three mutually perpendicular directions, namely, pitch, yaw and roll. Error-free functioning of control systems is very important for a successful mission. The ideal choice for the first-stage control would have been a nozzle that could be swivelled as required. But we did not possess the practical knowledge to move a nozzle for 100 seconds while it was continuously ejecting huge quantities of hot gases. Hence, an innovative mechanism for controlling the thrust direction was conceived. The control mechanism worked by injecting liquid strontium perchlorate through 24 valves mounted around the periphery of the rocket nozzle. We had only textbook knowledge of changing the direction of the thrust of the rocket using this method. Sridharan Dhas and team perfected the system in steps through several experiments. The initial trials were carried out in a 560-mm diameter sounding rocket. Using the data from those tests, the first-stage control system was developed. The proportional flow control valves and other mechanisms worked well and the efficacy of the control system was confirmed in the first static test of the PSLV's first-stage rocket. The thrust-vector control (TVC) system, as described earlier, controls the pitch and yaw directions. To control the rotational movement about the axis of the vehicle, small liquid rocket engines mounted on an electro-mechanical swivel mechanism were incorporated.

The third stage of the PSLV was designed using composite materials, which are strong yet light. Glass fibre had been used earlier. However, Kevlar fibre, being stronger, was selected for the PSLV. The Reinforced Plastics Centre (REPLACE) at the VSSC made significant contributions in indigenizing the composite technology.

Many important carbon-composite products required for rocket nozzles were also realized at REPLACE. The technology was later expanded to realize satellite structures, high-pressure gas bottles and solar panels, as also calipers for polio-stricken children as examples of societal use of technology. Dr C.R. Sathya and P.N. Subramanian were the pioneers in this area.

The third stage of the PSLV was based on a solid motor with high efficiency and optimized design, capable of a peak thrust of 26 tons. It was the second-biggest rocket of that class, after Boeing's Inertial Upper Stage in the USA. A number of new subsystems had to be developed for this stage, including flexible nozzle control. It was difficult to understand the behaviour of Kevlar motors under extreme conditions of pressure and temperature. During static tests, two motors failed consecutively.

Dozens of such path-breaking decisions were taken during the development of the PSLV after extensive reviews. But often, all the details may not be available. Still, a decision had to be made by taking calculated risks. Intuition played a major role on such occasions. The words of Professor U.R. Rao were always at the back of my mind, 'Even when one is crossing the road, one has to take a risk. Without taking risks, one cannot reach the desired goal.'

13

Taming the Workhorse

Developing the PSLV was a herculean affair compared to all the tasks undertaken by ISRO until then. Several new technologies had to be developed, along with new facilities for fabrication and testing. All these—from finalizing the specifications to designing, engineering and proving the technologies in detail—were really challenging. The teams at ISRO had no past experience or knowledge in many of the areas. Still, they achieved success in their tasks through sheer hard work and perseverance. Explaining that arduous journey will require hundreds of pages. A brief summary is given in these chapters, along with the technological challenges.

The tireless efforts during the ASLV development experience as well as the first two mission failures had taught us many lessons: finer aspects of the dynamics of a rocket's flight through the atmosphere; identification of the various mechanisms required for staging a vehicle; design of a heat shield that protects the satellite during ascent; understanding the effects of upper atmospheric winds on a long, slender rocket during its flight; and so on. The second ASLV failure had occurred while we were finalizing the designs of the PSLV subsystems. Design of most of the inter-stages and joints had to be revisited to improve the structural margins. A major re-examination of the autopilot design and implementation was also needed. Developing software for the digital autopilot system, while accounting for the complexities of controlling a vehicle with varying dynamic characteristics and achieving high accuracy in the attitude control systems, was challenging. Truly, the ASLV mission failures became the reference book and foundation for the development of the PSLV.

Evaluation of the performance of the ASLV motor cases had

pointed to the need to recheck the methodology of rocket design. The finite element analysis software needed for thermo structural analysis was simply not available to us due to embargoes. The awareness led us to develop new software that incorporated such models. This completely indigenous structural analysis software was named 'FEAST' and became just as good as any such imported software. Concurrently, the design for controlling the path of the rocket through the unstable region of atmospheric flight, identification of the changes needed in the control system and analysis of the structural dynamics of the launch vehicle were taken up. Incorporating all these requirements in the 6D trajectory simulation system was quite an involved task.

SEPARATION SYSTEMS

Many more complex hurdles had to be crossed before the PSLV's launch could be attempted. As the flight progresses, the dead mass of lower-stage rockets has to be jettisoned, which is a complex task carried out by pyro-operated stage-separation systems. While separating stages during the rocket's flight, adequate separation velocity between the stages has to be ensured. The series of operations during all stage separations have to be precisely controlled. Many sensitive parameters have to be measured and real-time decisions taken by the on-board computers to ensure effective separations without collisions. Sufficient redundancy also has to be provided for all these subsystems. The aerospace mechanisms and pyrotechnics groups at the VSSC shouldered the onerous task of developing the separation systems.

The satellite was kept within a heat shield to protect it from aerodynamic heating while flying through the dense atmosphere. The shield had two parts made of aluminium alloy and covered with protective thermal paints. Once the launch vehicle crosses the atmosphere, the heat shield halves had to separate. Simultaneously, it also had to split laterally into two using a linear-shaped bellow system, consisting of a highly explosive charge.

A number of pyrotechnic devices were realized for the ignition of solid motors and staging devices. The first stage of the PSLV used an igniter that was as big as a sounding rocket motor, burning about 50 kg of fuel per second. Appropriate safety measures were needed to avert any inadvertent ignition of the motor. A large number of devices like batteries with end-to-end redundancy were introduced to ensure reliable ignition.

Pyrotechnic technology development at ISRO was initiated at TERLS. In fact, a failed sounding rocket experiment conducted in the upper atmosphere using sodium vapour opened our eyes to the need for mastering this technology. Dr Kalam invited V.V. Babu, who was working in a defence establishment, and he, along with C.B. Kartha, created a humble pyrotechnic lab. It has since been expanded into a world-class facility. Developing the mechanism that releases a very high amount of energy within the fraction of a millisecond was the special challenge. No precise chemical or mathematical models were available. The empirical data derived from numerous experiments became the foundation for all later developments, including the mechanisms used later for cryogenic stages.

NAVIGATION, GUIDANCE AND CONTROL

The goal of the PSLV mission was to place a spacecraft precisely into a polar, sun-synchronous orbit. The SLV-3 rocket had worked using an open-loop guidance system, where the vehicle was commanded to follow a pre-stored flight path, resulting in a dispersion of around 100 km. For the PSLV, this was changed to a closed-loop guidance system. Here, the real-time position and velocity were measured and used to steer the vehicle to its destination.

The development of closed-loop technology, started during the ASLV project, was a real challenge, not just in terms of the design of the mission-planning algorithm but also in the development of an inertial navigation system, precise control systems and associated sensors, electronics, computers and software. The technology was central to missile development and was not available to us from any source. Everything had to be developed in-house, and the responsibility was given to the avionics group. A team led by Dr S.C. Gupta, N. Vedachalam and Dr V.P. Kulkarni worked on these sophisticated developments.

The inertial navigation system is vital in deciding the accuracy of the orbit achieved in launches. Inertial sensors were in their infancy at ISRO during SLV-3. The basic sensors are gyroscopes to determine angular rotation and accelerometers to measure acceleration. These data, in three axes, are used to compute velocity and position. Considering the importance of this technology, Dr Sarabhai had sent a small team, including N. Vedachalam, to train at the top-notch Draper Laboratory, then a part of Massachusetts Institute of Technology (MIT), USA, where they obtained some basic knowledge about these sensors.

The team's first goal was the time-bound development of a high-quality gyroscope for SLV-3, like the one used in Scout, the American vehicle. Embargoes prevented its imports, and in-house realization would have taken a very long time. Necessary special materials like beryllium and a hydrofluorocarbon liquid could not be imported either. The BARC initiated a cooperative effort and set up the necessary facilities at Wasi in Mumbai for developing beryllium components. As a contingency plan for SLV-3, a few units from France were to be imported. The decision to buy those instruments from abroad made it possible to launch the SLV-3 and ASLV on time.

The imported gyroscopes laid the foundation for very accurate gyroscopes and accelerometers of our own and also helped our team get better insights into inertial system development and testing.

A four-gimballed inertial platform was developed for use in the ASLV. Though the system was developed successfully and met the needs of the ASLV, the presence of several moving parts was always a worry. During the ASLV's development, N. Vedachalam and his team suggested using a strap-down system instead, which is more reliable and accurate—the sensors are fixed on a cluster attached to the body of the rocket itself, eliminating many moving parts. But the computational complexity was orders of magnitude higher and required very deep knowledge in basic dynamics and coordinate transformations. The computational load of the on-board computer system would also increase. Estimating the drift parameters of gyroscopes and accelerometers just before the launch was also an intricate problem to be solved.

Pursuing two development routes concurrently was expensive. Hence, a choice had to be made about the navigation system for the PSLV. The two-axis dry-tuned gyroscope was under development and not yet fully qualified. Still, we decided to use the more advanced and novel redundant strap-down inertial navigation system for the PSLV instead of the system proven in the ASLV. It was a risky decision. Everything had to be developed afresh. The efforts resulted in the realization of precise gyros and accelerometers, indigenously. The team, led by Dr S.N. Puri, carried out excellent work that resulted in a world-class strapped-down inertial navigation system. The injection accuracies achieved later confirmed that our decision had been correct.

N. Vedachalam can be described as the father of inertial systems in India. Our present success in this area is because of the innovative work carried out under his guidance. His deep interest in the field and sincerity helped us to cross all hurdles and realize the precise systems needed for our launch vehicles. He had promised the core project team that he would deliver a navigation system using only indigenously developed sensors. He kept his word to make the system available well in time for the PSLV. I recall many heated discussions between us on this topic, which ultimately paved the way towards a grand success. We have maintained a very good friendship throughout the years.

Initially, clean-room and calibration facilities for the development of inertial sensors and systems were built in the VSSC campus. Clean-rooms are enclosed spaces with access-restriction, where a high level of cleanliness is ensured by eliminating dust particles. They are essential for assembling high-precision components. When the demand for inertial systems increased, a separate unit called the ISRO Inertial Systems Unit (IISU) was set up in the Vattiyoorkavu campus, near Thiruvananthapuram. World-class facilities to develop state-of-the-art sensors were established there as the first of their kind in the country. The IISU has evolved as the birthplace of many advanced technologies like laser gyroscopes, micro-machined components and quartz accelerometers.

THE COMPUTERS

Finalizing the configuration of the on-board computers, which constitute the brain of the launch vehicle, was really tough. There were many options in front of us, starting with having a single unit for all the functions to the extreme idea of using quad-redundant units as in the USA's Space Shuttle.

We had used digital on-board computers first for the ASLV. The avionics group at the VSSC developed the computer systems to meet the stringent requirements of computing for the mission management of launch vehicles. Due to the very harsh import-related controls and embargoes, we only got very basic models of 8-bit microprocessors of the Motorola 6800 series. We developed a computer based on this chip using magnetic core memory and a hard-wired multiplication unit, which was then used for the autonomous digital control of the flight path and orientation of the launch vehicle. Due to capacity limitations, three computer units were used to implement the navigation, guidance and control functions for mission management. This configuration had the limitation that if any one of the units failed during the mission, it would result in a catastrophe.

A more robust configuration was evolved for the PSLV by adopting a cross-strapped redundant configuration. Here, the computational load was shared by three computers connected in series, and each unit had a redundant unit carrying out the same function simultaneously. Cross-linking the outputs between the prime and redundant chains ensured a successful mission even if any of the units failed.[1] This scheme, named as a series-parallel redundant cross-strapped system, was a unique technique developed for the PSLV. I am happy that I could guide the teams in this sophisticated area for the initial three years as head of the electronics division at the VSSC.

[1]Three computers connected in series were used in order to carry out navigation, guidance, control and sequencing functions, and made up the 'prime' chain. Similar three computers connected in series formed the 'redundant' chain. Cross-linking between the chains enabled the sharing of intermediate data. This was done to avoid the possibility of single-point failure.

Though the computer system was flight tested for the ASLV, the computational load and performance requirement for the PSLV were higher. The hardware interfaces and real-time software posed great challenges. Back then, 16-bit microprocessor chips were just coming out in the international market. We took the bold decision to build the on-board computers around such commercial chips. Concurrently, efforts were mounted at the VSSC to develop a microprocessor chip in-house. That effort finally culminated in an indigenous chip called Vikram, which is now being used for the PSLV and GSLV. D. Basu led the team, and T.R. Chidambaram, with whom I was associated right from the SLV times, served as my right-hand man for this activity. He was appointed as the chief advisor to the design team.

Designs were made using commercial components available in the market and screened in elaborate facilities. Each component and subsystem was tested extensively for performance and quality. Tests were also conducted under simulated environments of vibration, temperature, vacuum, etc., which would be encountered during flight.

SIMULATION, TEST FACILITIES AND OTHER SYSTEMS

Launch vehicle designers need precise information about the rocket's travel to space. Simulations of the rocket's flight based on the thrust, instantaneous mass, aerodynamic disturbances, etc., are carried out on ground computers to predict the trajectory. In the early 1970s, only limited facilities were available at the VSSC for the development of simulation test-beds and software. We had to be satisfied with 3D models at first, that is, the linear movement of the rocket in three mutually perpendicular directions. Such a simulation must capture the motion of the centre of gravity of the rocket as well, taking into account the thrust and other aerodynamic parameters acting on the vehicle.

To start with, a first-generation Russian-made tele-type computer at TERLS was used for such simulations. The system was used for the trajectory computation of sounding rockets. During the SLV-3, efforts were made to develop a simulation software that can capture not only the motion of the centre of gravity but also the angular movements of the rocket. Such an integrated model capturing motion in three directions helps assess the performance more precisely.

A more powerful and high-speed computer was required to solve the multiple equations of motion simultaneously, using the Fortran programming language. The VSSC scientists collaborated with experts at the TIFR to develop such a software, and ran it on a powerful IBM System/360 computer there. A few years later, the VSSC acquired an IBM System/360 computer of its own for such simulations. The software was enhanced by including more parameters like the dynamics of the control systems, disturbances due to wind, efficiency of the rocket motors, performance of the actuators and so on. This simulation software has since been extensively used for the PSLV and GSLV missions. The development efforts were initially led by Dr D.S. Rane, Dr R.M. Vasagom and Dr T.S. Prahlad, and the software was later perfected under Dr V. Adimurthy.

Unlike the ASLV, which used only solid propellants, the PSLV used a combination of solid and liquid engines. Several new features like pogo and slosh control had to be added. Pogo effect is the thrust modulation caused by oscillations in the engine due to liquid movement and the structural response; slosh is caused by the free movement of liquid propellants in the tanks and causes large disturbances to the attitude control. These effects make attitude control of the rocket more difficult. All these issues were systematically addressed through theoretical models and experimental verification by experts from the fields of fluid dynamics, structural dynamics and control systems.

The total control system for the rocket was also modernized using digital technology. The bold decision to move to a digital autopilot was taken at a time when the launch vehicles of major space powers like the Soviet Union, Europe and the USA still used analogue. But digital systems allowed complex algorithms to be implemented flexibly and make corrections to solve problems fast, without changing the hardware.

Developing the mission-control algorithm to manage the flight of the PSLV posed many challenges. Different schemes were discussed and tested using 6D trajectory simulation software. Finally, a novel control-and-guidance algorithm compatible with solid and liquid rockets used in alternate stages was developed for the PSLV. All the successful missions that could inject satellites into precise orbits stand testimony to the strength of that algorithm in later years. A modified version of the same software was used later in the GSLV missions as well.

A wind-tunnel test facility is required to determine the aerodynamic characteristics of a launch vehicle. The facility at the National Aerospace Laboratories (NAL) had been originally set up for aircraft and tests could only be done at speed up to three times that of sound. Launch vehicles typically achieve six times the speed of sound before leaving the atmosphere. Hence, the NAL facility had to be augmented to meet the PSLV's requirements. After the modifications, numerous tests were carried out at the NAL facilities before finalizing the aerodynamic parameters of the PSLV. Both the PSLV and GSLV models were tested there. The models, especially the GSLV, were also taken to laboratories in the Soviet Union for comparing and confirming various parameters.

Dependence on external resources for critical tests caused considerable delays. As the requirement for such testing was increased, I decided later, as the chairman of ISRO, to set up a modern hypersonic wind-tunnel facility at the VSSC to test models starting from low speeds up to 12 times the speed of sound. When a rocket moves up with such speed, a lot of heat energy is generated, raising the temperature of the exposed parts. Thus, the facility was to have the provision to simulate the heating too, up to 1,700°C. No support was forthcoming from other countries in setting up the facility, since it can also be used for testing missiles and space capsules re-entering the Earth from orbits. A small team of scientists led by Dr A.N. Subash and Dr S. Pandian designed all the necessary subsystems. Larsen & Toubro was our industrial partner. Though the work started in 2008, the facility became fully operational only by 2017. It is the third-largest hypersonic test facility in the world. It gives me immense satisfaction and happiness to think that this facility is sufficient to cater to all types of high enthalpy aero-thermodynamic tests that we may need for many years to come, including those for human spaceflight missions.

Coming back to the PSLV, the various electronic systems inside the rocket were assembled within small volumes, and interference between the various signals used was common. Many innovations had to be tried out to prevent the electromagnetic interferences. A team of young engineers under N. Narayanamoorthy worked day and night to rectify all the issues. V.P. Sandlas, project director for the SLV-3 continuation flights, and Dr M.Y.S. Prasad, who later became the director of the SHAR centre, were the pioneers of electromagnetic interference studies at ISRO. Special facilities were set up at the VSSC for measuring electromagnetic radiation and the effect on sensitive packages.

Thousands of parameters corresponding to the trajectory as well as the performance of each of the stages and subsystems during the flight of the launch vehicle must be acquired through the ground stations using telemetry tracking and command systems. Numerous sensors are mounted in each stage of the rocket for collecting the performance parameters. A central control unit in the EB integrates the data from various acquisition units and sends it to the ground using S-band transmitters. V.P. Sandlas, P. Anguswamy and U.S. Singh played crucial roles in this area. New telemetry stations were established at different locations at the launch site and along the path of the flight for receiving the signals. The ISRO Telemetry, Tracking and Command Network (ISTRAC) team led by K.V. Venkatachary was responsible for setting up the ground stations following international standards. He had joined TERLS along with me and had been moulded by R. Aravamudan.

Precision-tracking radars were established in the ground stations to follow the rocket in its flight independently. Aravamudan, leading a multidisciplinary team, took the initiative to develop the tracking radars indigenously since the technology was unavailable. The development efforts begun inside the old church building in Thumba led to the commissioning of C-band radar at TERLS and two more in Sriharikota. The technology was subsequently transferred to Bharat Electronics Limited (BEL). A wide network of telemetry and tracking systems was deployed to closely monitor the flight performance of the PSLV.

Facilities were set up to abort the launch in case of any dangerous deviation during the flight. This operation requires a telecommand system. The system I had developed for SLV-3 was still operational. Only its power level needed to be increased to cater to longer-range operations.

The data processing and display systems established at the SHAR were innovative and matched up to any modern launch centre in the world. A NASA team that visited Sriharikota was surprised to see the modern facilities there. Their own facilities were at least 20 years old!

DEVELOPMENT ROUTE WITH FACILITY SETUP AND INDUSTRIES

When work for the PSLV began, we did not possess the required laboratories or facilities. Hence, the first laborious task was developing these, such as the ISRO Inertial Systems Laboratory, which later evolved into an independent unit (the IISU), solid propellant plants, a mobile vertical integration facility for rocket integration, facilities to test liquid rocket engines, simulation setups, etc. All these were conceived and realized indigenously for the first time.

Right from the beginning, ISRO had adopted a policy of partnering with industries involved in manufacturing structures, chemicals, electronics, etc., and guiding them to achieve excellence. This practice was maximized for the PSLV project. We tried to make maximum use of the industrial resources already available, and in cases where they were not, new facilities were set up at the project's cost. In-house facilities were established only for critical technologies.

As briefly mentioned earlier, the VSSC took the initiative to develop materials like maraging steel and titanium alloys in collaboration with MIDHANI. Mishra Dhatu Nigam evolved as a major source for metals for all missions of our space programme, and the materials were successfully produced in large quantities. Balco Industries also contributed to developing aerospace-grade aluminium alloys for our launch vehicles.

Indigenous material development was indeed a major factor in making our space programme self-reliant. Dr P.P. Sinha was its doyen at ISRO. Very sophisticated alloys of steel, aluminium and titanium were developed under his leadership. The materials group set up by Dr Mukherji at the VSSC was the prime mover for developing these materials.

Propellant ingredients were another area in which industrial support was required. There were not many industries that could take up the production of ingredients for solid propellants in India back then. A plant to produce ammonium perchlorate, one of the important constituents of our solid propellant, was established at Aluva with the cooperation of the Central Electro Chemical Research Institute (CECRI) in Karaikudi. The HTPB-based propellant was developed by the in-house chemical group, and a pilot plant was set up in Thumba. Then the production was transferred to Andhra Sugars Limited, which produced fuels like unsymmetrical dimethylhydrazine (UDMH) and monomethyl hydrazine (MMH) for liquid rockets as well. N_2O_4 of high purity, an essential requirement as oxidizer for liquid rockets, was obtained from Hindustan Organic Chemicals Limited at Mumbai. Capabilities were established in all these industries for the production of space-grade products in the required quantities. K. Sitarama Sastri, Dr V.N. Krishnamurthy, Srinivasa Shetty, Dr Natarajan, Dr K.V. Ninan and others were responsible for developing the HTPB-based propellant and organizing the production. Dr Ninan and team developed a large variety of polymer compounds and organized the reliability and quality assurance set-up in the chemical area.

Synthesis and production of solid propellants was done by using in-house facilities since it would be dangerous if the technology fell into wrong hands. The Rocket Propellant Plant (RPP), established by M.R. Kurup at TERLS could make propellants needed for the SLV-3, which had a rocket with a 1-m diameter. Back then, only a 100-ton plant was needed. At this juncture, the vision of Dr V.R. Gowarikar has to be lauded. He foresaw the future need for larger diameter solid motors and established a facility that can handle up to 500 tons of propellant on the island of Sriharikota. The location was selected mainly because a large isolated area was available to ensure adequate safety while handling huge quantities of propellant. P.D. Majumdar and M.C. Uttam played key roles in establishing the facility. This plant was to become very important in the PSLV's development.

Later, when I was the chairman of ISRO, the green signal was given for a new 1,000-ton plant, the biggest in Asia. It was to meet the requirements for the GSLV and beyond. The challenge of setting up such a large plant with automated handling facilities and safety equipment was taken up by M.C. Dathan, who had to make several personal sacrifices in the process. Dathan became the director of the SHAR and, later, of the VSSC.

A major constraint during the PSLV's development was the lack of fabrication and test facilities for the 2.8-m-diameter hardware of the first stage. The SLV-3 and ASLV hardware, as mentioned earlier, measured 1 m in diameter, and, hence, the propellant casting, integration and test facilities available were also suited to that measurement. The new motor case with 2.8-m diameter needed machining and welded fixtures. Two companies, namely, Larsen & Toubro and Walchandnagar Industries, had suitable machining centres. They had the experience of producing 15CDV6 motor cases for the SLV-3 and ASLV too. Naturally, they were selected to undertake the required tasks, based on technology transferred from the VSSC.

As explained earlier, the 2.8-m-class motors for the first stage had to be made with maraging steel. The required facilities had to be newly set up at these industries. Maraging steel is a brittle material—even a minute crack can lead to a catastrophic failure. Special ultrasonic testing equipment was needed to detect even minute cracks. The VSSC worked with industries to set up the necessary X-ray and ultrasound equipment as well as to develop the techniques to interpret the data. These industries continued to manufacture maraging steel motor cases for the various PSLV and GSLV missions. Later, the facilities were augmented to take up even the 3.8-m-diameter motors needed for the GSLV. A.V. Hanumantha Rao, under the guidance of D. Eswaradas, contributed a lot to help develop these industries to adhere to space quality standards.

The metallic nozzles for all the stages were fabricated in industries. The processes of developing the inner thermal protection lining using carbon phenolic composite material, curing at high pressure and machining to the required contour were carried out at the in-house composite facility. Then the complex operations of lining the motor case with insulation and filling of propellant began. The special vacuum-casting facility ensured that there were no voids and air entrapment. Once that was done, the motor cases were cured at high temperatures and inspected to ensure integrity. The high-power neutron radiographic equipment used for detecting any defect was developed by the BARC along with the TIFR.

By coordinating all these efforts, segments for the first stage started coming from the industries. We were thrilled to see the five segments flawlessly assembled in a vertical assembly facility, taking care to ensure that the joints were sealed and then tilting to a horizontal position. The finished motor, nearly 30-m long and weighing 130 tons, was transported in a special trailer with a dozen axles moving like a caterpillar. The motor was then moved to a special test stand.

STAGE MOTORS AND STATIC TESTS

Rocket-motor performance is verified through static tests—tests conducted after anchoring the motors firmly to the ground. The motor being tested will be heavily instrumented for collecting data on various performance parameters for validating the propulsion as well as the structural and thermal designs.

Unlike other flight systems, rocket motors for different stages cannot be tested before flight clearance. The motors are not reusable. Hence, test sequences needed to be worked out to evaluate on ground the performance of motors identical to the flight units. Limited funds and time meant that only a limited number of tests were possible. Elaborate quality control and inspection processes were implemented for the flight motors to ensure the quality of the units manufactured.

Testing the PSLV's first stage with 125 tons of propellant needed a large facility to ensure safety. The SHAR was the obvious choice. Normally, such motors are anchored to the ground horizontally, with freedom for longitudinal movement, so that rocket thrust during the test can be precisely measured. However, since the first stage used a TVC system, the lateral forces needed to be measured too. Hence, a cradle-like structure in which the motor could be suspended, facilitating the measurement of forces in the pitch, yaw and roll directions (called the six-component test), was designed and developed.

The first-stage motor of the PSLV was finally static tested on 21 October 1989. A major milestone in the history of the Indian rocket programme! The performance was as predicted, and we were all overwhelmed with the success. Most of the systems worked as expected with some minor deviations. Based on the test feedback, some design modifications were made and the test was repeated successfully on 23 March 1991. The TVC system performed well, proving the design concepts and providing valuable inputs for the autopilot. Later, based on observations during the actual flight, the rocket underwent further optimizations, like reducing the wall thickness, increasing the propellant loading, etc. This followed the ISRO philosophy of making a conservative design initially to ensure reliability and then subsequently optimizing it based on mission performance.

Regarding the second-stage Vikas engine developed along the lines of the French Viking engine, individual parts and components were evaluated before integration in the new integration facility at Mahendragiri, Tamil Nadu. Finally, two integrated engines were ready by 1985. But our test facility was not yet ready. Hence, it was decided to take these engines to France for testing through a contract with the SEP, the liquid engine-development facility in Vernon, France. The engines performed extremely well and even the French experts applauded the success of the ISRO team's maiden efforts. Later, four more engines were tested at the vertical test facility specially developed for the purpose in Mahendragiri.

Establishing test facilities for the liquid engines needed quite a major effort. The Vikas engine uses chemicals such as UDMH and N_2O_4 as propellants, both of which are hypergolic and dangerously toxic. Static tests of such engines can be conducted only in uninhabited places. Hence, it was decided to set up the necessary test facilities in Mahendragiri, where large areas were available, away from habitation. Unlike solid rockets, which are tested in the horizontal condition, the large liquid engines must be mounted vertically for static testing. Creating a huge structure where the second stage could be suspended to withstand an upward thrust of 60 tons was arduous. Additionally, building storage tanks for large quantities of N_2O_4 and UDMH propellant and pumping them into the engine at the required pressure were difficult tasks. The principal test stand in Mahendragiri was commissioned in 1988, and all our Vikas engines and stages were subjected to full duration tests there. The fourth-stage engine had to be qualified for vacuum conditions along with a full-length nozzle. A huge vacuum chamber connected with a long ejection tube, which can ensure high vacuum around the engine, was created. The LPSC teams designed the liquid engine test facilities, and the fabrication was subcontracted to industries like FACT, Oil and Natural Gas Corporation (ONGC), NOCIL, etc.

Elaborate instrumentation was built in all the test beds for both solid and liquid motors. The test article was provided with close to 500 channels of measurement along with an equal number in the support facilities. Fully computerized data-logging systems, which were operated remotely, were established in all the test stands. Additionally, the command and control systems to operate the test sequences to ensure safety were also built and integrated. The enormous instrumentation allowed the qualification of our rockets with minimum tests.

The Vikas engine development was nearing completion. All systems necessary for readying the second stage of the PSLV with the engine had to be realized by us. The design of the tank to contain the corrosive fluids was completed by the LPSC team. Since the materials required weren't available in the country, it was decided to import a few tanks from Air Liquide in France, which had manufactured similar tanks for the Ariane programme. The tanks were realized on time and our engineers also obtained exposure to the entire fabrication technique.

As Hindustan Aeronautics Limited (HAL) had experience in fabrication using aluminium and composites for aircraft, the fabrication of these tanks for the PSLV was subcontracted to them. Though they were specialists in riveted aluminium alloy structures, they had no experience in welding using the special alloy. Initially, HAL was reluctant to undertake the work. But they agreed under the guarantee that ISRO would handhold them in the initial stages. A new facility was set up at the aerospace division at HAL in Bengaluru and was funded by the PSLV project. Together, HAL and ISRO carried out the design and realization of the facility. It later evolved into a major facility and became capable of fabricating most of the vehicle systems needed for the PSLV. Subsequently, it undertook the fabrication of the liquid stages for the PSLV and GSLV and also the cryogenic tanks required for the GSLV. Now the facility has been further augmented to integrate liquid rocket stages, with engines being supplied from other industries.

Several private companies like Godrej and MTAR and many small-scale industries played significant roles in the fabrication of the various engine parts needed for the Vikas engine. Initially, some parts were imported but they too were indigenized under the leadership of M.K.G. Nair.

After many verification trials and tests on individual components and the engine, the flight version of the second stage was finally fully realized, and two integrated tests were conducted in Mahendragiri. Every minute detail of the engine performance was monitored. The clearance for the flight stage was given only after confirming satisfactory performance.

Vikas—the liquid rocket engine developed for the PSLV—continues to be the largest in the country even today. It has proved to be a real asset for ISRO and is widely used not only in the PSLV but also in all variants of the GSLV. S. Nambinarayanan and his team were responsible for this commendable achievement.

FAILURE AND COURSE CORRECTION

The third-stage development had to overcome several hurdles. The motor case with Kevlar fibre and metallic interfaces showed differential expansion under a variation of temperature and pressure, which could be deciphered only after extensive tests and analyses using the FEAST software. The flex nozzle needed for the motor was being developed for the first time. Everything had to start from scratch. Our team with Rajaram Nagappa, Dr Radhamohan and Rajmohan struggled for several months.

The stage needed to be tested not only with respect to the thrust generated. Its capability to ignite in vacuum as well as the integrity of the nozzle for operating under high-altitude conditions had to be verified. A special high-altitude facility, integrating a huge vacuum chamber connected to an ejector tube, was installed at the SHAR for this purpose.

The first test failed. When the second test also failed, Professor U.R. Rao, who was closely monitoring the activities, wanted us to reconsider the development of an optimized solid stage and wanted to pursue the option of a single liquid stage replacing the third and fourth stages. We had earlier conducted a feasibility study of that option but had then dropped the idea since it entailed developing one more liquid engine of 3-ton thrust, which was risky and time-consuming. After quickly assessing the reasons for the failure, I assured Professor Rao that we would solve the problem within three months. Expansions of the Kevlar case and its metallic interfaces are dissimilar at high temperatures, and that was the primary reason for the hot gas leaking from the burning propellant. After extensive thermo structural analysis, the interface dimensions were modified. Additionally, an excellent idea from one of the technicians—adopting a self-correcting hot gas leak-sealing mechanism similar to the one used in domestic pressure cookers—was incorporated. The problem was solved once and for all! Five more tests were conducted to confirm the design adequacy, vacuum ignition, normal engine performance and high-altitude performance. Thanks to all these trials, the third stage has performed precisely in all the flights so far, emerging as one of the most reliable solid rocket stages in the world.

Modifying the 600-kg thruster, originally conceived as a roll control motor for the first stage, to a high-performance upper-stage liquid engine with maximum efficiency and the least weight was equally involved as the development of the third stage had been. Realizing a metallic nozzle extension that can withstand extreme temperatures of nearly 1,000°C was tough, but we were lucky to find some sheets of a suitable special niobium (known previously as columbium) alloy imported from the USA for our satellite programme. Those sheets came in handy for the initial development. Concurrently, our VSSC team worked with MIDHANI to synthesize the material indigenously. However, all sophisticated machines from various industries could not shape the material into the complex-contoured nozzle. Finally, a small firm of blacksmiths succeeded in carrying out what was required. Even today, the process is their close-held secret.

DEVELOPING FURTHER INDIGENOUS CAPABILITIES

Once our high-altitude test facility was ready, the fourth-stage engines were tested for several thousand seconds and the fourth stage with the twin engines was tested twice.

In addition to the rocket motors, a large number of subsystems and modules, such as the pulse-code modulation telemetry, C-band transponder, igniters, heat shield, etc., were being developed in parallel. Since several of these systems were not testable before the flight, sufficient tests on each module had to be worked out. The necessary environmental tests in hot and cold temperatures, for vibration and acoustics, and at high-altitude vacuum were also conducted. Special facilities were built to simulate various environmental conditions.

One of the complex facilities needed was to characterize the integrated full-scale rocket motor for the first stage. The nearly 30-m-long stage, weighing almost 130 tons, had to be floated on hydraulic bearings and excited with small electro-mechanical actuators at 20 locations along the length, with the response measured to determine the structural modes. Ideally, the whole vehicle should have been suspended during such measurements. But due to the physical limitations, the tests for the first stage were conducted separately and for the remaining stages together as a completed assembly. S.A. Palaniswamy and G. Muthuraman played crucial roles in realizing these systems.

A special drop test facility was designed and built by the Aerospace Mechanisms Group (ASMG) team for testing aerospace mechanisms, where zero-gravity conditions could be simulated for about two seconds. Separation tests of the heat shield and the various inter-stages were conducted there. It was another example where experts from different fields worked together to perfect a complex system.

Rocket hardware of large diameters could not be integrated at the Thumba complex. Hence, facilities for mechanical integration, electrical integration and checkout systems were established at Valiamala. One assembly bay was made for mechanical activities and another for electrical integration and testing. The latter was fully air-conditioned to maintain a clean environment for handling the delicate electronic assemblies and control systems.

The rocket motors are connected mechanically through inter-stage structures mounted with several electronic modules, pyro devices and control components. After acceptance tests, such modules were integrated into the inter-stages at the Valiamala facilities, and this was followed by integrated tests, including tests for withstanding vibration and shock. In fact, much of the equipment needed were not available from the USA due to embargos. Massive efforts were mounted to design and develop them locally. Finally, a system capable of simulating vibration levels in the range of 20–2,000 Hz on the test assemblies weighing up to 2 tons was developed by a team led by Palaniswamy and Muthuraman. Later, similar equipment was industrially manufactured as per ISRO's design and supplied to several strategic users in the country.

The most complex subassembly made was the EB, which was mounted around the fourth stage. It is literally the brain of the vehicle and houses various sensitive instruments like accelerometers, gyroscopes and computers for autonomous mission management, along with monitoring instrumentation, telemetry transmitters, transponders for tracking and the telecommand system. These are powered by a set of rechargeable silver-zinc batteries. Redundant power packs were provided for critical functions. Several problems related to interface and electromagnetic interference occurred initially, which were resolved with time and effort.

Finally, the entire assembly was tested in a simulated flight environment of vibration, shock and temperature. Three models of the EB were made—first an engineering model, followed by a qualification model and then the flight assembly. The EB for every mission must be tested for performance as well as for withstanding the necessary environmental conditions to ensure the reliability of the system for flight.

During the overall performance evaluation, a completely computerized checkout system, identical to the one at the launch pad, was used. This allowed us to validate the checkout system and software. The EB was connected to the inter-stages using harnesses identical to those used in the flight assembly. The entire vehicle checkout and countdown sequences were exercised several times. Afterwards, the EB and flight assemblies were subjected to environmental tests.

The EB is mounted on top of the fourth stage. Hence, the flight model of the fourth stage, with the EB integrated on it, was subjected to hot tests in Mahendragiri.

These development and qualification programmes took several years, mainly because the required facilities for the assembly and testing were being built in parallel. It was only by 1988 that all the required facilities for undertaking qualification tests of the rocket motors and subsystems were commissioned.

Bharat Electronics undertook the development of the avionics systems, though ultimately, it was not very successful. Today, some private agencies and Kelton provide support in fabricating electronic subsystems as per ISRO's designs.

The development of fluid-control system elements like valves, regulators and actuators also needed new facilities. These had been developed in small laboratories and temporary sheds on the Veli Hills for SLV-3. Sridharan Dhas, with only the experience of brief visits to the world-class facility of Moog in the USA in early 1970s, was the pioneer in this field. His ability to quickly grasp new technologies and use them practically led to the realization of fluid-control systems for solid rockets as well as unique and sophisticated control components for spacecraft and cryogenic engines. Various additions to the high-quality engineering labs and cleanrooms in Valiamala were made periodically, and today it has become a world-class facility, meeting the requirements of all our launch vehicles and satellites, thanks to the dedication and hard work by Dhas and his team. He has always been a good friend and colleague to me.

Efforts were made to subcontract the production of precision-fabricated parts to machine tool-manufacturing industries for control components and actuators in large quantities. The task was distributed among many small-scale industries in the country. Around 150 companies became ISRO partners in this area.

The uniquely complex tasks of the assembly and evaluation of hydraulic and electrical actuators for the second, third and fourth stages were carried out by the VSSC led by Dr B.N. Suresh. He is the designer of all the control and guidance algorithms used in ISRO's launch vehicles. His contributions to the development of control and guidance systems as well as for the overall review of launch vehicles are commendable. He served as the project director for the guidance and control systems for the PSLV and then as the director of the VSSC. He was the first director of the Indian Institute of Space Science and Technology (IIST), Thiruvananthapuram, and is now its chancellor.

Major effort was required to establish facilities for the integration, test and launch in Sriharikota. The assembly hall built during the time of SLV-3 could be used for the integration of strap-on motors, which were transferred directly to the launch pad. Integration of the first stage with assembly of the segments was carried out on the launch tower. The second and fourth stages were integrated in Mahendragiri before the final acceptance tests. The stages were then transported to Sriharikota. Integration of the third stage with the fourth required additional safety precautions due to the presence of live propellant in the third stage. A separate assembly hall with air conditioning and all safety features for propellant handling was built close to the launch pad for this purpose. The EB was integrated along with the fourth stage.

The control centre built for the ASLV was modified and new checkout terminals and large display systems were set up. While the control centre was located nearly 7 km away from the launch pad, a terminal room was built close to the launch pad for providing interface to the vehicle through umbilical cables. A data acquisition and command computer installed there communicated with the control centre through dedicated high-speed cables.

Establishing production facilities in-house and in industries, while enforcing stringent quality control, is not an easy task. Today, the fruits of those labours are being enjoyed by the country. Many of those industries are able to obtain international contracts as well.

A major part of the budget allocated to the project was spent in developing technology and establishing facilities. The remaining funds were hardly sufficient for making the expensive subsystems, namely, the development and engineering models, the qualification models used in subsystem-level tests and the units required for ground tests of the rockets. The only option was to optimize the number of models for the ground tests. Two full-scale tests were conducted on the first-stage solid motor, three full-duration tests on the second-stage liquid engine and six tests each on the third and fourth stages. This number was much lower than in other development agencies. In spite of this, the elaborate instrumentation set-up made for collecting details about the test performance and systematically comparing the data with the designed parameters helped us build confidence and validate the design and performance. The quality assurance team carried out an analysis based on the number of tests, and the overall system's demonstrated reliability computed for the launch was less than 20 per cent. However, our robust review mechanism gave us the confidence to proceed.

Open technical reviews are the main contributor for success at ISRO. After each stage of development tests, exhaustive reviews are conducted. To provide continuity, the review team remains the same, whether it is for reviewing the concept, preliminary design, critical design or final readiness of the subsystem for the mission. An integrated mission review is conducted at the final stage.

After the qualification tests and extensive review of the test results, clearance was given for preparing the flight systems. They soon started arriving at the integration facilities in Valiamala, Mahendragiri and Sriharikota.

With the assurance and confidence given by the various review teams, we decided to proceed with the first launch of the PSLV in early 1993.

14

The Last Lap and Beyond

Integration and testing of ISRO's rocket systems initially took place in Valiamala, except solid motors, which were integrated in Sriharikota, and liquid stages in Mahendragiri. After successful tests, all the subsystems were brought to the vehicle assembly building (VAB) at the SHAR.

The launch campaign starts with the arrival of the rocket motors and other subassemblies like the EB, control systems and heat shield at the VAB. The safety and health of each subassembly needs to be ensured when they arrive at the VAB and during integration. The subassemblies are connected to each other electrically, and integrated tests on the vehicle as a whole are carried out. After that, each subassembly is placed on the launch pad vertically one above the other in the required sequence to realize the whole vehicle.

Monitoring of all relevant parameters of the vehicle subsystems is interfaced to the ground checkout system, using a set of umbilical cables. The data acquired has to be analysed, and various control commands must be issued as per the predetermined time sequence using the checkout system before the launch. Such operations were tried out first for the ASLV. The activities would last for several weeks.

To protect the PSLV vehicle systems from the vagaries of weather, a huge steel tower, nearly 45-m tall and weighing about 3,000 tons, was built. The tower had air conditioning and modern lift facilities inside. The topmost section was provided with a clean-room to handle the spacecraft, which may contain sensitive optics and electronics. This building, called MST, was mounted on wheels, so that it could be moved away after completing the assembly, leaving the vehicle open for the launch. This unique set-up was the largest of its kind in India. People used to call it the biggest chariot in the country, as it could move!

INTEGRATION: MORE THAN AN ASSEMBLY OF PARTS

The integration of the PSLV starts with placing the base shroud on the launch pedestal. Then the five segments of the first stage are integrated one above the other. The preparation of segments and sealing are done with extreme care. Then the TVC tanks and strap-on motors are attached around the first stage. After that, the integrated second stage is brought in. Subsequently, the third and fourth stages are assembled along with the EB in the VAB and integrated as a composite over the second stage. All the pyros are then installed and cabling completed.

Once all the stages are integrated, the health of the vehicle as a whole is verified. If everything is normal, permission is given to integrate the satellite on top of the last stage. The heat shield is brought in two halves, placed around the spacecraft and assembled together using explosive-actuated bolts. In the first PSLV mission, called PSLV-D1, it took about 60 days to complete all these operations.

During the launch of SLV-3, these activities were controlled from a block-house, a few hundred metres away from the launch pad. All the required persons worked inside the safety of the blast-proof block-house during the launch. Since the PSLV propellant quantity was nearly 20 times bigger, this concept was not feasible. Safe distance during the final phase of the launch was computed to be 7 km. Hence, a new configuration was evolved.

A terminal building was set up close to the launch pad, physically connected to the rocket through umbilical cables. Systems for data acquisition and commanding were kept in the terminal building, which were digitally connected to the control centre 7 km away.

Development of the computerized checkout systems, configured for remote unattended real-time operations in the terminal building, was a challenge. Computers had just arrived in the country back then, and that too mainly for scientific calculations. No ready reference was available for the real-time computing and control necessary to ensure precision and speed. The configuration of the checkout system network conceived by John P. Zachariah, G. Raveendranath and Dr R. Vikraman Nair impressed even the visiting foreign specialists. Zachariah led the team for checkout system development for both the PSLV and GSLV. Such systems were then only in the process of being deployed even in developed countries. P.S. Veeraraghavan, who later retired as the director of the VSSC, did a tremendous job integrating all the activities of vehicle assembly, checkout and launch operations with his tireless efforts and innovative ideas.

During the countdown leading to the launch, a large number of launch vehicle parameters are observed and verified as being within limits. This is even more crucial during the process of filling hazardous liquid fuels and high-pressure gases into the rocket structures. The control systems in the vehicle must be subjected to tests to confirm proper functioning before launch. Drift parameters of the inertial system have to be calculated and must be uploaded to the on-board computers. Verifying the safety criteria, pressurizing the liquid stages and checking the sequencing circuits are among the other critical operations to be completed on schedule. Adherence to safety precautions must be ensured at all times. In case of any deviation or shortcoming, the operations have to be suspended and the countdown stopped. Implementing all these in real time, especially during the last 10 minutes, are carried out through a chain of computer networks.

The PSLV set-up was a hundred times more complex than that of SLV-3. Experts with deep knowledge about each system were observing the parameters from individual consoles during the various phases of the launch preparations. But during the last 10 minutes, thousands of parameters must be monitored and more than a hundred commands are to be issued and confirmed. Hence, the operations in the last 10 minutes were left entirely to the computers. Only the mission director was authorized to stop the countdown in case of an emergency.

All these operations for PSLV-D1 were completed by mid-September 1993. After thorough reviews of the tests results by experts in the Mission Readiness Review Committee and a comprehensive review by the Launch Authorisation Board (LAB), the final clearance was given. The launch sequence was initiated as per the countdown schedule. We were concerned about the weather in Sriharikota, as it would usually be fraught with cyclones, thundershowers and lightning during October–November, and September was a transition time. Still, we decided to start the final countdown.

Everything progressed as planned. But on the day before the launch, certain errors were found in a safe-arm plug—a system used to ensure the safety of the electrical instruments and pyro systems in the rocket. We could have ignored the errors since that system was not required during the launch, but we decided to rectify it before proceeding with the countdown.

LAUNCH

Early on the day of the launch, 20 September 1993, I visited the temple, mosque and church within the SHAR complex before taking my seat at the control centre. The subsequent three hours were a nightmare. All possible modes of failure were flashing through my mind. It was difficult to concentrate on the screen showing the progress of the countdown and data about the performance of each subsystem. Half the time, I was silently praying that nothing should go wrong. Fifteen minutes before the launch, the status of all subsystems changed to green. Status of all the ground stations was also clear. At last, the final moment arrived.

I turned the key authorizing the launch sequence and the last-minute operations by the computerized checkout system.

All the operations proceeded in an unbelievably smooth manner. It triggered a small sense of concern in my mind. My previous experiences had led me to coin a theory. The number of problems is a constant. If none are encountered during the preparation stage, then the issues may strike us during the flight.

Finally, the ignition command for the first stage was issued at 10.42 a.m. The first stage ignited and started its upward journey with a thunderous roar. The rocket rose majestically from the launch pad, leaving a trail of fire and smoke behind, tearing into the skies like an arrow spitting fire. It was an unforgettable sight. In a few seconds, the vehicle became masked by clouds. I did not have the opportunity to see this sight directly but saw it through the CCTV images in the control room.

The displays on the giant screens in the control centre were not as extensive as they are today. Different panels displayed important parameters as the fight progressed. The first panel showed the overall performance of the vehicle—parameters like its altitude, range, velocity, etc. The next one showed the major events during the flight. The panels in front of the executives showed the status of the critical parameters of their respective subsystems.

About 100 seconds into the flight, we could see that the first stage had completed its burn, both through the displays in the control room as well as through the display in the first-stage subsystem console. The second stage was initiated as planned and the vehicle was following exactly the path required. Everything continued to be normal until the second stage burn was completed.

The second stage then got detached as per the plan. Based on a real-time decision-making algorithm, the on-board computer gave the command for the ignition of the third stage. The rocket had by then reached beyond the atmospheric limits and was at an altitude of 250 km. We saw an increase in pressure in the third-stage motor as shown by the parameters listed in front of us and knew that the third stage had indeed ignited. However, within a few seconds, it became evident that something was wrong. Though the pressure–time curve confirmed normal performance, the vehicle was not gaining velocity as expected! Its orientation was not steady. It began a tumbling motion. The rocket's flight path started deviating. Just 500 seconds after the launch, the PSLV, along with the satellite, fell into the Bay of Bengal!

Just before impact, we observed the ignition of the fourth stage as well.

FAILURE AND THE AFTERMATH

I was devastated. The toil of nearly 3,000 people for 10 years had gone to waste. Everybody was speechless. I met my team members, who were anxiously waiting on the ground floor of the control centre. All the faces were sad, and a few of my colleagues were weeping. I kept my cool and tried my best to console them. Professor U.R. Rao tried to reassure me, but he, too, was very depressed. All the previous mission failures at ISRO flashed in my mind—the times when Professor Dhawan and Dr Kalam had met with failure during the first SLV-3 and when Dr M.S.R. Dev had suffered a roadblock during the ASLV flights. 'I too must face this, it is fate,' I told myself.

I reached the press gallery. Indian and foreign media were waiting anxiously. I didn't turn away. 'The mission has failed. All the subsystems worked well till the third-stage ignition. Although the rocket's performance was normal, we failed to move in the desired course. The reasons are not clear. We will have to analyse large volumes of data before we can pinpoint the reason for the failure, and we are starting the analysis immediately,' I told them.

Many questions were asked, including about the money spent. I answered them all. I explained how failures are not uncommon in space launches. The USA had failed three times before succeeding in a similar mission. Russia had tasted failure nine times. I assured them that we would identify the problems, rectify them and prepare for the next launch.

Only a broad picture of the performance was available at the control centre. After the press conference, K. Narayana, the range director at that time, took me to the range safety room. The elaborate parameter displays there served to support the range safety officer in the decision whether to allow the vehicle to fly. In this flight, during the third stage, the rocket had deviated widely from the desired path. Yet, the range safety officer had taken the bold decision to not give the command for destruction. Hence, the flight had continued, and even the fourth stage's ignition was confirmed before the rocket fell into the sea. Even though all the subsystems had performed normally, the satellite had failed to reach the orbit! What a tragedy! I couldn't control myself. I broke down, tears gushing out of my eyes, for the first and the last time in my official life.

The political leadership of the country trusted and supported us. They knew that ISRO was committed to its goals. Dr Kalam was the scientific advisor to the prime minister at that time. I immediately informed him about what had happened. He rushed to the launch site to be with us.

I used to visit the DRDO and meet Dr Kalam after every milestone during the PSLV's development. I would participate in the reviews of their missile development programme too. He would often praise me as the role model of a rocket systems engineer in front of his colleagues—a practice that would embarrass me greatly. We used to invite him to ISRO for important review meetings of the PSLV as well. After the PSLV launch failure, I met him in Chennai and we were driving to Sriharikota. I was explaining our first observations about the PSLV's failure to him when he suddenly asked the driver to stop the car. It was in front of the shop where we used to take tea on the way to the SHAR during the SLV-3 days. The shopkeeper recognized us and served his special tea as during the old days. Dr Kalam reminisced about his visit to Prime Minister Indira Gandhi after the SLV-3 success. He had neither a good coat nor suit and only had worn-out chappals on his feet for footwear! We had to get a shop to open at night in Chennai to buy a pair of shoes and a formal dress! While we were sharing old memories and sipping hot tea, Dr Kalam's security guards rushed in. They had not realized that we had stopped the car on the way, and they had gone 2–3 km ahead of us!

We reached the SHAR at almost midnight and Dr Kalam wanted to review the failure scenario immediately. We assembled several specialists who were fast asleep after many days of continuous work and presented the preliminary observations. He patiently listened and gave many valuable suggestions. He once again stressed the point that failures teach us more than successes.

His words gave us confidence to focus on the work ahead.

REVIEW: PINPOINTING THE ERROR

In spite of our disappointment, we pledged to recover from the setback. Professor Rao immediately set up a formal failure analysis committee, with the vice chairman of ISRO, Col N. Pant, as the chairman. Extensive reviews were conducted with the participation of experts from various ISRO centres and academic institutions. The reviews lasted nearly two months. The committee noted Dr Kalam's suggestions as well.

A lot of data from the on-board systems was available through telemetry within a short time after the launch. Many parameters were in analogue format, plotted on strip charts. Only a few were available in digital form. Reading each chart and converting the data into performance parameters was a herculean task. Subcommittees were entrusted with analysing the performance of each subsystem. Within a short span of time, the analyses were completed and reports were submitted.

The review committee held detailed discussions. No issue was found in the design of the vehicle subsystems. Even the performances of the third- and fourth-stage rockets were normal. The flight was quite normal until the third-stage ignition. Further investigations were initiated and simulations were carried out to recreate the events from that instant of the flight.

The primary reason was identified as loss of attitude control at the transition to the third stage. Several factors contributed in a strange combination to cause the failure. During the final phase of the vehicle integration, it was noticed that the actuators for the third-stage control had been assembled in the opposite direction. That was the starting point of the problems. That issue could have been solved in two ways. The actuators could have been pulled out and refixed in the correct direction. That would have needed several weeks of work and risked damaging the Kevlar composite motor case. The alternate suggestion was to make the corrections electronically through necessary changes in the control commands issued by the on-board computer, through changes in the software.

We had opted for the software change, which had seemed relatively simple on paper. The change had then been verified through digital simulation tests. However, when the solution had been finally implemented in the on-board control software, limitations posed by the 8-bit arithmetic of the microprocessor had not been taken into account. The most significant bit in the control command byte was taken to represent the direction of the command, and the remaining 7 bits for the magnitude. Nobody had realized the potential problem that could occur if, at any time, the magnitude of the error led to an overflow condition. In such a case, the direction could become erroneous.

There had been a particular period of no control during the transition between the second and third stages of the flight. The tail-off thrust in the second stage had caused large disturbances during the stage separation. The attitude error had increased during the short period of no control. The net result was that the magnitude of the error had become large and overflowed into the sign bit. This had reversed the direction of the corrective signal, leading to a positive feedback and the resultant tumbling of the vehicle.

Clearly, the failure had been caused by a strange combination of factors. If only any one of them had been absent, the flight would have succeeded. Later, the situation was simulated in a ground computer using the flight-observed condition of control transition to the third stage. The primary reason was the software implementation error in the on-board computer. If the control signals had been limited to 7 bits, the whole history of the Indian space programme would have been different. Sometimes, we think God is indeed playing with our lives.

REMEDIAL MEASURES

The quality control of software systems was evidently not as comprehensive as for other systems. More stringent control was necessary in the on-board software systems. Hence, a comprehensive plan was evolved for the configuration control, validation and quality assurance of the software for the first time in the history of ISRO. This was in the 1990s, when even international agencies were only framing a few guidelines in this area.

A new simulation facility that integrated the control hardware, on-board computers and a ground-based digital computer running the 6D trajectory program was developed for conducting virtual flights. This was also being done for the first time in the country. A team led by Dr K. Sivan, who later became the chairman of ISRO, was responsible for this unique development. This hardware-in-loop facility became the mainstay for all future launches, including the GSLV missions.

The cause for failures of the ASLV was our lack of understanding about interactions between the aerodynamic configuration, structural dynamics and control systems. Hence, many modifications and innovations had been attempted in this area for the PSLV. Experiments had been carried out using digital computers to improve the vehicle configuration and actuator performance as well as to avoid delays in issuing control commands. The structural response was measured on full-scale models. Appropriate digital filters were introduced to avoid interactions. The hardware used in the control system for each stage of the rocket, along with the on-board computers, the software and the inertial measurement unit, were tested as many times as possible to validate the mathematical models used in various simulations. During these tests, commands corresponding to different stages of the mission would be initiated from the ground computer network. By simulating the different stage performances, the effects of deviations in propulsion modules and other disturbing forces could be assessed.

The simulation tests have all the characteristics of real launch scenarios. They are also useful in identifying deviations in the performance when external disturbances occur beyond expected limits. Such 'stress tests' help us understand the reasons for failures and in finding solutions well before the actual flight. As a result of these tests, many corrections could be made in the on-board software. More than 1,500 such simulations were conducted before we cleared the next launch of the PSLV.

Precise documentation and supervision of all the work were conducted rigorously. A clear directive was given to not keep any activity secret. To avoid unauthorized changes in designs, a system was implemented so that all design details had to be clearly documented and audited by quality assurance teams. The required changes had to be presented to the Configuration Control Board for approval. This was an extremely difficult task practically, especially in an R&D environment, even more so in software, where everything is in the mind of the designer. Today, the well-established quality control and configuration control systems have been standardized. These are among the primary reasons for the high success percentage of ISRO missions.

THE SECOND FLIGHT OF THE PSLV: SUCCESS AND REVIEW

Within a year, PSLV-D2, the PSLV's next mission, was carried out on 15 October 1994. The rocket lifted off from Sriharikota, carrying the Indian remote sensing (IRS) satellite, IRS-P2. This time, all the stages worked perfectly. The navigation, control and guidance systems ensured that the satellite was injected into the precise orbit. Shouts of joy rose in the control centre. I came out of the control room and made a declaration of our success to the nation. I could see scientists, technicians and many other team members dancing outside. Representatives from Doordarshan and the BBC were among the media. The BBC gave a lot of importance to the launch and announced to the world that India had entered the Inter-Continental Ballistic Missile (ICBM) club! Dr K. Kasturirangan, who was the chairman of ISRO then, conducted a press conference. Dr Kalam congratulated me. 'Buddy, you have done it,' he shouted with childlike joy, and wanted his appreciation to be conveyed to all the team members.

I.K. Gujral was the prime minister at that time. The nation was going through a lot of difficulties economically and politically. In spite of this, ISRO was not affected. A congratulatory message reached us from Prime Minister Gujral. That night, we celebrated the success with a dinner for all team members at the SHAR. Tea parties were conducted and sweets distributed in all the other centres of ISRO.

In retrospect, I see that all the subsystems for the PSLV were realized by the tireless efforts, something like a *tapasya* (penance), of the 3,000-strong ISRO team, which comprised engineers, technical experts, administrative personnel and supporting staff, along with the participation of several industries and academic institutions.

The success in developing such complex technologies while adhering to all government rules and respecting time and budget limits became a new chapter in management theory. No wonder ISRO has been touted as a model for other government organizations.

Almost all the centres of ISRO had contributed to the development of the PSLV in one way or another. But it was the VSSC, LPSC, SDSC, ISAC, ISTRAC and IISU that made the most significant contributions in developing infrastructure, evolving technologies and delivering subsystems for the flight.

The transparent review mechanism created for the PSLV proved to be a boon for the design and development of many multidisciplinary missions that used cutting-edge technologies. In developed countries, such missions are usually conceived by government-owned space agencies and developed in commercial aerospace industries. Control is exercised through cash compensation for work and penalties for liabilities in case of failures or delays. A transparent government set-up that works with shared responsibilities without any blame game is a unique achievement of ISRO. Technological challenges are the motivators for the employees, not monetary returns.

The multitier project-management system developed for the PSLV programme was also unique. In each project, the project director has the overall responsibility and decision-making power for technical, financial and administrative matters related to their area. As explained earlier, the project director is helped by the PMB and reports to the management council, which is chaired by the director of the lead centre of ISRO, under which the project functions. The management council is the highest authority for project activities and reports directly to the chairman of ISRO. This management system cuts across multiple layers of hierarchical management systems and eliminates red-tapism. Once the Space Commission approves a mission by defining its goals, schedule and budget, all the development activities are left to the above management structure. The centres and facilities provide technical and infrastructure support through a matrix system of management.

Coordination among launch vehicle centres, the project and ISRO HQ was a major controlling aspect. The role played by my best friend and colleague D. Narayana Moorthi as the director of the LVPO is unforgettable. He was the eyes and ears of the chairman of ISRO and maintained extremely cordial relations with all centres and projects. We had started our careers together working on the SLV-3 project, under Dr Kalam. After the SLV-3 project's completion, he was deputed to Washington, D.C., as ISRO's liaison officer, where he worked to strengthen our relationship with NASA. After returning, he had a short stint at ISAC. When Srinivasa Shetty took voluntary retirement, Professor Rao appointed him as the director of the LVPO. In that capacity, he worked with three chairmen—Professor Rao, Dr Kasturirangan and me. Moorthi always had the knack for foreseeing problems and working with the concerned people to obtain the right solutions. He helped me especially to solve inter-centre problems during the PSLV development. During my tenure as the chairman, he was instrumental in starting several new initiatives, especially our cooperation with Russia. He was virtually the conscience keeper of Dr Kalam, who would discuss various issues with him, starting from the SLV-3 days until his demise. Even after leaving official posts, he continues to be a source of great strength to me.

The programme management function for the PSLV was implemented by R. Ayyappadasan Pillai, P. Ratnakara Rao and their team. Successful completion of more than 16,000 activities related to system development, testing and facility establishment culminated in the launch. It was simply impossible to create a conventional PERT chart manually with all these events for monitoring and control. Although Ayyappadasan Pillai created a computer program, the network established through dial-up telephone lines was unreliable even for voice communication and, hence, inadequate for real-time decision-making. The development teams were reluctant to reveal details too, especially when something failed. The scheme turned out to be only partially successful. However, the system that was started for the PSLV has been perfected and is being used today.

The administrative functions were decentralized for the launch vehicle projects. Each project had its own teams to support the activities of logistics, procurement, accounts and stores. This helped with speedy implementation, as in the corporate sector. P.S. Nair had started the administrative wing of SLV-3. Many youngsters who worked there, including P.G.M. Chettiyar, D. Srinivasan, M.C. John, etc., later evolved as administrative leaders at the VSSC and other major centres. Their dedication and sincerity of service were really laudable. There were many other such people. I can never forget the services of D. Ushakumari, who was my personal assistant starting from the PSLV days until I left the VSSC. I am thankful to people at the VSSC, such as K.P. Nandakumaran, G. Sivanandan, K. Raveendran Nair, M. Balakrishnan and S. Vijayanatha Kurup, and those at the LPSC, such as P. Sasikumar, who supported me in official matters. Indian Space Research Organisation has reached the niche where it is today due to the cooperation and selfless work of all such colleagues.

AFTER PSLV-D2

The success of 1994 erased the bad memories of the first failed launch. We gained a lot of confidence from the textbook performance of that mission. One more launch with an IRS satellite on board had to be conducted as per the plan. Once that was also successfully carried out through the next launch (PSLV-D3), the PSLV developmental project was concluded. It had been conceived and was delivered into my hands as a baby by the great chief designer Dr Srinivasan. I am lucky that I had the opportunity to nurture it into a mature well-behaved adult, setting a sort of a record for low-cost and reliable access to space.

By the time the PSLV's development missions were concluded, ISRO had evolved into a big organization, with five major centres and as many smaller units, spread all over the country, from Mahendragiri to Shillong.

A series of continuous PSLV launches followed the developmental flights, to cater to both national and international users. By then, subsystems of the PSLV were being realized in more than 300 large- and small-scale industries. Indian Space Research Organisation handled specialized areas like avionics, inertial systems, control systems, pyro systems, propellants, mission software and vehicle integration fully in-house. Once this scheme became operational, the periodicity of launches increased to four per year. That was the situation when I left ISRO. Today, the periodicity has increased to one launch per month. Subsequent project directors like R.V. Perumal, S. Ramakrishnan, N. Narayanamoorthy, George Koshy, P. Kunhikrishnan, B. Jayakumar and R. Hutton played major roles in achieving this growth. The decision to work with industries has proven to have been the right one.

The first successful launch of the PSLV in 1994 put a satellite weighing 850 kg in a polar, sun-synchronous orbit. In subsequent launches, a disciplined approach was undertaken to continuously improve subsystem performance. Eventually, the payload could be almost doubled. Through step-by-step improvements in propulsion, structural elements, electronic systems and other subsystems, the rocket can now take satellites up to 1,500 kg to polar, sun-synchronous orbits.

The PSLV has become ISRO's workhorse, evolving into one of the most reliable satellite launch vehicles in the world. After the first failed mission, it has had a continuous stream of 39 successful launches, and has made a total of 56 launches, with 54 of them successful as on January 2023, as I write this book. It is used not only for launches into polar orbits but also to geostationary orbits to a height of 36,000 km. The configuration of the PSLV can also be changed depending on the weight of the payload to be carried. Over the years, the rocket has successfully placed the IRS series of satellites in accurate orbits. It was the launch vehicle used for Chandrayaan-1 mission as well as for the mission to Mars. Orbiting the Indian navigation system constellation in geostationary orbits was also carried out by the PSLV.

An innovative multiple launch adapter was developed to enable launch of multiple spacecraft in a single mission. The satellites could also be launched into multiple orbits. During my time as the chairman of ISRO, 10 satellites were launched in orbit in a single mission. Recently, using this same technology, 104 small satellites were placed in orbit in a single mission, through which ISRO set a world record.[1]

I cannot help being anxious on one account. The lifespan of small satellites is typically very short. In a few years, they will be dead and become space debris, detrimental to satellites working in the various orbits. Right now, nearly one lakh such parts are present in the near-Earth orbits. Space debris will only increase further in the coming years. Proper mitigation measures need to be

[1]'ISRO Sends 104 Satellites in One Go, Breaks Russia's Record', *The Economic Times*, 15 February 2017, https://bit.ly/32vpx9L. Accessed on 26 April 2023.

established to reduce the debris and dispose of the satellites after they become non-functional.

The launch costs of our missions are much less than that of many other countries. This gives us an advantage in the international market. Today, in addition to meeting the requirements of the country, ISRO is able to undertake commercial and competitive launches for the international community.

The development of the PSLV helped the country achieve self-reliance in SLV technology. The technology was developed in-house by the efforts of our scientists and technologists. It also created a new work culture. Lessons learnt from the PSLV were employed to improve the design of the GSLV as well.

I could not only lead the PSLV development but also put my signature in all its dimensions, in every nut and bolt—I consider this as a great achievement in my life. The highest praise I received after this achievement was from my guru, Dr Kalam. Once he and I appeared together in a children's programme. One child started to heap praise upon Dr Kalam as usual. He stopped the child, pointed at me and said, 'SLV-3 developed by me is small compared to the PSLV, which is 20 times bigger. The father of the PSLV is sitting by my side!' He further stated that he is proud of his shishya overtaking the guru!

On another occasion, my name had been considered for an award, and there was some opposition. The issue was that I had not published any scientific papers. Dr Kalam had been present in the selection committee. He had lifted the photograph of a PSLV launch in his hands and asked, 'Can anyone say how many papers are equal to this?'

Apparently, nobody had any more objections afterwards!

15

Towards the GSLV and Cryogenics

With the PSLV, India attained self-sufficiency in launching Earth-observation satellites. However, we continued to depend on other countries to launch heavy satellites to geostationary orbits. A satellite in the geostationary orbit, which is a circular orbit above the equator, has an orbital period equal to the Earth's rotation period of 23 hours and 56 minutes and, hence, appears stationary in the sky from the Earth. In the mid-1970s, a feasibility study for building and launching the Indian National Satellite System (INSAT) series of geostationary satellites had commenced, and studies on possible configurations for such a launch vehicle had been carried out under the leadership of Dr R.M. Vasagom. A few of our engineers had obtained some exposure to American launch vehicles. A semi-cryogenic stage using liquid oxygen and kerosene, similar to the one used in the Delta launch vehicle, was considered. But the work did not progress as our focus was on the development of a solid rocket system. It was unwise to diffuse our efforts by investing them concurrently in several fronts.

Germany had taken the lead in research on liquid rockets during the Second World War and had perfected the technology. Kerosene was the fuel used, with liquid oxygen as the oxidizer. When the War ended, the rockets as well as the German technical experts were captured and shared between the USA and Soviet Union. Afterwards, both countries developed powerful rockets based on V2, the German rocket, for their missiles. Germany can be called the birthplace of modern rocketry. All missiles hitherto developed by Western countries are further chapters of that German story. Dr Wernher Von Braun, who led the development of the huge Saturn rocket for the Apollo mission, was one of the experts.

During the Cold War, rockets were competitively developed for military purposes by the two factions. To increase the payload capability of satellite launchers, NASA began to use liquid oxygen and liquid hydrogen. The Saturn rocket, which took man to the Moon, used both semi-cryogenic and cryogenic engines. The Soviet Union and the USA acquired cryogenic technology first. Many years later, France and China also entered the arena.

These countries first developed rockets for military purposes and later converted them to satellite launches. India is the only country that developed rocket systems to orbit satellites for civilian applications. Our first SLV was SLV-3, which used only solid motors. We did not have much experience then in liquid rockets.

BIRTH PANGS OF THE GSLV

The GSLV development project continued to be in cold storage until the successful flight of SLV-3. When Professor U.R. Rao took over as the chairman from Professor Satish Dhawan, he appointed a committee for evolving a configuration and development plan for the GSLV. R. Jeyamani chaired the committee. The design studies were led by Dr S. Srinivasan, the director of the launch vehicle design group.

Professor Rao used to conduct frequent reviews of the project. At one of these, Nambinarayanan and his team from the LPSC presented a configuration using only liquid engines, similar to the French launch vehicle Ariane-4—a four-engine cluster of Viking engines for the first stage, a single engine for the second stage and a new 12-ton liquid engine for the final stage. Although the configuration looked sleek and efficient, no one wanted to put all their eggs into the one basket of liquid engines, which had to be developed from scratch!

By this time, the configuration of the PSLV, with a 125-ton solid booster and a second stage using Vikas engine, had been confirmed. Dr Srinivasan proposed the addition of strap-on motors to achieve the geo-mission. Concurrently, building on the indigenous experience in solid propulsion, another proposal was put forth by the VSSC, with solid motors for all the stages. During those discussions, both

Nambinarayanan and Dr Srinivasan would argue strongly, neither yielding to the other. People made fun of them saying, 'Their fight is like that of cats fighting for sweetmeats!' Both were, no doubt, driven solely by their limitless sincerity and passion for advancing technology and ensuring the success of the project.

As a compromise, Dr Srinivasan proposed a first stage with two Vikas engines and using two solid boosters of the PSLV as strap-ons. But the liquid team was unyielding. They said that most of the details of Ariane were available for a four-engine configuration, whereas for a twin-engine, they would have to start everything afresh.

In hindsight, one can see that Dr Srinivasan's proposal was the right one. The idea was to make a core stage using two Viking engines, along with the already developed PSLV solid booster around it as strap-ons. The second stage of the PSLV could be used as the second stage for the GSLV. The final stage was to be a 12-ton cryogenic engine, similar to the French one. This configuration would have made it possible for us to take 3.5-ton satellites to geostationary transfer orbits 20 years earlier! Instead, we spent a lot of time developing the complex GSLV Mark II with seven rocket engines and the cryogenic stage from the Soviet Union! Later, a configuration with two engines for the first stage and two big, solid strap-ons was adopted for GSLV Mark III and has proven to be efficient and reliable.

Coming back to the GSLV, finally a configuration of compromise was reached, using a mix of solid and liquid rockets: a solid booster of 2.8-m diameter, surrounded with four liquid strap-on rockets 2 m in diameter. The strap-ons used an updated version of the PSLV second stage and had to burn for an extra 40 seconds after the booster shut off. Managing the control transition was tricky. A liquid core stage flanked by solid strap-ons was the norm for launch vehicles internationally. This unique configuration of the GSLV was the result of the trade-off formula by Professor Rao, pacifying both the solid and liquid lobbies. Many made fun of it and commented that it was like the cashew nut being outside the fruit. As you know, the nut is inside the fruit in most cases.

A Vikas-engine-based second stage, similar to the PSLV's second stage, was selected. Initially, an upper-stage configuration of a solid apogee–perigee motor was proposed. After extensive deliberations, a single stage using a cryogenic engine was finalized. Thus, a three-stage configuration with a total height of 49.13 m and weighing 414.75 tons at lift-off was finally confirmed for the GSLV. Some had the apprehension that reliability of this configuration would be low, as it used seven propulsive stages.

Among chemical propulsion systems, hydrogen burning with oxygen is the most efficient and does not produce any harmful gases that may pollute the atmosphere. But these gases cannot be carried in rocket motor chambers due to the large volume and high pressure requirements. Hence, they are stored in liquid form at sub-zero temperatures. This is how the cryogenic rocket came to be named.

Since we lacked the confidence to develop a highly efficient cryogenic stage within the required time frame, international bids were invited for acquiring a cryogenic stage for the GSLV. The USA and Japan possessed the technology, but they did not respond due to embargos. France quoted ₹1,000 crore but was unwilling to part with the technology. The Soviet Union, on the other hand, made a bid for ₹235 crore, payable with Indian currency, and agreed to transfer the technology.

Based on these factors, ISRO and Glavkosmos, the Russian space agency, signed an agreement in 1991, by which both cryogenic engines and technology were to be provided by the Soviet Union. However, India had to develop the electronic systems for engine control. The engines had been developed long back for a manned mission to the Moon by the Soviet Union and had not been flown yet. The electronic systems were outdated. We proposed to use very modern microprocessor-based controllers.

Nambinarayanan was appointed as the director of the project responsible to operationalize the contract with the Soviet Union for acquiring the cryogenic engines and technology. R. Jeyamani took charge as the project director for the GSLV project.

Let me dwell a little on the early days of developing cryogenic technology at the LPSC. Well before signing the Russian contract, some efforts had been initiated for developing the cryogenic technology indigenously. A study team had been working at ISRO since 1982 under the leadership of E.V.S. Namboodiri. The team of Indian scientists who worked in France under Nambinarayanan as part of the SEP agreement between the two countries had gathered a lot of information on the technology. The turbo pump and thrust chamber were the crucial items. One person was totally engrossed in its development of turbo pumps: N.K. Gupta. S.C. Ghosh was working on development of an injector and thrust chamber. They had developed a preliminary design of a 12-ton thrust cryogenic engine. A 1-ton thrust engine was made using gaseous hydrogen and oxygen and was tested for 200 seconds. After two years, a 12-ton thrust chamber using a special oxygen-free copper developed in collaboration with the CECRI was fired successfully for 20 seconds. In March 1991, a test firing for 150 seconds was carried out. An experiment conducted in June 1993, using both hydrogen and oxygen in liquid state, failed. The first successful test of an engine using both hydrogen and oxygen in liquid state was in November 1995. By February 1997, a 12-ton thrust engine could be fired for five seconds. The very next year, the duration increased to 50 seconds. Putting all our faith in the Russian contract signed in 1991 virtually killed our in-house initiative. If only those efforts had been continued, India would have developed the capability several years earlier!

However, many of the materials and technology developed came handy later during the indigenous design and development of the 20-ton cryogenic engine.

The breakup of the Soviet Union in 1991 changed not only the course of world history but also the story of the Indian cryogenic rocket development, causing a major change in the administration. Industries and research institutes now belonged to several states and the scientists became citizens of different countries. Most of the scientists wished to migrate to the Western world, especially to the USA.

RUSSIAN TECHNOLOGY

I visited the Soviet Union for the first time in 1972. Everything was then under the government's control. One had to stand in a queue for half an hour to even get a cup of soup. All restaurants would close by 10.30 p.m. If we were even a little late, there would be no dinner. Once, we went to see the famous Russian circus and it was 10.48 p.m. by the time we returned to the hotel. The restaurant door was closed. Looking through the glass doors, we could see food heaped on the tables. But the door keeper said, '*Nyet*!' (No). We had to turn back disappointed and settle for an apple and some water for dinner. For any luxury item, one had to stand in a queue from the previous night itself. I used to buy some local items as gifts for Radha whenever I went on foreign trips. The Soviet Union was the one country from which I had to come back empty handed.

After 1991, the restaurants became more like the ones in Western Europe, and the prices sky-rocketed. Everything had to be paid for in dollars. There was a saying that people used their worthless ruble notes to fill pillows! Once I exchanged $100 and got lakhs of rubles in exchange. The government began to print 1,000-ruble notes later and devalued the currency. Many business people made unbelievable profits, but the poor were devastated. Anti-social elements had a field day. Once, I saw an Indian student being kicked on the head by *goonda*s (thugs) who looted him. Hotels received security threats. Head load workers began to extract 'looking charges', similar to the custom prevalent in Kerala. Compensation demanded on the pretext of providing additional security, without any service, for the first cryogenic engine being taken from the factory to the airport was US $50,000! We were unable to pay and lost a lot of time. Most of the technical experts who used to interact very freely with us earlier became reticent. I had always found Russians to be honest people who would do anything for their friends. After the breakup, their attitude changed. It was as if a deep fear that someone was always watching gripped them. However, a few were ready to disclose details in exchange for money.

I could feel the depth of the damage caused by the transformation. Managers of many factories producing strategic products declared themselves the owners of those factories. As the economic situation degenerated, many institutions went bankrupt. One could see Russian citizens, who had once walked with their heads held high, now begging on the streets. Many desperate scientists began to approach representatives of foreign countries, trying to sell their products and services at a much-reduced price. A software engineer came to meet me secretly in a hotel to sell his product along with its source code. It was an aerodynamic simulation software, and the price was so low that we immediately obtained the money in dollars from our embassy and made the purchase. Another scientist came to sell ion thrusters that could be used to stabilize satellites in their orbits. We purchased these cheaply too.

When some scientists approached me to sell a gyroscope based on the principle of Doppler shift created by rings of laser beams, I was greatly surprised. Those optical laser gyroscopes were state-of-the-art! The scientists were ready to give the device along with the technology, and the price was one-tenth of a similar American product! We immediately arranged for the purchase. All the necessary approvals were obtained after we returned to India.

My plan was to get the gyroscope modified as per our requirements by Vedachalam, our specialist in inertial sensors. However, when I informed Dr K. Kasturirangan, who was the chairman of ISRO, he wanted to entrust the task to Dr T.K. Alex of the Laboratory for Electro-Optic Systems (LEOS), which was engaged in fibreoptic gyros. But things did not progress well. I then took the equipment to Vedachalam, and he was able complete the task. He studied the technology and developed a laser gyroscope of our own, which performed 10 times better than the Russian-made one. All the required facilities were also established. The work was carried out at the IISU in Thiruvananthapuram. Today, our advanced launch vehicles use this instrument and reach their destinations very precisely.

Many countries seized the golden opportunity after the collapse of the Soviet Union. Technology flowed from there to China, North Korea, Iran and even Pakistan. But India did not capitalize on this chance as much as it could have. 'I have informed many heads of departments in India about these rare opportunities. But nobody took any initiative! The USA and European nations are taking everything away. You alone are trying to take something for India!' the then Indian ambassador Ronen Sen once told us with disappointment. Sen maintained very good relations with ISRO scientists. Whenever we approached him for a solution to any issue or to get foreign currency in an emergency, he made immediate arrangements. The accounts would be settled later after obtaining the necessary permissions. Thus, we could get hold of a number of vital technologies at a cheap price.

The Soviet Union had three major organizations engaged in space research. These were located in Ukraine and Georgia, and the facilities were better than the American ones in several areas. But with the breakup, everything was disintegrated. Research funds were drastically reduced. This led to a downslide in the quality of the systems and the USA climbed to the first place in space technology. Boris Yeltsin, the successor of Gorbachev, was not a good administrator, though he had led the agitators well. It was only after Vladimir Putin, the erstwhile chief of the Russian secret police, became president that Russia began to slowly come out of the rut. Even then, without the old Union countries, the intellectual and capital resources were considerably reduced, and it was difficult to regain the past glory.

The fall of the Soviet Union seriously affected our cryogenic engine dreams. Yeltsin succumbed to the American pressure to rescind the contract with India for the supply of engines. The transfer of technology was forbidden. Only fully integrated engines would be given—that too at a higher price, to be paid in US dollars! The bargaining started. Finally, we had to rewrite the contract omitting the clause for transfer of technology. Russia agreed to provide two flight-ready engines and two more for ground tests. The price was ₹325 crore. Further, three more flight-ready engines could be provided at ₹180 crore each.

Since the way for technology transfer was closed, everybody was finally convinced about the urgent need for indigenous R&D in the area.

16

A Fictitious and Tragic Tale

The passion of S. Nambinarayanan for cryogenic technology is laudable. After the development of the Vikas engine, he set his eyes on cryogenics. In France, he gathered a lot of information on the cryogenic engine used in the Ariane launch vehicle. The team under E.V.S. Namboodiri even prepared a preliminary design and development plan. N.K. Gupta and S.C. Ghosh were the other key players. Nambinarayanan played a central role in technology acquisition from Russia as well. A team under the leadership of Gnana Gandhi was making the necessary efforts in Moscow towards that and even succeeded to a great extent.

When the Russian agreement for transfer of cryogenic technology was cancelled, ISRO had no other option but to prepare its own development plan. Professor U.R. Rao cleared the proposal for indigenous development of cryogenic engine in his last year as the chairman. Nambinarayanan would have been the natural choice for undertaking the task of developing the engine. But he became entangled in a false spy case that derailed his entire scientific career.

The second PSLV mission emerged as a stupendous success. Many people, both inside and outside the country, were envious of the achievement. Many of them highlighted that India has achieved the capability to develop ICBMs through the PSLV. This meant that India now could potentially become a military power. It was no surprise that this achievement gave Western countries, the acknowledged leaders in satellite and rocket technologies, the jitters. As a result, sanctions were tightened by these countries against the supply of high-tech instruments and technologies to ISRO. We, in turn, after internal discussions, decided to prioritize indigenous development of cryogenic technology.

It was at this juncture that headlines appeared out of the blue in the media, screaming about espionage activities with direct impact on national security allegedly taking place at ISRO![1] The 'spy case', as it came to be known, literally shook ISRO and state as well as central governments.

ARRESTS: ALL HELL BREAKS LOOSE

It started with news reports on 21 October 1994 about the arrest of two women from Male in connection with a spy case, hinting that a few ISRO scientists had contacts with them. The next day, the Malayalam daily *Kerala Kaumudi* reported that one of them had connections with a scientist in the PSLV project and that a middleman for Russian contracts from Bengaluru had introduced them to each other.[2] This shocked hundreds of scientists at the VSSC, LPSC and other centres of ISRO, and cast a shadow of doubt over them.

In the following month, officers of the Kerala Police came in search of D. Sasikumar, a senior engineer working at the VSSC, presumably on the basis of the deposition of the lady from Male, Mariam Rasheeda.[3] The intelligence bureau relayed this information to Delhi. However, they could not get much from questioning him. Meanwhile, Sasikumar wrote to the chairman of ISRO, explaining his position.

On 21 November, he was placed under police arrest, and a special investigation team started questioning him. He later revealed to me the physical torture he had to undergo in custody. Even then, he refused to own up to a crime he did not commit, only saying that he was an expert in mechanical fabrication and didn't know any technical details of cryogenic engines.

---

[1]Fathima, Azeefa, 'The Real-Life Story of Nambi Narayanan, the Scientist Madhavan Plays in Rocketry', *The News Minute*, 2 July 2022, https://bit.ly/3znG3Ks. Accessed on 30 March 2023; S. Nambinarayanan, *Ormakalude Bhramanapadham (In the Orbit of Memories)*, Current Books Thrissur, 2017.

[2]'What Was the ISRO Spy Case, Involving Scientist Nambi Narayanan?', *The Indian Express*, 3 December 2022, https://bit.ly/3oEVk7S. Accessed on 24 April 2023.

[3]Ibid.

The media began to craft countless stories. The daily *Mathrubhumi*, which had initially restrained itself, joined the others. I called them and pointed out the misunderstanding and highlighted the mental anguish that their speculative reports were causing to ISRO scientists.

'Sir, it is a question of survival,' said an acquaintance from the editorial department. 'The circulation of *Manorama* increased by 10 per cent after it started reporting on the spy case. How can we lag behind?' No one realized that many families were devastated due to these colourful and fabricated media reports.

Nambinarayanan was arrested on 30 November 1994.[4] A cloud of sadness descended over ISRO when news of the arrest broke out. It was simply unbelievable! Dr Kasturirangan was also disturbed. Nambinarayanan was jailed for a month-and-a-half. Though subjected to intense physical torture, he survived, and the investigating agency did not find any evidence incriminating him.[5] Still, he was named as the fifth accused in the case filed by the Kerala Police.

At this time, the investigation agency leaked the news that they were about to arrest 12 more scientists, including Dr A.E. Muthunayagam. Immediately, I went to ISRO HQ and met the chairman. I talked to him for over four hours and convinced him that no such espionage had taken place or can take place and that it was all purely fabricated. A joint secretary to the DOS tried to say that it was a case of national security violation and we should keep away. However, my arguments were finally accepted. Dr Kasturirangan rushed to Delhi, met Prime Minister P.V. Narasimha Rao and apprised him of the facts. He immediately ordered a CBI (Central Bureau of Investigation) inquiry, averting further damage.[6]

---

[4]S. Nambinarayanan and Arun Ram, *Ready To Fire: How India and I Survived the ISRO Spy Case*, Bloomsbury 2018, p. 22.

[5]Ibid. p. 37.

[6]S. Nambinarayanan, *Ormakalude Bhramanapadham* (*In the Orbit of Memories*), Current Books Thrissur, 2017.

IN SEARCH OF THE TRUTH

What is the truth about the cryogenic technology documents that Nambinarayanan and Sasikumar are supposed to have leaked to foreign countries? At that time, we had only prepared a rough outline for the cryogenic engine and had elementary knowledge of the subject. How could something that did not exist be leaked? Additionally, many truckloads would have been required to carry documents corresponding to even a single rocket engine as all the records then were in print. Drawings and details about thousands of parts would have to be physically copied and loaded into the trucks, with no electronic media. How could this happen inside ISRO centres, which are manned round the clock by the Central Industrial Security Force guards?

Presumably following the prime minister's directive, the CBI swung into action. They obtained details from the Kerala Police and visited the LPSC and the VSSC. I met them for over an hour and explained the matter. Meetings with the scientists were arranged. The team members visited the design offices and documentation centres and talked to the people. The investigation continued for nearly three months. Finally, after detailed investigations, the CBI concluded that the case was fabricated.[7] In the meantime, the Kerala Police also publicized stories alleging the involvement of Raman Srivastava—the then inspector general of police and a close associate of the chief minister of Kerala, K. Karunakaran—in the case. It was rumoured that they made the allegation that Prime Minister Narasimha Rao's son was also involved in the case and that the CBI was being used as a pawn to save Rao's son and Karunakaran![8]

After a lengthy court battle, Nambinarayanan and Sasikumar were acquitted of all the charges.[9] The National Human Rights Commission directed for a compensation of ₹1 crore to be paid. However, the Government of Kerala gave only ₹10 lakh at that

---

[7]Fathima, Azeefa, 'The Real-Life Story of Nambi Narayanan, the Scientist Madhavan Plays in Rocketry', *The News Minute*, 2 July 2022, https://bit.ly/3znG3Ks. Accessed on 30 March 2023.

[8]Ibid.

[9]Ibid.

time. Nambinarayanan took the matter up in the Supreme Court and finally won the case.[10]

I understand that Siby Mathews, the leader of the Kerala Police investigation team, who retired as a director general of police for Fire and Rescue Services, still stands firm in his belief that the case was genuine.[11] In a case filed by Nambinarayanan against him, the Supreme Court directed in 2018 that a compensation of ₹50 lakh must be paid to him immediately as an interim relief.[12] I had several occasions to discuss this topic with Mathews. What I understand is that perhaps if the statements made by the scientists interviewed by him were included in the case diary, the outcome would have been very different. But my question is, how can senior and honest police officers remove such statements from the diary if they were so important? If there were fears about the lives of the people who had made the statements, the police could very well have provided protection! Nothing of the sort was ever done! I appreciate Mathews' candour in owning up to his mistakes. I am sure that it is the lack of critical analysis and understanding of the facts and an effort to cover up his mistakes that makes him still believe that the spy case was real.

The whole story is explained in detail in Nambinarayanan's autobiography titled *Ormakalude Bramanapadham* (*In the Orbit of Memories*).

In fact, the case was fabricated by some groups with vested interests. The primary goal appears to have been to demoralize ISRO, which was about to make great strides with its workhorse launcher, the PSLV. Another objective could have been connected to Kerala politics, the aim being to unseat Chief Minister K. Karunakaran. A few second-rung Congress leaders in Kerala were disturbed by the gradual political rise of Karunakaran's son Muraleedharan. These leaders may have wanted to stop the latter in his tracks and made

---

[10]Ibid.

[11]Balan, Saritha S., 'I Was the One Who Was Victimised in ISRO Espionage Case: Former Kerala DGP Siby Mathews', *The News Minute*, 7 June 2017, https://bit.ly/3Gbq71O. Accessed on 3 April 2023.

[12]'What Was the ISRO Spy Case, Involving Scientist Nambi Narayanan?', *The Indian Express*, 3 December 2022, https://bit.ly/3W6Fwpd. Accessed on 13 January 2023.

the father a scapegoat in the process. This was alleged as the reason to pull in Inspector General Raman Srivastava into the case.

Finally, Karunakaran lost his position and A.K. Antony became the chief minister once again. Cherian Philip, a prominent politician and confidant of Antony, surely knows all the inside details. It is heartening to see that the media organizations have now retracted their previous stand and are reporting facts.

As I write this, Nambinarayanan has succeeded in his legal battle that stretched for nearly 25 years. The Supreme Court declared him innocent. In August 2020, the state government paid him an additional compensation of about ₹1.3 crore. The Court had also directed that the amount should be recovered from the police officers concerned.[13]

Nambinarayanan still believes that some foreign agencies played a key role in the whole drama to demoralize ISRO at the peak of its performance. He convinced the Supreme Court about this view. The Court has ordered further inquiry into the matter.

It is sad that an eminent scientist had to fight in several courts over a quarter of a century, spending all his savings, to establish his innocence. I hope our democratic set-up and judiciary will ensure that such things never happen in the future.

[13]'Nambi Narayanan Gets ₹1.3 Cr. Additional Compensation', *The Hindu*, 11 August 2020, https://bit.ly/3wtJUEA. Accessed on 25 January 2023.

17

The LPSC and a Swadesi Cryo

The period after the first PSLV flight witnessed changes in the top management of ISRO—Dr Kasturirangan took over as the chairman.

Dr K. Kasturirangan completed his doctoral research under the guidance of Professor U.R. Rao at the PRL. He then joined ISAC, Bengaluru, and led the development of the IRS satellites. He was appointed as the director of ISAC when Professor Rao took over as the chairman of ISRO. He contributed significantly to the development of satellite technology in the country.

Dr Kasturirangan, assuming the post of the chairman of ISRO, built upon the basic facilities and all the critical technologies Professor Rao had developed, following the true ISRO culture. He implemented programmes with a cautious approach, averse to taking any undue risks. Thus, most of the missions were successful. His eventful tenure at ISRO lasted till 2003, when he was nominated to the Rajya Sabha. Many used to say that he had a 'magical hand' that could turn anything into gold!

Some murmurs were heard when Dr Kasturirangan was appointed as the chairman, while Dr A.E. Muthunayagam and P.P. Kale were the contenders. Later, Professor Rao helped Dr Muthunayagam get the post of the secretary to the Government of India, to head the newly formed Ocean Development Department. Kale was given a higher responsibility as the director of the VSSC, the largest and the lead centre for launch vehicle development.

AS DIRECTOR, LPSC: FORGING UNITY

I was the project director of the PSLV until the second launch, which demonstrated the first successful mission. That was the time when Dr Muthunayagam left the LPSC. Nambinarayanan would have become the director of the LPSC, but the infamous 'ISRO spy scandal' thwarted his chances. He was shifted to ISRO HQ and took voluntary retirement soon. Sasikumar was posted to SAC in Ahmedabad, and he too retired a little later. Consequently, I was appointed as the director of the LPSC in November 1994. The LPSC was then at a crucial stage of new developments. I had to both manage the LPSC and take the cryogenic technology development forward. I had never imagined that the responsibility would fall on my shoulders!

Some people had doubts about a director with a background in electronics and experience in vehicle integration and management leading the liquid propulsion centre. I studied rocket development carried out in various countries and tried to understand the details of this less-familiar field. My understanding of the basic scientific principles and ability to logically analyse any matter and make decisions came in handy. My approach was to break down issues into small elements, solve each of them and then reintegrate everything. I am sure we can solve any issue in this manner. The formula of applying 80 per cent technical knowledge and 20 per cent intuition was often useful. Wrong decisions can lead to catastrophes. But that fear has never deterred me from going ahead.

The first thing I noticed was that the work culture at the LPSC was not very healthy, with a few groups working with selfish motives. I tried to bring in unity by ensuring that as the director, I did not align with any of the warring factions. First, a decision was taken to strengthen the management council by including 12 senior scientists as members. It enabled open discussions in the council on all matters and solutions to technical and managerial issues. The many factions at the LPSC slowly dissolved and everybody was brought together. An understanding that the LPSC's goals were more important than personal interests took root. The open discussions benefitted me personally as well, giving me a good understanding on different aspects of liquid rocket technology.

The support I got from five or six key people proved crucial. V. Gnana Gandhi played a critical role in the cryogenic development. My friend Sridharan Dhas, with his sharp intelligence and technical acumen, was a pillar of support. E.V.S. Namboodiri, M.K.G. Nair, Kasiviswanathan, Mohammed Muslim, Ramamurthy, N.K. Gupta and others were key players. M. Annamalai and N. Gunasekharan held the fort at the Mahendragiri and Bengaluru units. K.L. Valliappan handled satellite propulsion. C.G. Balan was a master of satellite engines. Within a year, work started moving like a well-oiled machine in the LPSC. In retrospect, I think the defining factor was my approach of giving equal importance to everyone in the team, integrating not only technologies but also the multidisciplinary experts. This was a unique management technique that I had learnt from Dr Sarabhai and Dr Kalam.

THE LONG ROAD TO INDIGENOUS CRYO

In the early days, we could freely roam around in the Russian laboratories and test facilities during our visits. But when our contract was rewritten after the collapse of the Soviet Union, the discussions were confined to conference halls and the scientists became reticent. It was hinted that the American agents were everywhere. As a result, other than the sketchy information that we obtained during the early days, we could not get details of cryogenic technology from them. Nambinarayanan and Gnana Gandhi believed that we had already obtained nearly 80 per cent of the details along with the drawings. But later, we found that the design details were based on an old engine, and the one being prepared for our flight had undergone several changes.

When we tried to seek clarification, some Russian scientists talked comparatively freely. But many did not share exact information and a few said misleading things. The collaboration with Russians dwindled to a mere commercial contract. Even though we could depend a little on the overall design of the engine, explanations for the how's and why's were not available. Therefore, cryogenic rocket technology had to be painstakingly developed in-house.

The indigenous design, on hold since the Russian contract

finalization, was resumed. A new initiative was started for developing a 7.5-ton engine similar to the Russian one. Our engineers recreated a design using whatever specifications and details were available. The Russian design used a turbo pump working at 45,000 rpm. Faster pumps need greater precision as well as special materials for their manufacture. We examined the Russian rotor—it seemed to be made of a strange mixture of metallic elements. Some manufacturing details were available, but nobody had any clue about the materials used. The materials were unlikely to be available in the international market either. It was clear that even if we asked for details, the Russians would not part with full information. Mishra Dhatu Nigam, which had developed maraging steel for the PSLV, agreed to develop some of the materials for our cryogenic engine. These efforts were fully supported by the materials group at the VSSC.

Next was the development of the thrust chamber, which had to withstand extreme temperature and pressure conditions. Our design was based on a special-grade pure copper having good conductivity. However, the Russian design had used a special stainless steel double-walled elaborate construction. Any leak would lead to a big explosion! A six-axis machining centre was imported from Japan to ensure precise machining of engine parts. An induction furnace capable of reaching up to 1,500°C had to be put inside a vacuum chamber to integrate the parts. We could finally build a thrust chamber that was even better than the Russian one!

The next major challenge was the development of a turbo pump for hydrogen and oxygen, both in liquid form. Hydrogen and oxygen would be burning at one end of the turbo pump, with cryogenic fluids at the other end, resulting in a high temperature gradient. Creating a seal to avoid the mixing of fuels and a suitable material for making the turbine, which must rotate at the high speed of nearly 50,000 rpm, were challenges. The design team wanted to make a fresh design using material available from the international market. I conducted several reviews and, considering the complex thermostructural needs, converged on Russian materials, which were difficult to obtain. Fortunately, during a visit to Russia, I managed to buy six sets of such materials. These materials were later indigenized at MIDHANI.

As PSLV mission director at the console at the mission control centre at the SHAR for a PSLV launch in 1994. From left: Dr P.S. Goel, Col N. Pant, K. Narayana, Dr K. Kasturirangan and I.

Courtesy: ISRO Archives

With Dr Kalam (second from left) at the SHAR in front of PSLV-D3 before the launch on 21 March 1996. Also seen are D. Narayana Moorthi (extreme left) and M.C. Uttam (extreme right).

Courtesy: ISRO Archives

The setting of the launch: PSLV-C2 on the launch pad in Sriharikota in 1999
Courtesy: ISRO Archives

During a review meeting at the VSSC in the late 1990s. With the chairman Dr Kasturirangan (extreme left), Dr Srinivasan (second from left), Dr S. Vasantha (third from left) and others
Courtesy: ISRO Archives

A light-hearted moment: With S.M. Krishna, the chief minister of Karnataka (centre), and Dr Kasturirangan (right) in Bengaluru in 2002
Courtesy: ISRO Archives

With the poetic prime minister: Presenting a model of the satellite Resourcesat-1 to Prime Minister Atal Bihari Vajpayee at the Prime Minister's Office in 2004. Dr Goel is on the left.
Courtesy: ISRO Archives

With a visiting Russian delegation led by Dr Anatoly Perminov (third from left, front row), the chief of the Russian space agency at ISRO Satellite Centre (ISAC) in 2004. Dr Goel is to my left, followed by P.S. Sastri.
Courtesy: ISRO Archives

In constant pursuit of new technologies: During cryogenic-stage development at the ISRO Propulsion Complex in Mahendragiri, c. 2005
Courtesy: ISRO Archives

During an event at the VSSC in 2005. Seated are T.N. Seshan (extreme left), Dr Kalam (second from left), Professor M.G.K. Menon (third from left) and others, with Mrinalini Sarabhai at the mic.
Courtesy: ISRO Archives

The importance of lucid explanations: With an Italian minister at ISAC in 2005
Courtesy: ISRO Archives

Making international friends: With NASA president Dr Michael Griffin (right) and Dr Suresh (left) at the VSSC in 2006
Courtesy: ISRO Archives

A universal passion for space: My wife Radha and I with astronaut Sunitha Williams in Hyderabad in 2007
Courtesy: ISRO Archives

A successful experiment: The capsule from the Space Capsule Recovery Experiment (SRE) being brought in from the Bay of Bengal near Chennai with the help of the Indian Navy and Air Force in 2007

Courtesy: ISRO Archives

An international network: Addressing an International Astronautical Congress (IAC) session in 2007 in Hyderabad

Courtesy: ISRO Archives

A head-to-head with Dr Keiji Tachikawa, president of the Japanese space agency at the IAC, Hyderabad, in 2007

Courtesy: ISRO Archives

Extending the hand of friendship: With the chief of Arianespace Jean-Yves Le Gall (left), and Francois Auque (centre) of Airbus Space in French Guiana in 2007

Courtesy: ISRO Archives

When ISRO's technology and industrial facilities collaborate, both parties benefit. It does away with the need to add to the in-house production facilities, which is generally cheaper in the long run. The high-quality production technology implemented by the industry helps in the realization of aerospace components for other applications as well. Companies that had worked with us on the Vikas engine collaborated with us again, such as MTAR, Hyderabad, and Godrej, Mumbai.

A hydraulic mechanism was used to regulate the thrust of the Vikas engine by controlling the fuel flow into the engine. To make an electronic controller like the one the Russians used, flow meters and electrically controlled valves that work at cryogenic temperatures were needed. Developing control valves working at room temperature was difficult. Indeed, the first SLV-3 failure was caused by such a component. Under cryogenic conditions, the complexity increased exponentially. In spite of all challenges, we succeeded in realizing all the parts within ISRO.

The Russians had used analogue control. We changed it to microprocessor-based digital control and proved it with the Russian engine. The same scheme could be used later in our indigenous engine as well.

The cryogenic liquids vaporize when they flow over hot surfaces. Hence, the initial flow would be an unpredictable mix of liquid and gas. It took multiple trials to learn to control the fuel and oxidizer flow exactly at the time of ignition. Often, it takes hundreds of tests to understand such matters. We avoided that path and used mathematical models to simulate the process in computers and optimize it.

Scientists like Dr K. Ramamurthy and Dr V. Narayanan invested a lot of time in the preliminary studies. The latter built a comprehensive theoretical model simulating all aspects of the engine and validated it using the Russian data. This theoretical model was used for predicting the performance of the Indian engine. The actual performance obtained during the test was a perfect match with the theoretical simulation. Today, we can make predictions with textbook precision on each indigenous engine. That we could evolve such a liquid engine model for the first time in India was indeed a great achievement.

COMING CLOSER TO REALIZATION

Some more subsystems had to be realized—a gas generator to drive the turbine, electronic controllers to integrate the operations as well as electro-magnetic valves and sensors. The Russians had given us only very rough ideas. Realizing the parts to suit the exacting performance requirements was a formidable task.

Materials that work under cryogenic temperatures were the primary challenge. The VSSC scientists joined with MIDHANI experts to prepare and test nearly 60 different metal alloys. The next problem was to realize the various engine parts using these materials. Such designs can only be made using complex thermostructural analyses. Sridharan Dhas took up the challenge. He had earlier developed similar parts for the PSLV's second-stage Vikas engine.

Mahendragiri was home to most facilities for integrating and testing cryogenic engines. The first step was making liquid hydrogen and liquid oxygen. Hydrogen was produced by cracking naphtha. Pure hydrogen was chilled to liquid temperatures through several stages of compression and expansion and then cleansed, which took nearly 15 days. The plant was a completely indigenous design, and many chemical power plants and instrumentation industries were involved in setting it up. We were all overjoyed when liquid hydrogen was realized for the first time in India.

A special clean-room had to be set up where the engine parts could be examined and integrated. The atmospheric humidity and temperature had to be precisely controlled, and even minute particles of water or dust had to be kept out.

The next task was building a test stand with facilities for filling liquid hydrogen and liquid oxygen into storage tanks kept at some distance from one another. Pipes bringing these cryogenic liquids to the engine, mechanisms for controlling the temperature and pressure, nitrogen shields to ensure safety, computerized systems for acquiring data and for sending thousands of control commands—all these had to be readied. The LPSC engineers, led by M. Annamalai, realized the systems precisely. A huge tower was also set up to fix the engine and stage. We succeeded in developing all such systems in-house.

These developments were completed within the span of two years.

When Russian scientists were taken to Mahendragiri and shown the complex activities, they were stupefied. They said that our modern computer-controlled facilities were a thousand times better than theirs!

I had many occasions to visit Russian manufacturing and test facilities as part of the contract signed with them. Many of these replicated factories from the Second World War. The machinery in many of the labs was outdated by more than 50 years! Still, they could come out with very complex rocket parts—this was indeed amazing. I once heard a comment: 'If one part is required, we will make five of them and choose the best one.' The military discipline of the erstwhile Soviet Union governed the technical experts and workers. Everything was precisely documented and reviewed at specific milestones. Their test stands and instrumentation set-ups were archaic in comparison with ours. But when dedicated scientists and technicians work together, success follows, even with such facilities.

The cryogenic engine parts started to arrive from various industrial plants. Many failed the initial tests, either due to lack of precision in fabrication or faults in the materials used. However, all the issues were rectified, and the subsystems were brought to Mahendragiri.

Dedicated hard work for the next six months resulted in the realization of our dream—the first Indian-made cryogenic engine. Since this Russian-model engine could only be tested in the fully assembled mode, we got ready for such a test.

At first, the engine was operated briefly. The test duration was gradually increased to 800 seconds. Once, a fire broke out all around the engine. We had a really hard time finding out the reason. It turned out that a gas-generator part did not match exactly with another, which had caused hydrogen to leak and, hence, caused the fire. It took three to four months to correct the errors and repair the damage to the test stand. The cryogenic technology department of Indian Institute of Technology (IIT) Kharagpur helped us analyse the engine performance in order to pin-point the reasons of failure. We also brought in a few Russian technical experts to the reviews.

The initial tests were followed by readying four more cryogenic engines. I remember that work went on day and night in Mahendragiri during those days.

The final test was scheduled at night. Hydrogen line chilling is a time-consuming process.[1] The operations were carried out inside a two-storeyed structure, which looked like a complex chemical plant. Hundreds of sensors as well as good-quality night-vision cameras were employed for ensuring safety during the whole process.

The LPSC HQ was in Valiamala during cryogenic engine development. It had another unit in Bengaluru, in addition to the test centre in Mahendragiri. The Bengaluru unit is mainly involved in developing propulsion systems for spacecraft even today.

I used to visit Mahendragiri every week to review the activities there. I had to focus not only on the realization of the cryogenic engine but also the computer systems and interface software used for controlling the tests. Another priority was resolving the issues that cropped up while integrating engine parts. V. Gnana Gandhi, the project director, would be in Mahendragiri along with his colleagues and would bring experts involved with both the engine and test facility to the meetings. Such discussions involving all the people concerned helped greatly in understanding the issues and finding real-time solutions to problems. He had experience of working at the SEP, France, and the Russian cryogenic development centre, and was a thorough expert in the technology.

N.R. Vishnu Kartha played a crucial role in realizing the cryogenic engine's parts. Rigorous hard work in Hyderabad and Mumbai resulted in the realization of all the complex parts. The subsystems were the responsibility of different groups. Gnana Gandhi and Associate Project Director Mohammed Muslim were engrossed in consolidating all the activities. Things were so complex that dozens of issues would come to my table every day. It was a real headache to analyse each and find solutions.

I would leave home at 8.30 a.m. and return only by midnight. Once all the administrative matters were dealt with by 10.00 a.m., it was time for technical discussions until noon, followed by visits to labs and workshops. Lunch at 1.30 p.m. used to be followed

---

[1] Liquid hydrogen at cryogenic temperature has to flow through the pipelines during the test. Before admitting the liquid hydrogen, the lines have to be cooled to cryogenic temperatures. This is known as hydrogen-line chilling.

by a review of critical issues 2.00 p.m. onwards. If any tests failed during the day, the failure analysis used to start by 8.00 or 9.00 p.m. The frequent travels were an ordeal—to Mahendragiri once or twice every week and to Bengaluru at least once a month.

All staff members had the full freedom to call me whenever they had a problem, irrespective of how busy I was. No one was denied a meeting for want of a prior appointment. I tried to attend to issues immediately as far as possible. The commutes between home and office were spent in chalking out the day's work plan. After reaching home, I would retire for a good night's sleep, keeping all issues aside for the meantime.

TOWARDS THE FINISHING LINE

The engine was ready in two to three years. But a lot of work was still needed to make a rocket stage that could replace the Russian one. The primary challenge was the light-weight aluminium storage tanks and the insulating materials that could maintain the low temperatures needed precisely, so that hydrogen and oxygen remained in liquid form. None of the aluminium materials used in the past had worked at such low temperatures, so a special alloy had to be developed. Sheets and forgings were prepared by entering into a contract with the Indian company Bharat Aluminium Company.

The next challenge was to convert the sheets into a cylindrical tank of 2.8-m diameter. The special tools and welding equipment required were realized by the HAL aerospace division led by N. Gunasekharan. Many parts had to be fabricated using a very modern three-axes machining centre. Delicate welding was needed to integrate the sheets together. Next, we developed special plastic foam to cover and insulate the tanks from the outside heat. The chemical composition was developed under K. Sitarama Sastri at the VSSC, and the mechanism to coat the tank with it was set up in Mahendragiri.

We had only a rough outline of the various components required to control the fuel flow from the tank to the engine. In-house development of each item, from designing based on detailed specifications to precision manufacturing, was indeed a huge effort. But our engineers accepted the challenge. The parts were fabricated at different places and were brought to Mahendragiri.

The pipeline had to be made with special composite materials. We had already used composite materials for SLV-3. Pyro-operated valves were needed to ensure safety till the time of launch. We had developed a small valve for use in control systems and satellites earlier as well. But now the requirement was for valves, 100–150 mm in diameter, that had to work at cryogenic temperatures. This difficult task was shouldered by the pyro technology group at the VSSC under V.V. Babu, a pyro expert selected by Dr Kalam. C.B. Kartha led the efforts. The activities initiated inside a little shed at TERLS then evolved into a big laboratory that could develop several types of pyrotechnic devices. The products developed there have been used to separate rocket stages, open heat shields, deploy satellite solar panels, control liquid or gas circuits and a hundred other applications. Still, stepping into the arena of cryogenic technology components was quite a daring endeavour.

To cut a long story short, we developed and qualified all the subsystems for the cryogenic engine and stage, using our own knowledge and the capabilities of smart, young scientists, engineers and technicians—all educated in Indian institutions. That is something we can rightfully be proud of. Since we did not have the freedom to file for patents, as space falls within the strategic sector, many such opportunities were lost.

Finally, the engine was qualified through many experiments and tests for a cumulative duration of 7,500 seconds. Our confidence increased manifold.

It took a full nine months to make a cryogenic stage ready for flight. It was already 2009. Twelve long years had passed to reach the finishing point. But we may recall that the French had taken 15 years for the same and Russia had taken 20 years! If we did not have to contend with the American sanctions, we would have worked even faster.

In retrospect, had we accepted Nambinarayanan's suggestion about getting French technology instead of the Russian, we could have built our engine in 60 per cent of the time we took, as the French version was simpler. Indeed, when I was the chairman of ISRO, we decided to follow the French gas generator model for the high-thrust cryogenic engine for the GSLV Mark III launch vehicle.

I am happy that I could participate in the indigenous cryogenic engine development programme right from the beginning. The support of the chairman of ISRO and my other colleagues was crucial in the successful development of the stage in the 12-year time frame. It was during my tenure as the chairman later that efforts towards obtaining formal approvals and development for the 20-ton cryogenic engine were prioritized. I consider the development of a totally indigenous 20-ton cryogenic engine as a substantial achievement.

Today, India has developed and proved cryogenic technology by itself. The USA and Russia did not give us the technology, perhaps fearing that it may be used in missiles. It is important to note that cryogenic engines cannot be used in missiles. These fuels can be filled only about four to five hours before launch. Hence, a notice of at least five hours is needed for launch. Such leisure is not available in the case of missiles, which need to be launched at short notice.

REFLECTIONS ON THE LPSC DAYS

I was the LPSC director for a total of four years. I was able to lead a number of crucial developmental activities. The first 7.5-ton cryogenic engine is a good example, which I explained in detail. The most exciting moments in those years were when the first drop of cryogenic fluids started flowing and the first flame of the cryogenic engine was seen. As the director, I could contribute to establishing the basic infrastructure, including production and storage facilities for liquid hydrogen and oxygen, the test stand and a state-of-the-art data acquisition and control centre for engine and stage tests. With the committed efforts of M. Annamalai and his team as well as industry participation, these could be established and have become valuable assets to the organization. The end result was the successful development of indigenous cryogenic engine for GSLV Mark II and a higher thrust cryogenic engine for the more recent heavy-lift launch vehicle GSLV Mark III.

Facilities for developing electric propulsion were set up during my time as well, and prototypes of a small 10-newton engine were fired. Contracts were signed with many industries for fabricating important parts needed for liquid engines as well as fluid control components. We also strengthened capabilities in the theoretical modelling of propulsion and combustion phenomena and evaluation of instability problems, among other developments, including comprehensive simulation software for cryogenic engines. Dr K. Ramamurthy and Dr V. Narayanan contributed greatly in these activities.

Although the LPSC's main mandate was the development of rocket technology, we initiated experiments to see whether a bus could be run on hydrogen, which is predicted to be the next-generation fuel. It has no harmful emissions and only water vapour as exhaust! While hydrogen could be injected directly as the fuel, there were several safety issues. Instead, I suggested using fuel cells producing electricity through hydrogen and atmospheric oxygen to power the direct-current (DC) motors that propel the bus. I believe that this is a good milestone in our path towards pollution-free vehicles. We carried out a joint project with Tata Motors for running a bus totally on hydrogen. The concept was successfully demonstrated.

I could perform well as the director of the LPSC not because of my expertise in propulsion but by keeping my eyes and ears open in all technical reviews and motivating experts to put in their best efforts. I was a totally content man when I left the LPSC.

I had succeeded Dr Muthunayagam as the director of the LPSC. As the PSLV project director, I had several opportunities to interact with Dr Muthunayagam. We always maintained good relations. Dr S. Vasantha took over as the director of the LPSC after me followed by N. Vedachalam. After him, R.V. Perumal took charge. He had earlier worked as the project director for the PSLV and GSLV. I found in Perumal a structural engineer with very deep knowledge of overall rocket systems. I always respected his expertise in solving technical issues.

Dr A.E. Muthunayagam used to call me 'Kalam's man'. I took it as an honour, as Dr Kalam was one person who loved me from the heart, was a dear friend who stood by me in every crisis and an expert at pointing out the right path to take during times of confusion.

18

Back at the Mother Centre

In 1999, I assumed the charge of the VSSC, Thiruvananthapuram, as its director—a very exciting milestone and a moment of pride for me. Memories from joining Thumba and the subsequent years flooded my mind. There is no comparison between TERLS of those early times and the VSSC of today. The infrastructure then was so primitive that rocket systems were transported to the launch pad on bullock carts and bicycles! Today, the VSSC has world-class research facilities.

Directorship of the VSSC was a position that my guru Dr Kalam could not adorn since he had to leave for the DRDO immediately after the SLV-3 launch. By the time I assumed that office, he had become the chief scientific advisor to the defence minister, concurrently holding the post of director general of the DRDO. He was extremely happy to hear about my appointment and wished me success, assuring all support as well.

The staff strength of the VSSC was around 6,000 then, the largest among ISRO centres. The VSSC had a well-structured and organized set-up, which made my job simple. It was bubbling with activities, being in the thick of preparations for the first launch of the GSLV. I focussed on accelerating the ongoing missions and innovating new technologies for the future.

Directors tend to get little time for technical work, owing to responsibilities like personnel management, recruitment, budgeting, public interactions, and so on. Several issues come to the director's table daily, for redressal. Management of interpersonal problems among the scientists, technicians and administrative staff was one of the most difficult tasks, while integrating the different activities of the VSSC, like research, design, fabrication, testing and advance planning for the future. Amidst all these, the director has to also find time to review technical issues and guide the teams to find solutions.

AN INHERITED STYLE OF MANAGEMENT

The VCMC, with heads of the different departments (deputy directors) as members, assisted the director in the overall management of the VSSC. The Space Centre Council (SCC) was another technical group, where, in addition to the deputy directors, 20 group directors at the VSSC were also members. Then there was the Space Scientific Committee (SSC) with all division heads and administrative chiefs as members. Each group had typically three or four divisions. One group exclusively dealt with programme planning and evaluation. The system had been in place right from Dr Brahm Prakash's time.

The SSC started off with about 60 members and grew to nearly 120 in my time. The hall where meetings of the SSC used to take place, the SSC conference hall, did not have the capacity to seat so many members. Walls had to be demolished, both physical and mental, to extend it.

The VCMC met every Friday afternoon to discuss matters like the progress of activities, issues faced by the groups and the status of each project. All major financial decisions of the VSSC were taken in those meetings. If any special matter had to be discussed, the people concerned would also be invited to the meeting. The SCC met once every two months and conducted technical reviews. The SSC met every month and discussed the progress of projects and day to day issues. Such systematic reviews led to the smooth functioning of the VSSC.

Heated arguments were a normal feature of these meetings. Everyone could freely raise issues about or question the presentations being made. A director's success lies in not taking any sides in such passionate discussions. My role model was Dr Brahm Prakash, the first director of the VSSC. He had a very effective style of management: He did not talk much in such meetings. He would just listen to everybody, holding a lighted cigarette. I still remember an occasion during a very heated debate when he absentmindedly lit the filter end of the cigarette! He would not announce the decision immediately at the end of the meeting for debates on controversial topics. Instead, he would meet all the stakeholders separately later in the evening and communicate his decision. I thought this avoided impulsive decisions, which are often driven by the vocal power of individuals rather than logic.

An annual plan would be made well in advance defining the goals of and resource allocations at the VSSC. Sometimes, mid-course corrections would be required. Such matters deserved the director's close attention. Most decisions were taken through a consultative process after accounting for the different viewpoints and resource constraints.

All ISRO activities are carried out under strict supervision. Control mechanisms have evolved over the years. The unique style of Dr Sarabhai, with broad-mindedness and scientific temper, coupled with industrial management expertise, is still visible in ISRO's culture. I think a majority of management training programmes follow a Western style, which may not suit an R&D organization like ISRO, where the work environment is unique. Most of us at ISRO did not have any formal management education. However, our leadership skills were sharpened through association with great leaders like Dr Sarabhai, Professor Dhawan, Dr Brahm Prakash and Dr Kalam.

I had understood the need for effective human resource (HR) development during the early days in my career itself and had submitted a detailed proposal to Dr Sarabhai about giving a three-month-long training to all new recruits at TERLS. He liked the idea very much. Unfortunately, he passed away before it could be implemented. No one took the initiative later to pursue it. When I became the director of the VSSC, I initiated a three-month training programme in 2001, where people from other centres could also participate. The training was held at three levels: entry, mid and senior. I was determined that everyone, especially the youngsters, should get exposed to the various aspects of the space programme without going through arduous on-the-job learning. Those efforts later culminated in establishing a separate training wing at the VSSC for HR development, catering to the whole of ISRO.

The VSSC had nearly 1,200 employees in Group C and D categories of central government employment. They worked in administration, canteen, stores, as drivers in transport services, etc. Although there were no formal trade unions at the VSSC, the employees were in three groups guided by different political parties. Welfare-related issues were resolved through the Joint Consultative Machinery (JCM), with representatives from the management and the employees. I tried to make the JCM more effective through open discussions cutting across party lines.

Only once did an employee' strike happen in ISRO. That was during the initial days of the organization, and it was about shifting Professor U.R. Rao's satellite division from Veli to Bengaluru. An employees' union led by the Congress leader Vayalar Ravi tried to prevent the transfer. Professor Rao did not budge. The satellite wing was shifted to the Peenya industrial estate in Bengaluru and later evolved into the present-day URSC.

While I was the director, many discussions focussed on the need for novel and diverse projects. An important idea being considered was about space vehicles that could be brought back to the Earth and reused, like the American Space Shuttle had been. We knew we had a long and hard way ahead if we wanted to realize such vehicles in India. As a beginning, a technology demonstrator project named 'Recovery and Reusable Experiment' was initiated.

Sending a man to space and developing new technologies that would greatly reduce the cost and effort of launches were some of the other new initiatives. Studies on the new technologies required were initiated. Energy systems for space applications were also being developed at the VSSC with silver-zinc and nickel-hydrogen cells. Foreseeing future needs, development of lithium ion and fuel cells was also initiated.

The biggest obstacle in developing simulation software was the unavailability of powerful computers at the VSSC. Let alone supercomputers, we did not even have access to regular personal computers! Hence, a project was formulated to develop a powerful computing system based on parallel computing. Good-quality commercial personal computers were sourced from supermarkets in the Gulf and Singapore, and were interfaced together to form a parallel computing system, matching a supercomputer with the speed of 1 TB/s in capability. This short-cut method yielded a system with one-fifth the power of the most powerful such computers in the world at that time. The hardware was soon ready, but developing the software was no simple job. However, our engineers, who were experts in modelling, worked day and night and emerged successful.

Simulation software used at the VSSC needed to be strengthened. Dr K. Sivan took up the challenge. Born into an ordinary family from a remote village in the Kanyakumari District, he had to overcome many challenges before completing his MTech degree. He joined ISRO in 1982 and was posted to the PSLV project. He became the chief designer of SITARA—a comprehensive 6D trajectory-simulation software developed without any external help. Dr Sivan later rose to the position of the chairman of ISRO.

Aerodynamic characterization is very important in rocket development. Earlier, we had to queue up at NAL in Bengaluru for such tests. I wished to change this. We started efforts to set up a full-fledged laboratory in Thumba. The lab at NAL had been realized with international collaboration. But at the VSSC, we were building it ourselves. The lab was 90 per cent ready by the time I quit my job. The plasma jet facility required for testing materials was another of my favourite projects. Another was air-breathing propulsion engines that would suck in oxygen from the atmosphere outside and use it as oxidizer for propulsion. Since oxygen need not be carried, the engines would become lighter.

Along with these projects, we considered moving away from hazardous and toxic propellants to non-polluting combinations. Cryogenic technology using hydrogen and oxygen was under development. But again, using large quantities of liquid hydrogen for the booster stage posed several problems, including high cost. The alternative was semi-cryogenic technology, which uses liquid oxygen and kerosene or methane. Such engines had already been proven in several American launches. Studies were initiated and, during my visits abroad, I kept looking around for technologies.

The Soviet Union had developed high thrust engines and had conducted three launches using them. After the dissolution of the Soviet Union, Ukraine acquired the technology of the 200-ton thrust engine developed for the Zenith rockets. We entered into a contract with them later during my term as the chairman of ISRO. However, the USA soon raised objections. But the head of the research centre in Ukraine was bold and agreed to give us three semi-cryogenic engines along with all the technical details. Unfortunately, my own successor to the office of chairman of ISRO annulled this contract, maybe due to fear of earning the wrath of the USA. Later, S. Somanath restarted the programme when he took charge as the director of the LPSC. I had observed, even during Somanath's involvement in the PSLV project, that he had the technical and managerial spark required for advanced projects. He had led the GSLV Mark III project before taking charge of the LPSC. Currently, he is the chairman of ISRO.

After the contract with Ukraine was signed, the plan was to develop the semi-cryogenic engine indigenously and take it to Ukraine for testing. Even though the development of the required test facilities in-house was initiated a long time ago, progress was hindered due to the 'policy paralysis' that happened during the second United Progressive Alliance (UPA) government.[1]

In my initial days after joining TERLS, Dr Kalam used to take his jeep to some shops in nearby Kulathur and somehow get some snacks for us when we worked during the nights. But today, we have air-conditioned canteens at the VSSC. The food is subsidized. Nowhere else are full meals provided for less than ₹10! Once I asked our canteen manager how this was possible. It turned out that the food served during the seminars and workshops regularly conducted at the VSSC could be priced high, thereby making up for the loss on the regular food. A nice arrangement that benefits both the employees as well as the canteen management!

GSLV: AVERTING A DISASTER

During my tenure as the director of the VSSC, the most memorable event for me was the successful launch of the GSLV. In case of

---

[1]Vaishnav, Milan and Danielle Smogard, 'A Devil Called Policy Paralysis', *Carnegie Endowment for International Peace*, 17 May 2014, https://bit.ly/40IJOFF. Accessed on 27 April 2023.

the GSLV, the first experimental mission was successful, unlike the SLV-3, ASLV and PSLV, where the first launches had tragic outcomes.

The development of the GSLV was indeed very challenging. Most of the subsystems were developed and qualified by our expert teams at various ISRO centres. The launch was scheduled for 28 March 2001. The first-stage motor of the GSLV was similar to that of the PSLV. The different segments of the motor were fabricated by external industries and brought to Sriharikota, where solid propellant was filled into the segments. The stage was then prepared by vertically stacking the segments. Four L40 liquid stages used as strap-on rockets were integrated in Mahendragiri, and the four stages were brought to Sriharikota for assembly to the core first stage.

The second stage of the GSLV was similar to that of the PSLV. It was also brought to the MST in a fully assembled condition. The EB was assembled over the Russian cryogenic stage and fully tested. All the facilities needed for preparing the cryogenic stage and filling the propellant into the rocket had been realized indigenously. A communication satellite weighing 1,540 kg was built at the URSC in Bengaluru, brought to Sriharikota and assembled inside the heat shield of the launcher, which was developed solely by ISRO.

The final tests were conducted by connecting the rocket to the control centre, located 7 km from the launch pad. All systems for acquiring data from the rocket and ensuring its safety were set up in a terminal building situated near the launch pad. The data were sent to the control centre using long fibreoptic cables. In the control centre, a chain of 24 computers continuously analysed and displayed the data corresponding to the different systems of the rocket. In this way, its health was examined critically and accurately by the specialists. Filling of cryogenic fuel into the stage started on the day before the launch, as this can only be done very slowly.

With everything going well, we reached the final minutes of the countdown. During the automatic launch control phase, in the last 10 minutes, the rocket is entirely controlled by a set of powerful computers that examine thousands of parameters indicating the health of all the systems. If anything abnormal is found, the countdown is stopped. Then the experts intervene, identify the issue and solve it before the launch activities are resumed.

That day, everything was going smoothly. I had a nagging doubt that something may go wrong. The countdown reached the last 10 seconds. The strap-on motors (called L40s) had to be lit 3.80 seconds before the countdown reached zero. The checkout system had to confirm that all the four motors were functioning satisfactorily and were generating full thrust, before the first-stage booster rocket could be ignited.

The four strap-on engines, which belong to the 'zero stage', were lit at the exact time. Three seconds went by. Suddenly, the warning that one of the L40 engines was not developing the required thrust flashed. The automatic launch control system immediately intervened and stopped the countdown. The L40 engines were shut down. The ignition command was not given, and, thus, a huge disaster was averted. At once, all the rocket systems were commanded to 'safe' mode, so that no further operations took place.

Everybody was shocked and disappointed that the launch could not take place. But we heaved a huge sigh of relief that no great damage had happened. Had the launch proceeded with one L40 underperforming, the mission would have ended in a catastrophe!

Dr Kasturirangan, Mission Director R.V. Perumal, Jeyamani, range directors and experts from other ISRO centres and I were all present. An expert team chaired by Jeyamani, the chairman of the LAB, discussed the issues. Disappointment mixed with relief could be seen on all the faces during the meeting. Dr K. Kasturirangan did not hide his relief that a huge loss to the nation had been prevented.

The fuels in the cryogenic and liquid stages of the rocket were drained by remote control. The details from the ignition of the strap-on motors to the break in the countdown were obtained from the control centre computers. These, along with the data about the rocket systems obtained through the telemetry systems, were examined thoroughly.

The underperformance of one of the L40 engines was reconfirmed. Close examination revealed that not enough concentrated nitric acid had been pumped into the gas generator, which is needed for operating a turbo pump of the engine. Without sufficient oxidizer, the turbo pump was not able to generate the required speed. As a result, less fuel was pumped into the engine, leading to the diminished thrust.

The powerful computers, the large amount of data available and the sharpness of our engineers made it possible to ascertain the cause of the failure within a day. To conclusively establish the root cause of the issue, the Vikas engine needed to be detached from the L40 rocket, and all parts examined closely. This could be undertaken only in the specially set-up assembly line in Mahendragiri. But it would have taken a week to take the stage by road to Mahendragiri and back. The analysis in Mahendragiri would have required even more time! Clearly, it would be at least two months before another launch attempt could be made. Then we realized that since corrosive propellant had already been filled in all the liquid stages, the tankages had to be used within one month!

The only way was to prepare a makeshift clean-tent at the launch centre itself and to disassemble and check the rocket inside it—a risky operation. Any propellant remaining in the stage would be dangerous to the people handling it. Any particle entering the rocket from outside would later affect its functioning. We proceeded with extreme caution.

Careful review revealed tiny lead particles hindering the oxidizer flow into the gas generator. But how had these particles entered the plumbing? A similar issue had occurred in an Ariane rocket two years earlier. The rocket had flown some time before the problem had manifested, and it had fallen into the sea. The parts retrieved from the sea had been closely examined. A small piece of cotton waste, used for cleaning, had got stuck inside and caused the damage. Even today, it is not confirmed whether it was an accident or sabotage. Not surprisingly, we also had such doubts.

Our engineers went to the factory where the engine had been fabricated and examined the process-sheets documenting the relevant information. For easier handling, the pipes had been filled with lead, which has a low melting point, to help retain the shape while bending, instead of sand, which had earlier been used for the same purpose. Once a pipe was properly formed, it would be heated to remove the lead. In this particular engine, a lead particle had remained, causing the problem.

This explanation for the failure was satisfactory. Such a trivial issue had stopped a huge mission in its tracks! A new tube and other systems were immediately arranged and we proceeded with the preparations for the next launch.

The experts went through the recommendations of the failure-analysis committee and the subsequent corrective actions, and gave permission for the launch. The launch was scheduled for 18 April 2001—just two weeks after the first attempt.

This time, the launch was a complete success. All the rocket systems performed normally. The stages ignited and separated in sequence, exactly as intended. The performance of all the stages before the cryogenic stage was normal. The Russian-made cryogenic engine then ignited and performed normally, but the fuel depleted earlier than expected. The engine provided a specific impulse for 454 instead of 458 seconds, as intended. This demanded more fuel to be consumed for developing the required thrust. It was the first experimental flight of the engine.

The satellite could only be injected into an orbit 3,000 km lower than the intended altitude of 36,000 km. The deficiency was rectified using the liquid apogee module (LAM) engine in the satellite, but it reduced the life of the satellite by about two years.

There are many limitations to putting satellites into geostationary orbits. The best locations for conducting such launches are near the equator, far from densely populated areas. French Guiana, just 5 degrees south of the equator, is ideal. Sriharikota, our space port, is 13 degrees north of the equator. Countries like Sri Lanka and Thailand fall within the ground trace of the rocket as it travels nearly 5,000 km to reach the injection point. What if the rocket disintegrates during the launch and its parts fall on populated regions? This is always a point for worry. The international directives insist that the number of flights over populated areas, oil mines or oil rings in the ocean should be minimized even if they fly higher than 100 km. Avoiding the airspace above some of the land mass is not feasible. So we select flight paths that avoid populated zones to the maximum extent possible. The government concerned as well as the air and sea transport authorities are put on alert. Thankfully, none of our launches have faced such issues. There have been a few cases of rockets disintegrating during the initial launches by Russia and China. Since these countries possess vast land masses with little or no population, they did not have to give any explanation to the outside world.

A PERSONAL EMERGENCY

I faced a major health problem during a visit to Moscow for the cryogenic stage review. I felt some uneasiness in breathing, which subsided after some rest. As soon as I returned to Thiruvananthapuram, I went for a thorough check-up, which revealed that five blood vessels taking blood to my heart were blocked to a great extent. Dr Kalam was in touch with me and sent all the relevant details to Dr Trehan, a leading heart specialist in Delhi and his close friend. The latter concluded that an open-heart surgery was the only option and wanted me to rush to Delhi for the procedure, promising to make all support available. However, noting the difficulties in taking treatment so far from my family, I explored the options available nearby. A super-speciality hospital had just been commissioned in Kochi by the spiritual leader Mata Amritanadamayi.

Given that the hospital was new, many people were not happy about me going there. However, after studying the track records of the chief cardiac surgeon Dr Shiv K. Nayar, I decided to undergo surgery at that institute. My wife Radha and son Jayakrishnan accompanied me. After the surgery, the doctors allowed me to return home within a week. In a month's time, I returned to the office. I was extremely impressed with the efficiency with which I was taken care of at Amrita Hospital by Dr Nayar and Dr Haridas. Dr Kalam also came down to the hospital to visit me.

After many years, I was invited to inaugurate a PET (positron emission tomography) scan instrument at Narayana Hrudayalaya, Bengaluru. Dr Devi Shetty suggested a novel way for the inauguration: I underwent a complete scan, and he showed me the 3D picture of my heart—the remnants of my surgery in 2000 were still intact. Much gratitude to the expert hands of Dr Nayar!

FURTHER FLIGHTS

The second experimental flight of the GSLV was conducted in 2003. It successfully placed the Geosynchronous Satellite-2 (GSAT-2) satellite in a geostationary orbit. Afterwards, the first operational launch of the GSLV was conducted in September in the same year. The first Indian satellite for educational purposes, EDUSAT, was launched in that mission. However, the second operational launch of the rocket failed to put the INSAT-4C satellite in its intended orbit. While its failure analysis was ongoing, the INSAT-4CR had to be launched. Our workhorse, the PSLV, was used with some modifications for a completely successful launch.

The first launch of the GSLV using the indigenously developed cryogenic engine, christened GSLV Mark II, conducted in April 2010, failed. The cryogenic engine did not ignite. Another launch using the Russian cryogenic engine was attempted in December in the same year. This time, the rocket lost control in the first stage itself. Sensing danger, the range safety officers issued a destruction command, disintegrating the vehicle. Later, in 2014, the first successful launch could be achieved using the Indian-made Mark II cryogenic engine. Indian Space Research Organisation has developed and launched 13 GSLV rockets until 2018. Five of these were GSLV Mark I using the Russian-made cryogenic engines.

Failures in space missions are not uncommon. Many countries have failed not only in their first missions but in subsequent missions as well. Even the Space Shuttle, the pride of the USA, failed two out of 135 missions. Even the best launchers have faced failures in the range of 10 to 15 per cent in their missions. The failure rate of ISRO is below 10 per cent. The main reasons behind this are the meticulous reviews and the ability to learn lessons from failure, ascertain the root causes for failures and take corrective actions.

The first SLV-3 mission had failed due to a very simple cause—debris got inside a valve and prevented it from closing. An error while translating the digital autopilot code into the computer's assembly language cost us the first flight of the PSLV mission. The first launch of indigenous cryogenic engine failed due to a foreign particle creeping inside the bearing of the turbo pump. Simple errors during fabrication or testing led to these failures. Strict quality control is the solution to such problems. We have put in place systems for ensuring quality—right from the design stage to selecting materials, fabricating, testing and integrating all the subsystems together. Missions in later years could achieve continuous successes thanks to the efficacy of these systems.

We can be proud that ISRO has never faced any problem due to design or technology deficiencies. Indeed, we have developed technical know-how that is undoubtedly world class.

I was the PSLV project director when the GSLV configuration was being evolved. Later, as the director of the VSSC, a project report for the next-generation GSLV, Mark III, had to be prepared for government approval. There were several opposing arguments. We were also thinking about man-rating a rocket to prepare it to lift a human crew. It was difficult to achieve this goal with the old GSLV Mark II configuration. So we revisited the configuration to increase the payload and reliability.

A. Rajarajan, a senior ISRO engineer and composite specialist, suggested using a composite honeycomb to fabricate the heat shield for GSLV Mark III. Nobody accepted this idea in the beginning. But Rajarajan and his team worked hard to make a model. Now, a fully honeycomb-based heat shield is used in GSLV Mark III rockets, saving a lot of weight, time and effort.

A very painful event transpired on 3 January 2002, when I was the VSSC director: Professor Satish Dhawan passed away. A great personality, Professor Dhawan had added onto the foundation of the Indian space programme laid by Dr Sarabhai. During his tenure as the chairman from 1972 to 1984, all the present-day institutions of ISRO were established. He set up many major facilities and centres at Bengaluru, Shriharikota and Mahendragiri. The perfect mix of an academic, professional engineer and philosopher, he instituted a management system and the kind of environment where young people like Dr Kalam could grow and flourish. Not long after his death, ISRO's launch centre in Sriharikota was rechristened as the Satish Dhawan Space Centre to immortalize his memory.

DR KALAM AS PRESIDENT

I was the director of the VSSC when our beloved Dr Kalam was appointed to the highest position in India—the president of the country. The entire nation rejoiced, keeping aside all political and cultural differences. Many celebrations were held at the VSSC. The wave of happiness that spread over Thumba was extraordinary—the place where the great man had spent a significant period of his life, where every grain of sand carried his signature.

Not long afterwards, Dr Kalam visited the VSSC—his first visit as the president of India!—to unveil the life-size statue of his guru, Dr Vikram Sarabhai. We received him with great happiness. His eyes were twinkling with joy. 'Coming to the VSSC is like recharging my batteries. You fill me with the sheer abundance of your ideas,' he declared and the audience erupted in loud applause. After the meeting, he mingled with the crowd, disregarding warnings from the security staff.

After the public meeting, he met with senior scientists of the VSSC. He mainly talked to us that day about air-breathing propulsion, one of his dream projects, which can reduce launch costs tenfold. He stressed the practicality of the technology and exhorted us to surmount the tremendous technical challenges needed to achieve it. He was very pleased with the visit and went back happy.

When Dr Kalam was the president, he used to call me while preparing the technical talks to be delivered at major research institutions. His behaviour on such occasions was always very informal. The pleasantries would be over in four or five sentences. The discussion would then shift to scientific and technical topics. Sometimes politics also would make an entry.

Once he became the president, Dr Kalam's travels naturally became restrained. Before that, whenever he would come to TERLS, he would stroll on the Thumba beach at night, often with me accompanying him. He used to become very nostalgic and would visit the old places, like the bishop's house, which used to be our office. Once back at the guesthouse, there would be a loud call of 'Chandra!' The canteen employee Chandran would immediately appear with a glass of his favourite beverage—buttermilk!

Dr Kalam loved to visit an institution for children with disabilities, run by Father Felix at Vazhuthacaud, whenever he was in Thiruvananthapuram. Once, he took me along for a programme there. He had penned a poem on the flight from Delhi. He requested me to quickly translate it to Malayalam. After the meeting, he asked the children to read it. It was obvious that he loved those children as his own. The sight of those children singing and dancing with Dr Kalam, forgetting all their troubles, is still fresh in my mind.

The scheduled date of retirement from ISRO for both Dr K. Kasturirangan and me was 31 October 2003. Two months before that, in the beginning of September, there was an unexpected development. Dr Kasturirangan was nominated as a member of Rajya Sabha by Prime Minister Vajpayee. We were overjoyed at this rare achievement bestowed upon a space scientist.

Rumours circulated about Dr P.S. Goel succeeding Dr Kasturirangan at ISRO. Dr Goel was the director of ISAC and had worked closely with Dr Kasturirangan from the beginning of ISAC. He also had the advantage of having two more years of service left. His name was first in the list of possible successors submitted to the prime minister by the outgoing chairman. In other departments, normally, the additional secretary holds charge if the secretary leaves. This was not the practice at ISRO or the DOS.

Meanwhile, I received a directive from the prime minister's principal secretary Brajesh Mishra: 'Take charge as the chairman of ISRO and come to Delhi urgently and meet me.' It was the first time in history that the director of a centre had been asked to take over as the chairman of ISRO!

19

Holding the Reins of ISRO

I had no idea about what was in store for me when I reached Delhi to meet Mishra. Only six weeks of my service were left, and the rules normally did not permit extension of service. I did not have a godfather who could have recommended me for higher positions either.

'We are not going to leave you,' Mishra said as soon as he saw me. 'The government has decided to deviate from the norms and extend your service by two years!' I was being appointed as the secretary to the DOS and the chairman of ISRO! The relevant papers had been faxed to the prime minister, who was on a visit to Tashkent, and he had immediately approved the same!

I was overcome with mixed feelings when I left Mishra's office. What may have prompted them to pick me for this very important role? I had no personal connection to Prime Minister Vajpayee. When he had come to Sriharikota once for a PSLV launch, I had explained the PSLV and its missions to him. I had told him that the PSLV can take a small spacecraft even to the Moon. He had been poetic in his reaction, 'The Moon looks so beautiful from the Earth. Lovers compare their beloved's face to the Moon. I wonder how it will be once we reach there and get a closer look.'

I had previously had only a few direct meetings with him and had found him to be a patient listener and a calm and decisive person. Nothing could perturb him. He had a deep awareness of many things and could grasp things and make decisions quickly. On another occasion, I had been invited for an official dinner for foreign dignitaries hosted by Prime Minister Vajpayee. The ease with which he conversed with the visitors on international matters was amazing.

Such opportunities are not rare for top officials of ISRO. I had earlier interacted with Indira Gandhi, Rajiv Gandhi and P.V. Narasimha Rao. When Rajiv Gandhi had come to Sriharikota for a PSLV launch, I had accompanied him to the launch control centre. He had the curiousity and keenness of a jet pilot while asking about the computers in the rocket and the autopilot systems. I had found him sharp and able to quickly get to the crux of any matter.

Narasimha Rao had visited the SHAR during an exhibition organized by ISRO. I had been his guide during the visit. He had been very enthused to know about the computer systems developed by ISRO and asked several questions. This had been when the US-made computers were just making their way into India. Answering a query about why ISRO should develop its own computers, I had mentioned the need to overcome the international embargos slapped on ISRO's launch vehicle programme.

'Yes sure, we must become self-reliant in technology. We must develop whatever we are lacking today, irrespective of the cost,' he had agreed.

Perhaps it was my recognition as the project director of the PSLV—the vehicle of pride for India—that had drawn the attention of Brajesh Mishra and others. Mishra was a broad-minded, action-oriented and brave person. He must have picked my name from among a few others and recommended me to the prime minister.

As soon as Prime Minister Vajpayee returned from the foreign trip, he called me. After small talk and introductions, he gave me some advice. 'Mr Nair, you must focus on how the rockets and satellite technologies can benefit the poor people of our country. The efforts of ISRO should not be merely for developing technical know-how and getting prominence in the international arena. Problems of our ordinary citizens must be solved using space technology. I will extend full support to such initiatives.'

His words, in line with Dr Sarabhai's vision, illuminated my path throughout the six years that I served as the ISRO chairman.

'A CROWN OF THORNS'

Dr Kalam called me as soon as he came to know about the posting. 'Buddy, it is a well-deserved one by all means. Congratulations!' he said. Then he continued, 'Don't forget that it is a crown of thorns. Be extremely careful whenever you undertake any action or take decisions. There could be people who are envious of your achievements. Your success lies in taking them also along with you.'

'You are always a source of strength for me,' I replied. 'I shall disturb you whenever I am in trouble. I shall need your advice to resolve issues, just as I have in the past.'

The virtuous guru that he was, Dr Kalam gave me strength and succour throughout my tenure. But did I correctly understand the many dimensions of his warning? Later experiences have made me wonder about it. I have seen people who declared undying affection for me and acted as humble supporters, who later backstabbed me. I can only pity their ignorant and thoughtless actions.

A big reception awaited me at ISRO HQ. Nearly 500 people, including both the administrative and scientific staff, were gathered there and most were well known to me. They greeted me with great joy. I could feel a festive spirit in the air.

R.Y. Yashoda, private secretary to the chairman, had kept everything ready. My friend S.K. Das, who was additional secretary, was with me when I signed the appointment papers. I then met scientists from the different programme offices and senior DOS officers and discussed the immediate activities to be focussed upon. Dr K. Kasturirangan was busy winding up, and we could only have a brief discussion. I promised him that I would continue the programmes he had been pursuing.

Yashoda had looked after the affairs of the chairman's office since Dr Kasturirangan's tenure. She rendered splendid service as personal secretary to me and continues the good work for my successors as well, having served with six incumbents in more than 25 years. She was adept at ensuring seamless interfaces with New Delhi offices, including the Prime Minister's Office (PMO), often donning the role of a public relations officer. She efficiently oversaw all the affairs in the office and could deftly dig out the paper trails of any matter, however old.

The ISRO HQ is situated at New BEL Road, Bengaluru, opposite the IISc campus, and was built during Professor Dhawan's term. Only the activities of the satellite wing were a little alien to me, though I was quite fluent in satellite technology due to my inherent interests in electronics and communication.

MANAGEMENT OF ISRO/DOS

Let me briefly explain the structure of the top management at ISRO/DOS.

The DOS is an administrative set-up that comes directly under the prime minister and is headed by the secretary to the DOS. A secretariat functions under the secretary to implement government policies. An additional secretary, joint secretary and supporting staff focus on approving the budget, carrying out large value procurements and deploying HR.

The responsibility of conceiving and managing all space-related activities lies solely with an apex body called the Space Commission. Full government powers related to space activities are delegated to the Commission, which approves both short-term and long-term goals and the annual budget for the DOS. It meets at least once every quarter to review the progress and take corrective measures if required. Financial approvals for large projects are also given by the Commission. Initially, members of this Commission were the principal secretary to the prime minister, Cabinet secretary, finance secretary and two senior technical experts. Later, it was expanded to include the Minister of State in the PMO and the national security advisor (NSA). At that time, even ministers could approve only projects worth up to ₹50 crore. However, the Space Commission's limit was ₹150 crore! The Commission also has complete authority to take financial and personnel-related decisions as well as to monitor the planning and implementation of projects for the Indian space programme. No big bunches of files need to be sent to other ministries or the Cabinet. Only policy changes and projects requiring budgetary allocations exceeding ₹150 crore need to be submitted for Cabinet approval.

Indian Space Research Organisation may be termed as a virtual organization and is headed by the chairman of the Space Commission. The ISRO Council, consisting of the directors of the major ISRO centres, helps the chairman to realize the organization's goals. It meets at least once in three months to review the programmes of ISRO, devise solutions to outstanding issues and prepare the annual budgets for all the centres. Antrix Corporation Private Limited commercially markets the technological products and services developed by ISRO.

The custom has been to appoint one person to simultaneously head all three institutions, namely, the DOS, Space Commission and ISRO, which ensures unity of command and helps avoid conflicts.

Officers of central administrative services head many R&D organizations in India. However, the posts of the secretary to the DOS and chairman of the Space Commission have always been held by technocrats. Officers of the administrative wing support them. This unique structure has been the main reason for ISRO's exceptional successes. This is the same for the Council of Scientific and Industrial Research (CSIR), the AEC and the DAE.

When I was the chairman of ISRO, my dear friend and a senior from the BARC training school, Dr Anil Kakodkar, was the chairman of the AEC. We maintained excellent cooperation and friendship throughout and jointly worked on common policy matters in the two departments. A very close personal friendship evolved between Dr Kakodkar and me, perhaps because our working styles and perspectives were similar. We both believed in striving towards indigenization and self-reliance in technology domains.

Thus, it can be seen that the chairman of ISRO has to don multiple official roles concurrently. However, being the secretary to the DOS is the main responsibility. This entails preparing Cabinet notes, interacting with other departments and periodically informing the progress of activities to the prime minister, among others.

Since ISRO HQ and the DOS functioned from Bengaluru, a branch secretariat was set up in Delhi to interface with the Delhi offices, the Planning Commission and the PMO. However, everything concerning R&D is supervised by the chairman of ISRO. A 'scientific secretary' and programme directors in different areas support the chairman. Their main job is to critically analyse scientific and technical development activities, bring issues to the notice of the chairman, plan long-term goals and support communication with the centre directors.

The DOS operates from ISRO HQ and used to have only three or four officers. However, this was not a problem for me. Right from the beginning, many brilliant IAS officers like T.N. Seshan, M.A. Vellodi, S.K. Das and S.V. Ranganath rendered stellar services to the DOS. S.K. Das served at the DOS for more than 20 years culminating into his role as the member (finance) for space and atomic energy. With his extraordinary brilliance and memory, he helped me foresee problems and solve complex issues with the government. Ranganath's extraordinary efforts in implementing a special incentive scheme for the employees of ISRO have to be highlighted. He succeeded after wrestling with and taming many stalwarts in the finance ministry and the PMO.

Indian Space Research Organisation works on R&D activities for rockets, satellites and applications through a number of different centres under it. It has five main centres. The centre for satellite development, the URSC, is in Bengaluru; the VSSC, LPSC and IISU are in Thiruvananthapuram. Space Applications Centre, which develops payloads for the various satellites, including those for Earth observation, is in Ahmedabad. The SDSC in Sriharikota is the spaceport of India, from where the big rockets are launched. National Remote Sensing Centre in Hyderabad, the satellite tracking station in Hassan and ISTRAC in Bengaluru are the other major centres.

The chairman of ISRO is responsible for appointing, through a peer-review process, capable technocrats as directors of all these centres and units. The management philosophy gives the director full freedom in the activities at the respective centres.

MILESTONES ON THE JOB

The annual budget of ISRO was ₹2,500 crore when I became the chairman. The tremendous government support ensured nearly 25 per cent annual growth, enabling us to accommodate new initiatives. By 2009, when I was superannuated, the budget had increased to ₹ 6,300 crore. Only 20 per cent was spent on day-to-day affairs, including lab maintenance, equipment replacement and salaries of the nearly 15,000 employees. The rest was spent entirely on R&D, application programmes, launch vehicle projects and satellite-related activities.

In line with ISRO policies, my goal was to utilize indigenous industries for as much work as they could undertake and to empower them further by developing the basic infrastructure. Nearly 60 per cent of the budgeted amount was spent through Indian industries, thereby building a national base in high-technology manufacturing. Today, more than 200 small and large industries work for ISRO missions, employing more than 10,000 people.

A meeting of ISRO's science programme was scheduled at National Atmospheric Research Station in Gadanki near Tirupati the day after I took over as the chairman. I instructed my staff to prepare for the meeting. One of the staff officers approached me and advised, 'Sir, it has not been many days since you took charge as the chairman. The science programme is a new area for you. Why not postpone the meeting to a later date, so that you can get fully informed about all the relevant matters?'

The suggestion was not acceptable to me. I went through the agenda and found that I was familiar with the items. I told him, 'I must face the meeting one day or the other—the sooner, the better. Let the meeting go ahead as scheduled.'

I had opportunities to interact with many national and international scientists right from my days at TERLS and, hence, was familiar with atmospheric science, ionosphere studies and phenomena like X-rays and gamma-rays. I found no reason to get perturbed about interacting with space science experts.

The meeting was conducted and went well. I could handle it. The staff officer met me after the meeting and said, 'Sir, you did extremely well!' I just smiled. This incident helped boost my self-confidence. I remembered Professor U.R. Rao's words to me, 'If your fundamentals are strong, you can address any scientific or technological issue.'

The first time I participated in an important satellite launch—an INSAT-series satellite—as the ISRO chairman was in French Guiana. Usually, we reach the launch station a few days before the launch.

However, because of other commitments, I reached a day later than scheduled, after a long trip via Paris. Although the reviews had already concluded, the Ariane space team conducted one more brief review and summarized their results and actions. The launch was authorized only after I, representing ISRO (Ariane's customer), concurred with the actions.

There, I met Yannick d'Escatha, the president of the CNES, the French space agency. He had earlier led the French nuclear programme. The intimate friendship that we formed on that day continues till date. During a short break in the countdown, Yannick showed me around all the facilities at the launch complex. Several inputs gathered during that short exposure on integration, moving to launch pad, elaborate arrangements made for weather monitoring, forecasting of thunderstorms, etc., were useful while designing our new launch complex for GSLV Mark III.

The INSAT-3E satellite was launched successfully by the Ariane-5 rocket, and I came back to India immediately after the launch. The satellite had reached a geosynchronous transfer orbit—an elliptical orbit at a distance of 200 km by 36,000 km from the Earth. The orbit is determined by the master control facility in Hassan, which also tracks the satellites. Commands are given from the ground to the satellite for raising the orbit through a series of firings of the LAM engine in it, to finally reach the intended circular geosynchronous orbit at an altitude of 36,000 km.

The first orbit-raising operation had to be executed on the day after the launch. I had just reached Paris from Kourou. I contacted the control centre in Hassan and learnt that the initial engine firing operations had succeeded. I reached Bengaluru the next day, after continuous air travel of 27 hours, and immediately left for Hassan by car. Other orbit-raising operations on the satellite were carried out subsequently. After ensuring that the satellite was positioned at the correct orbit and was functioning fully well, I returned to Bengaluru.

COMMUNICATION SATELLITES: A BRIEF HISTORY

Dr Vikram Sarabhai was of the belief that we can create revolutionary changes in communication by using geostationary satellites. As early as 1975, an experiment was conducted that brought television programmes to villages in central India using the geosynchronous satellite ATS-6, an early NASA satellite borrowed for this purpose. The satellite was positioned over India, giving coverage to remote areas in Maharashtra, Karnataka and Madhya Pradesh. Nearly 5,000 villages with literacy levels less than 10 per cent were selected for the experiment.[1] Large dish antennae were set up to receive transmission of satellite television programmes covering issues like bad effects of alcohol, cruelty inflicted on women and children, citizen responsibilities, hygienic living habits, etc. The experiment, called the Satellite Instructional Television Experiment (SITE), was a tremendous success. The UN assessed it as the best social development effort conducted using space technology. These successful experiments demonstrated the advantages of satellite communication for societal development. Unfortunately, Dr Sarabhai was not with us by then to share the happiness.

Considering the advantage of using geostationary satellites for communication coverage over the entire country, Dr Sarabhai laid the foundation for the development of the INSAT. Initially, we did not have the capability to design and realize such sophisticated satellites. Hence, ISRO collaborated with the American company Ford Aerospace that built a communication satellite following our design and launched it. Indian Space Research Organisation boldly incorporated communication, weather monitoring and TV broadcasting within one platform in INSAT-1, though contemporary agencies used separate satellites for each. The first launch was in a US-made Delta rocket. However, the satellite had only a lifetime of six months compared to the planned three years. A second satellite INSAT-1B launched in 1983 failed within a few months. Both had a few technical problems, which were fixed based on the failure analysis. Subsequently, INSAT-1C and ID were launched. Using these satellites, services like telecommunication, TV broadcasting and weather forecasting were deployed in the country for the first

---

[1]Galloway, Howard L. Jr, 'Satellite Instructional Television Experiment (SITE) Reports from the NASA Resident Representative in India', *Goddard Space Flight Center*, May 1976, https://bit.ly/43ovUdN. Accessed on 28 April 2023.

time. The concept of design and technology proven in this series of satellites helped us perfect all our subsequent communication satellites.

The INSAT-1C and 1D satellites were planned to be launched using the Space Shuttle, which had been developed to take humans to space and to construct the International Space Station. The Government of India and NASA had decided to send my friend P. Radhakrishnan as an astronaut in a shuttle mission scheduled for 1988, intended for launching our INSAT satellite. Radhakrishnan had started crew training activities as well. But the Columbia shuttle mishap changed the plan and his space travel was cancelled.

All four INSAT-1 satellites were built in the USA. But that scheme was discontinued for many reasons, including the embargo on advanced technology imports. This led us to build the INSAT-2 series in India and launch it with the European Space Agency's (ESA's) Ariane rocket. After putting many communication satellites in orbit in this manner, ISRO developed the GSLV Mark II rocket, which was capable of launching satellites weighing up to 2 tons in the GSAT series. But the requirements have increased subsequently with the demand to launch even heavier satellites. The rocket GSLV Mark III has been designed to satisfy these increased demands of our user community.

P.P. Kale and Col N. Pant played significant roles in the development and operationalization of communication satellites. A. Bhaskaranarayana, an expert in satellite communication technology, contributed as the programme director of satellite communications at ISRO HQ. He also supported me as the scientific secretary for a few years. He drew the masterplan for deploying satellites to meet the communication needs for civilian and military applications.

INSAT-3E

The satellite INSAT-3E was the first to be launched after I became the chairman. Soon after the launch on 28 September 2003, it began to develop problems. A solar panel got stuck during deployment. The many avenues we took trying to solve the issue led nowhere. We were all dejected, wondering what to do next. Then one of the young engineers in the team spoke up, 'The panel's side experiences temperature below zero degrees as it is now turned towards the coldest direction. Perhaps that is the issue? Why don't we turn it towards the Sun?'

We were ready to try anything. As a last resort, control rockets were fired to turn INSAT-3E towards the Sun and kept that way for five hours. When commanded again, the solar panels opened up promptly! The satellite began to perform normally and obey commands from the control centre. Greatly relieved, we all returned from Hassan.

After three weeks, the solar panel on one side stopped supplying power, possibly due to a short circuit in the power bus, and it could not be corrected. This meant that the satellite had to survive with half the power for the remaining part of its life.

When I went to Delhi to inform the prime minister about the matter, I met Brajesh Mishra first. 'Madhavan, what happened?' he asked. I explained the issue in detail. 'The solar panels are used for generating electricity in the satellite. The connection from the solar panels passes through a slip-ring assembly. There are panels on both sides. The failure is possibly due to a short circuit in one of the slip rings. Only a detailed investigation can give the exact reason.'

'Wasn't there any redundancy?'

'The slip-ring assembly can cause a single-point failure in both panels. So any problem in that can lead to malfunction in solar power distribution.'

I had not finished talking when he asked again, 'Isn't it an error in the design?' Before I could explain further, he consoled me. 'Don't worry. Such things happen when you do something new. You correct the designs for the future and carry on!'

Only an enlightened bureaucrat can respond like that. Such people possess that extraordinary capability to understand and solve issues without making a fuss.

I could not see Prime Minister Vajpayee during that visit and, hence, went to Delhi again after a fortnight. I met him there and explained the details. Mishra must have already briefed him on the matter. He was very friendly and forthcoming. 'Don't worry, such problems do happen when we do new things. Just be careful that the mistakes are not repeated,' he told me. I remembered that ISRO culture dictates exactly the same thing.

Later investigations revealed that the failure was due to arc tracking, initiated by high-energy particles from the Sun causing a fire in a bunch of power cables.

In hindsight, the whole issue had a few positive outcomes too—I obtained extensive exposure to spacecraft design. It revealed deficiencies in design reviews as well as in quality and reliability management. Most of the designs were kept secret by specific project teams. There were individual projects for different spacecraft, with designs being modified every time by new teams. This prevented sharing knowledge and experience. Based on these inputs, I made several remedial systemic changes.

At one point, satellite designs were fully dependent on imports. Due to embargos, launch vehicle designers had no choice but to develop everything indigenously. This is one reason why the VSSC evolved as a technology leader among ISRO centres. Most of the rocket subsystems are designed in-house and fabricated by local industries. It is heartening to know that satellites have now achieved 40 per cent self-sufficiency in indigenous development.

On another occasion, an orbiting INSAT satellite lost the capability to orient its antenna towards the ground station because of a faulty Earth sensor, an instrument required for the operation. Without precise control of orientation, the communication link could not be maintained. The issue was finally solved innovatively. Signals sent by the satellite to the Earth were caught using four antennae kept far apart in north, south, east and west directions on the ground. Variations in the signals caught by these were analysed and used to control the satellite. Abandoning a satellite with 12 working transponders midway was simply out of the question. It turned out that the satellite could be utilized for its full working life and for seven more years!

In those days, the INSAT control centre at Hassan was led by Dr M.Y.S. Prasad, who was passionate in evolving and implementing new ideas. He had made stellar contributions in electromagnetic interference management and quality control for the SLV-3 project. He had also managed ISRO's office in Paris for some time. He served as the director of the SHAR before retiring. Development of synthetic aperture radar capable of tracking multiple objects simultaneously for the first time in India was one of his great achievements at the SHAR.

One person who gave me unstinting support in all my endeavours at ISRO was S.K. Das, additional secretary to the DOS. Earlier, I used to meet him during ISRO Council meetings. Our first meeting must have been in 1992. Preparations were ongoing at the time for the launch of one of our satellites using an Ariane rocket. The French team was in Bengaluru. The launch vehicle community also used to participate in such meetings, and I was there. During dinner after the meeting, I was talking to the French engineers when I heard a voice from behind: 'Who is Madhavan Nair? I want to meet him. I have a feeling he is going to be the future chairman of ISRO.'

I looked around. There was S.K. Das, the then joint secretary to the DOS. He met me. His conversation, laced with humour, attracted me.

Years later, when I reached Bengaluru to take charge as the chairman, he reminded me, 'Remember, I had a premonition that one day you would land here!'

20

New Visions and Missions

Towards the end of the 1960s, studies for SLV-3 had begun at Thumba under Dr Kalam. One day, sizeable debris from a rocket fell in an unpopulated area in Rajasthan. Locals alerted the nearby Border Security Force personnel, who observed that it contained the remnants of a satellite. Without wasting any time, they packed those and sent them to Thumba. Dr Kalam found the debris very interesting. The module was part of a satellite from the Soviet Union, which was at the forefront of rocket technology in those days. The payload remnants revealed instruments, including a camera for taking pictures of the Earth and sending the film cartridge back to the planet. Dr Kalam called M.K. Abdul Majeed, who was then building the foundations of aerospace mechanisms at ISRO and was passionate about technologies dealing with recovering objects from space.

Majeed studied the equipment closely and generated detailed drawings—a case of reverse engineering. Digital cameras were not in vogue back then, and the Russian camera was a conventional one that used a bromide film. When the satellite was in orbit, the camera would be commanded to take pictures of the Earth. The film capsule would then be ejected and get de-orbited to re-enter the Earth's atmosphere. In the final phase of the return journey, the capsule would be slowed down by a parachute system and captured by a helicopter.

While satellite debris was being studied, some people expressed doubts about possible atomic radiation emitted by the equipment. Immediately, the payload remains were buried under the ground.

This event was the starting point for our own Space Capsule Recovery Experiment (SRE) later.

SPACE CAPSULE RECOVERY EXPERIMENT

As many as 16 countries used the regular American Space Shuttle launches to send scientists and instruments to the International Space Station to conduct experiments under microgravity and bring back the resultant samples. However, India was denied that opportunity because the USA refused to include us in the 16-member club. Consequently, the question about how our Indian scientists could conduct their own microgravity experiments in space came up.

If we launch a capsule using a rocket to a high altitude, say 300 to 400 km, following a ballistic path and allow it to fall back to the Earth, microgravity conditions would be created inside the capsule for about 10 minutes during its free fall. Could meaningful experiments be conducted during that short duration? To prove the concept, in the early 1970s, a capsule and its launch using a Centaure rocket was envisaged. Majeed, V. Sudhakar and I explored the options, made a capsule and launched it. It returned, but landed in the sea. In those days, we did not have the technology to retrieve it from there. We sought the help of the French space agency, as they had the facility to locate and recover capsules in Kourou, South America. The next launch was from Kourou and the capsule was successfully recovered from the sea, brought back and examined closely.

That successful mission was the forerunner for the SRE, conducted using a PSLV rocket. The aerospace mechanisms group at the VSSC under Majeed evolved this project. A project team was constituted in 2001, led by A. Subramoniam. The government formally approved the project in 2005. It was supported by various other national agencies, such as NAL, Armament Research & Development Establishment, Terminal Ballistic Research Laboratory, Naval Science & Technological Laboratory, IITs, the Air Force, the Navy, the Coast Guard, etc.

When the capsule passes through the Earth's dense atmosphere on its return, a tremendous amount of heat is generated due to aerodynamic drag. The capsule velocity at 300 km altitude is about 29,000 km/hr, which has to be reduced to 360 km/hr using the drag offered by the special aerodynamic shape of the capsule. During this time, a lot of the kinetic energy gets converted into thermal energy, and the tip of the capsule experiences a temperature of nearly 3,000°C.

Design and development of a complex structure with an optimum insulation system to withstand this heat was the biggest challenge. A special thermal protection system was designed to protect the capsule from extreme heat during re-entry.

The SRE capsule was as tall as a man, weighed 555 kg and had a sphere-cone-flare configuration. Instruments for conducting two important scientific experiments were placed inside. One was to study the half-crystal growth occurring when molten metal is cooled under zero-gravity conditions. The experiment was carried out jointly by the IISc and Banaras Hindu University. The second experiment was on a study of micro-structural changes of the mineral hydroxyapatite, conducted by National Material Laboratory along with a Japanese agency.

The PSLV had a payload capacity of about 1,200 kg for this mission. A Cartosat-2 satellite and the SRE module were the primary satellites accommodated in a specially designed dual launch adapter. Two other small satellites, the Indonesian Lapan-Tubsat and Argentinian Nano-Pehuensat-1, for amateur radio communication, were riding piggyback. The satellite orbits were different, making mission management more complex.

The SRE had an autonomous navigation, guidance and control system during its orbital phase and de-boost operations. Many innovative techniques were employed in the total design. At an altitude of about 100 km, the capsule's re-entry into the Earth's atmosphere had to be achieved by the autonomous control and guidance scheme. The angle of entry, the speed during re-entry, deployment of the parachutes that would help it land gently on the surface of the Earth, the radio signal blockage that would occur as a result of extremely heated air in proximity with the capsule and other factors posed significant challenges. Numerous simulation studies were conducted, considering the different possibilities, before finalizing the design of the re-entry trajectory and all the structural elements. Our scientists were able to resolve these demanding issues and made the capsule ready by the end of 2006.

THE LAUNCH OF PSLV-C7

The rocket PSLV-C7 was prepared to launch four payloads, including the SRE capsule. Every PSLV launch causes reverberations of joy and pride in me, especially when the rocket carries such historical payloads into orbit.

The scheduled launch date was 10 January 2007. The rocket was ready at the first launch pad in Sriharikota. Exactly at 9.23 a.m., the rocket lifted off with the payloads. Nobody had any doubts about the success of the launch. The C7 was expected to become the ninth successful flight of the PSLV. All the attention and anxiety was about the subsequent re-entry and recovery of the capsule. Would the capsule successfully surmount all the challenges and return in 12 days? We remained glued to the computer monitors in Sriharikota.

When the rocket reached an altitude of 638 km, Cartosat-2 was injected into the designated orbit. Next to get in orbit was Nano-Pehuensat-1. Then, it was the SRE-1 capsule's turn. It was put into an orbit at the height of 635 km. Soon, Lapan-Tubsat also reached its intended orbit.

The SRE module started orbiting the Earth under conditions of zero gravity. The planned microgravity experiments were performed successfully. The capsule was controlled using magnetic torques, so that the microgravity conditions were not disturbed.

The next 10 days and nights passed smoothly. It was time to make a change in the capsule's orbit to get its ground-trace above Chennai as a prelude to the commencement of the re-entry and recovery operations. On 20 January, the capsule was repositioned into a repeating elliptical orbit.

The D-day of re-entry was 22 January. Tension was visible on the faces of all the scientists. In spite of meticulous planning, there was apprehension since everything was being attempted for the first time. The operations started at 9.00 a.m. The closed-loop guidance system was working normally. The capsule reached the exact location for re-entry at the required velocity and angle of entry. It was 9.17 a.m. The capsule started descending at a fiery velocity of 7,900 m/sec. I examined the telemetry data. Everything was okay. However, the situation changed in the next instant. No signal was forthcoming. We waited with bated breaths. Was the capsule still on its way down? Seven seconds passed. At exactly 9.25 a.m., we started receiving signals again with no major deviation from the designated path. The capsule was moving southwards from the North Pole.

The scientists at ISTRAC were busy calculating the re-entry trajectory from real-time data. The capsule was expected to reach 100 km above the Earth with the required velocity and angle of entry. The Lucknow ground station was now continuously receiving the telemetry data from the capsule. Ten more minutes passed. The capsule was now descending vertically. The scientists waited for the parachutes to activate. The crucial period of highest heat around the capsule was now imminent. Soon, the capsule would be engulfed in a sheath of plasma as a result of the heated air, which would black out the data transmission! It occurred after three minutes. The capsule was now falling from 90 to 40 km. No data could be detected from the capsule. Our anxiety peaked. What was happening? Was the capsule safe? Did the torrid heat burn it to ashes? Were any of the instruments damaged? These questions flashed in our minds.

All this time, the Indian Navy ship *Sarang*, with a Chetak helicopter on board; the Coast Guards' speedboat *Gemini;* and a Dornier aircraft of the Indian Air Force were waiting, fully equipped and ready, near the designated area, 140 km off the coast of Chennai, where the capsule was expected to splash down. Expert swimmers from the Navy were ready for the dangerous mission. They had all been briefed extensively about the challenges involved. Even superpowers like the USA and the Soviet Union had failed in their initial attempts at re-entry. If India could manage to taste success in this maiden mission, we would create history! Everyone was fired up by that thought.

It was 9.40 a.m. We started receiving signals from the capsule again! All of us jumped up with joy. There were smiles and applause all around. The mission had passed through the most critical part of re-entry. I could feel the tension slipping away. But one more job remained, in which we had no prior experience—bringing the capsule ashore from the ocean. Messages were flashed to the Army, Navy, Air Force and Coast Guard teams. Members of the coordination team became vigilant.

Two more minutes passed. The capsule was now barely 5 km above the sea surface. Sriharikota could no longer receive the signals directly. The Navy ship started receiving signals. All three parachutes in the capsule opened precisely at the designated time, and its velocity began to reduce rapidly. In the next instant, at exactly 9.47 a.m., it touched down on the surface of the sea, in a location very close to the intended one. Immediately, the float was inflated. It carried an ultra-high frequency beacon to precisely identify its location. The Dornier aircraft was circling in the sky by then, waiting for signals from the capsule. None were forthcoming. Once again, we were all disappointed.

Ten minutes passed. Perhaps, the beacon had malfunctioned. How were we to locate the capsule in the vastness of the sea? Without locating it, how could it be retrieved? We racked our brains. Only if the capsule was shown to the world would the scientific community believe that we had brought it back from orbit! The captain of the Dornier was asked to search thoroughly near the predicted location and inform if anything was spotted in the sea. He immediately swung into action and crisscrossed over the suspected area at low altitude. One hour passed. At last, the colour of the dye marker and the reddish-yellow floatation system of the capsule were spotted in the sea!

As soon we learnt that the capsule was safe, I came out of the control room in Sriharikota to rush to the Chennai port by road, along with other senior colleagues. Both President Kalam and Prime Minister Manmohan Singh were informed about the success.

It was now 10.50 a.m. The pilot flew the aircraft towards the orange spot in the sea. Nearing the body, it became very clear—yes, it was indeed the SRE capsule! He informed everybody. The exact location was computed and shared with the rescue ship and boats, all of which started on their missions. Shouts of joy could be heard across all ISRO centres.

The Chetak helicopter from the Navy ship reached right above the specific location. Any fuel remaining in the capsule could spread in the sea and make it dangerous for the people approaching to pull it out. The scientists in the helicopter had to ascertain that there was no such danger. They minutely examined the sea surface and gave the green flag. Immediately, both the ship and boat reached the capsule. Master swimmers jumped into the sea and tied the capsule to additional floats. The *Gemini* pulled it to the *Sarang*. The people from the ship's deck lifted the small capsule carefully with a crane and placed it on the deck, thereby writing a new chapter in the annals of the Indian space programme.

The capsule looked perfectly alright, undamaged. Our happiness knew no bounds. Dr Kalam called and I could clearly hear the joy in his voice. 'Well done, buddy, well done!' he said.

The *Sarang* reached the Ennore port at 6.00 p.m. We were all waiting anxiously on the dock. The crane aboard the ship gently placed the capsule on a truck on the shore. The capsule had returned and looked the same as when we had launched it in orbit, except some surface charring, as expected! Of course, detailed examinations had to be carried out in Sriharikota.

The recovery mission was a complete success! No further delay was required to announce it to the world. The global media made it big news. *Aviation Week*, a major magazine in the field, wrote a cover story on the SRE-1 success.

The capsule was taken to Sriharikota and examined thoroughly. As suspected, the ultra-high-frequency antenna had not worked. The instruments used in the microgravity experiments were sent to the respective laboratories. Banaras Hindu University informed us that the first experiment was a complete success. However, the second experiment, funded by ISRO, had not gone as expected. Twelve days turned out to be insufficient for it.

With the spread of the news about the success of SRE-1, we received many requests for similar new missions. It was the relatively low cost of the mission that attracted foreign players. Usually, at least $100 million would be required, but we could do it for US $10 million. Sadly, Indian scientists did not seem very interested in conducting more such experiments. Hence, nothing happened for a while. There were suggestions to send a dog to space inside the SRE-1 capsule, like the Russian dog Laika. But I didn't think it was the right thing to do. The dog would probably not be able to withstand the impact of the launch. If it died during the launch itself, nothing would be achieved. Hence, that idea was dropped.

A MANNED MISSION?

The technical know-how required for the SRE experiment is more than what is required for an intermediate range ballistic missile and far more complicated than launching satellites. Consequently, the technologies achieved in such missions become useful in many diverse areas. The capabilities needed for taking a man to space and bringing him back to the Earth are very similar. Indeed, the SRE-1 mission demonstrated that ISRO had achieved the technical capability for bringing back a manned capsule from space.

During one of my visits to Russia, I discussed with Dr Anatoly Perminov, the head of the Russian space agency, the possibility of collaboration for a manned mission. I could establish a firm friendship with Dr Perminov during my first visit to Russia after taking charge as the chairman. The Russians had been using a capsule called Soyuz to send as many as three people to orbit and bring them back, and had completed a few hundred missions. He agreed. We immediately constituted a 12-member team to work out a collaborative programme with the Russian space agency. Dr Unnikrishnan Nair S., who had been the director of the study project; P.S. Sastri, the LVPO director; and D.R. Suma, the LVPO associate director were among the members. The Russian facilities for manned missions were opened before us with detailed explanations.

I worked with Dr Perminov towards strengthening space cooperation. We continued our friendly relations while working together at the International Academy of Astronautics (IAA).

India required a deeper collaboration with Russia. Training the first batch of Indian astronauts needed help. Technologies for flight support, food, waste management and spacesuit had to be shared. Help was also needed to set up a space simulation facility in India. These were our requirements. After discussions, we signed two contracts with the Russians for the development of life-support systems and spacesuits.

A total of 5,000 scientists were required to work on such a mission in India. The expense, estimated in 2010, came to ₹12,000 crore. The project report was approved by the Space Commission and submitted to the prime minister for the final clearance. He was very much interested in the mission. He referred the proposal to Dr Montek Singh Ahluwalia, the vice chairman of the Planning Commission, for expert advice. According to Dr Ahluwalia, it was indeed the next logical step for India to put a person in an orbit around the Earth and bring them back safely.[1] The expense could be met from the returns of the experiment. In any case, compared to the technological advancement and scientific outcomes expected from such a mission, the expense was very modest. Since we did not possess a Space Shuttle, one of our rockets was to be used for the purpose of launch. We made a detailed presentation to Dr Ahluwalia and he agreed.

A discussion with Rakesh Sharma, the first Indian astronaut, who had travelled to space on 3 April 1984 in a Soviet rocket, was our next step. He shared the experiences of his space trip with us and happily agreed to help us in the astronaut training process. His demeanour was very friendly. 'You go ahead fearlessly. The mission is entirely possible for ISRO. I promise all the help that I can provide,' he assured us.

We then got an appointment to meet the prime minister. Members of the SRE-1 project team, human spaceflight design team and heads of different ISRO centres were part of the group that went to meet him. Many top officials like the principal secretary to the prime minister, the NSA and Professor Roddam Narasimha, member of the Space Commission, were with him.

Professor Narasimha spoke affirmatively about our proposal. 'The estimated expenses for the mission are very meagre. The outcomes of this mission can directly benefit our people,' he said. Prime Minister Manmohan Singh also seemed excited about the mission. 'We are not behind anyone in space technology. It is necessary that the tempo is maintained,' he said.

---

[1]Ramesh, Randeep, 'India to Launch Its First Astronauts into Space by 2015', *The Guardian*, 23 February 2009, https://bit.ly/3LKw5tC. Accessed on 1 May 2023.

He appointed a committee with Dr Ahluwalia as the chairman to review our proposal in detail. Dr R. Chidambaram, Professor Roddam Narasimha, Professor M.G.K. Menon, Professor Yash Pal and Dr M.S. Swaminathan were the members. Dr K. Radhakrishnan, who was later my successor at ISRO, was the secretary.

The detailed report of the Ahluwalia Committee determined that the human spaceflight programme was quite necessary. It also stipulated that along with developing the capacity for human spaceflights, space robotics had to be developed. Research on bio-astronautics, space medicine and astrobiology had to be strengthened in universities and research organizations. Maximum industrial participation had to be ensured from the start.

The Committee concurred with the choice of GSLV Mark II for the initial flights for the journey of a two-member team to space. However, it noted that the GSLV Mark III rocket, scheduled to make its first launch in 2010–11, was expected to be able to carry a 10-ton payload, enabling three people to go to space and spend as much as 30 days there.

A test plan was made, including tests for the crew module's re-entry into the atmosphere and three unmanned missions before the final manned mission. Our project report also included a detailed blueprint for raising the reliability of the rocket systems, development of various subsystems, such as the crew module, systems for environment control and life support, spacesuit, a crew escape system as well as systems for setting up the infrastructure for an astronaut training centre, a new launch pad and new mission control centre. The Committee also highlighted the great advantages of a human spaceflight mission for the Indian industrial sector and, thereby, to the common man. About 30,000 employment opportunities would be created in public and private spheres, both directly and indirectly. A total of ₹12,400 crore would be poured into society. National progress resulting from the industries' technical advancement was an additional benefit. In the words of the Committee, 'Accelerated development of India's scientific and technological capabilities by attaining state-of-the art expertise is vital in our journey towards becoming a developed nation.'[2] The Committee highlighted the resulting social and economic progress and benefits for defence and security. It also spoke about the enthusiasm this project would generate in the youth and how that would increase the number of youngsters interested in space technology. The Committee concluded:

> A big country like India cannot keep herself away from the technological leaps such missions provide. The country cannot afford to become backward in technical capabilities. The number of youngsters who aspire for a job in the aerospace sector is now coming down. The thrill of a human spaceflight mission will enthuse students and attract them to challenging scientific and technical disciplines. Taking these factors into consideration, along with the accepted goal of further building up our Space sector, the committee feels that the need for a Human Spaceflight programme is undeniable.[3]

It also asserted that the main goals identified for ISRO by Dr Sarabhai in 1972 had already been achieved. 'The next task is to take that vision forward. ISRO has already acquired the strategic technical capabilities for Space flights through PSLV and GSLV rockets. We have the most modern remote sensing and communication satellites. The Space capsule recovery mission in 2007 has also laid the foundation for human Spaceflights.'[4]

The Ahluwalia Committee's recommendations were included in the project report. It was then discussed and approved in a Space Commission meeting in September 2009. The next step was getting the Cabinet's approval for the ₹10,000-crore project. That task should have been pursued further by my successor to the chair of ISRO. Unfortunately, the project did not proceed further for several years and was put in a deep freezer. The Russian contracts were cancelled.

The GSLV Mark III rocket had its first successful flight while I was writing this memoir. A 3.5-ton heavy communication satellite

---

[2] *Indian Human Spaceflight Programme: Recommendations of National Committee*, private report, 16 March 2009. See https://bit.ly/45IUDeL. Accessed on 5 June 2023.
[3] Ibid.
[4] Ibid.

called GSAT-19 was put into a geo-transfer orbit. All the new rocket systems including the C-25 cryogenic stage worked exactly as planned. A launch vehicle had performed precisely at its first launch itself, for the first time in the history of ISRO. I called up scientists at ISRO and congratulated them. I reiterated the hope that the launch success would accelerate the future plans of the rocket as well as ISRO's plans to take humans to space.

I am happy that subsequently, in 2017, Dr Sivan, the then chairman of ISRO, had the courage and convinced the government about the need for human spaceflight. Prime Minister Modi has given approval for the Indian Human Spaceflight Programme.

It is never too late. We are moving up the ladder in the exclusive space club of nations.

21

More Services to Society

Dr Sarabhai's vision was to use the technology of the space programme to improve the life of the common Indian. As the chairman of ISRO, I considered it as my primary duty to continue that endeavour.

Aryabhatta and Bhaskara were the first satellites built in India and launched with Russia's help starting from 1975. The resolution of images sent by Bhaskara was such that we could only identify objects bigger than an end-to-end measurement of 1,000 m. The technology improved over the next few decades, and today, our satellites can recognize objects measuring even less than 1 m across. The Indian fleet of active Earth-observation satellites now includes Cartosat, Oceansat and Radarsat, among others.

Satellite-based communication, television broadcasting, cartography and weather monitoring can be effectively used to meet the needs of the common man. Professor U.R. Rao and Dr K. Kasturirangan had created several such schemes. They had established remote sensing application centres in many states. I am fortunate that I could take these programmes forward.

MEDICINE, EDUCATION AND KNOWLEDGE

Experiments in tele-medicine had begun with the second satellite Bhaskara. Once, an employee at ISRO was undergoing treatment for heart disease. We sent his electrocardiogram (ECG) reports to a far-off hospital as a test case. Next, the medical reports of a patient from a remote village were sent successfully to a super-specialty hospital, where a specialist provided expert consultation.

Much of our population still resides in villages without modern facilities for medical treatment. During my tenure, I tried to prioritize tele-medicine projects. I increased its budget allocation from ₹10 crore to ₹300 crore. Specialty hospitals, such as Narayana Hrudayalaya in Bengaluru; Amrita Institute of Medical Sciences in Kochi, Kerala; Tata Institute in Mumbai; and Military Hospital in Delhi, were connected to several hospitals from the Northeast, Andaman and Lakshadweep Islands and Wayanad District in Kerala that were brought under the project. By the time I left office, nearly 350 hospitals were connected, including several mobile units.

Since no readymade equipment was available back then to acquire patients' data for tele-consultation, ISRO developed and deployed custom-made medical software, computers, diagnostic equipment like digital ECGs, satellite-based communication systems in remote villages and teleconference systems to communicate with specialist doctors, as part of the tele-medicine network. A small antenna and satellite transponders helped to bring everything together. Monitoring and control of the network were effected through ISRO's hub station, which facilitated real-time video conferencing and data transfer.

The patients' details could be sent either in real time or through offline modes. At first, only one patient–doctor interaction could take place. The facility was expanded, so that a patient would be able to interact simultaneously with multiple specialists at different locations. This multi-point system is now fully operational, resulting in considerable savings for the poor in the villages, who would otherwise need to travel large distances for such services. The system has also provided connectivity to distant islands and mountain regions as well as for the defence services to provide medical services to remote camps in the border areas, to connect to naval ships from their HQ, and so on.

Tele-education was the next public-utility project that we undertook as an extension of the SITE of 1975. Expert and experienced teachers are lacking in our country, especially for students in village schools. A system was evolved to enable students in remote villages to access classes by expert teachers and interact with them. The scheme is now being used to benefit both students and teachers.

Solar panels were installed for power generation in remote locations that did not have good electric supply so that the communication systems could be used. Many schools in the Malappuram District in Kerala were connected with the tele-education network in 2006. Even though we were ready to expand the service to all of Kerala, the government did not show much interest. Later, the scheme evolved into the popular Kite Victers education channel of today. In Haryana, several thousands of schools across the state were linked using the EDUSAT satellite, which was exclusively commissioned for tele-education.[1] It has been used for teachers' training and management courses, as well as for connecting leading institutions like the IITs with less privileged engineering colleges. In June 2022, during Covid-19, the central government announced the launch of 200 tele-education channels across the country. Tele-education has become the mainstay today. Satellite links are now needed only for the remotest of areas, since fibreoptics and mobile towers can provide connectivity in other places.

Remote sensing is the primary area where the fruits of ISRO's labours have benefitted the common man. Earth-observation satellites are performing valuable service for agriculture workers, fishermen and planners. Dr K. Kasturirangan pioneered the design and development of these satellites at ISAC and developed various applications while he was the chairman of ISRO. Dr V. Jayaraman was his right-hand person.

Survey data on India's natural resources is being provided by our satellites right from the start. The data is useful for monitoring various cultivations, assessing their health and estimating agricultural yield. Farming communities use them extensively. Recently, some experiments were conducted on precision farming. The crops in even small holdings can be identified and suitable action can be recommended to maximize productivity.

Observations on the ocean-surface colour, ocean temperature and wind patterns enable the prediction of areas where large schools of fish may assemble. Fishermen can then be directed to those locations, saving fuel and time. This scheme has almost doubled the catch.

---

[1]As per ISRO progress reports.

Monitoring forest coverage, forest fires, etc., helps preserve forest areas and enhance greenery in the country. Observing water bodies and floods and detecting underground water sources improves water management. All these applications have become intrinsic to our national life today. India is a unique country where such services are provided free of charge.

We implemented watershed development programmes in six districts of Karnataka as a pilot project. Agriculture and other human activities wholly depend on water from ponds in the interior regions. By using Earth-observation data, new water sources could be located. The land was fully mapped, and suitable farming methods as well as social forestry projects were implemented with the participation of the local people, voluntary groups and the district administration. The World Bank provided a few hundred crore for a project in Karnataka called Sujala. In an assessment after three years, the income of the farmers was found to have nearly doubled! In fact, the whole society benefited.[2]

Such projects were implemented through ISRO's Regional Remote Sensing Centres in Bengaluru and other places in various states.

NARENDRA MODI'S ENTHUSIASM

Gujarat has made maximum use of ISRO's services from the beginning. When I visited Ahmedabad after the Chandrayaan-1 mission, technology enthusiast Narendra Modi was the chief minister. He invited me for a breakfast meeting at his official residence to discuss how space technology can be utilized for developing Gujarat. I gave many concrete suggestions, which were accepted readily. He fully supported setting up a state centre for remote sensing applications in Gujarat. He was also the first chief minister to use satellite communication for his monthly review meetings through teleconference with district collectors.

The then chief minister also asked me about the Chandrayaan-1

---

[2]Milne, Grant, 'India: Karnataka Watershed Development "Sujala" Project', *South Asia: Rural Livelihoods—The People Sector,* https://bit.ly/3TRXfBq. Accessed on 29 March 2023.

mission. I informed him that we had found water on the surface of the Moon.

'There are references in the Puranas about the presence of water on the Moon. But there was no scientific proof at that time,' he said.

'Yes, you are right, Sir,' I said. 'There were no scientific explanations at that time. Now, our scientists have confirmed it with direct observation at close quarters via Chandrayaan-1 and announced it to the world for the first time.'

I elaborated how knowledge could be obtained about cultivated lands, rivers and forest wealth through satellite data and utilized for creating sustainable development programmes. The chief minister immediately insisted on executing such a system in Ahmedabad. Within six months, we implemented a scheme to bring information from all the districts and panchayats through satellites to Ahmedabad and use it in developmental projects as well as to ascertain the progress of the activities periodically. Chief Minister Modi would often visit and personally review the project implementation. He spent several hours studying the satellite pictures of the state to understand the potential effective use of land and water resources. No wonder Gujarat has emerged as the most efficient state in agriculture and water resource management. It is worth recalling that Dr Sarabhai, the father of this concept, also hailed from Gujarat.

Before the 2014 General Elections, I had submitted a detailed write-up about the new age in space technology and how science and technology can be utilized to benefits the people. In his first Independence Day speech, Prime Minister Modi mentioned many of those ideas, especially about using space technology for national development and improving quality of life. I felt happy and proud to hear that. Later, I learnt that he had organized a meeting with secretaries of all the central government departments to discuss about the use of space technology in their respective activities. No wonder the person who, as the chief minister of Gujarat, had striven to utilize space for the common man in his state also wished to implement such schemes at a national level.

However, such projects were not pursued by my successors at ISRO. The net result is that even today, there is a large gap between the potential of space applications vis-à-vis the actual realization.

MITIGATING DISASTER

Another application of satellite technology is in disaster management. The geostationary orbit enables observation of cloud coverage as well as other parameters of cloud formation and movement above the Earth. Special cameras for this purpose were instrumented, starting with our INSAT-1 series of satellites. We launched a satellite exclusively for weather monitoring too, named after Kalpana Chawla, the Indian-born astronaut who met with a tragic end in the Space Shuttle disaster. Data obtained from this satellite and other INSAT satellites are relayed every hour to the weather monitoring stations, facilitating accurate predictions of weather patterns for the next 48 hours.

Pictures of clouds from space can show low pressure above the high seas, which turn into cyclones, as soon as they form. Using these pictures, weather scientists are able to accurately calculate the speed, direction and impact locations of cyclones. The methodology has been perfected to provide advance warning to people and decision-makers even 48 hours before the events, allowing time for the necessary evacuations, mitigation and rescue operations. In case of floods, satellite images provide vital information about inundated zones to where relief materials and services can be rushed. Satellite communication can relay such information to every nook and corner of the country.

Earlier, thousands of lives were lost whenever cyclones demolished the coastal regions of Andhra Pradesh and other places. The damage caused to houses, farmland and equipment was severe. But things have changed with the advent of our remote sensing satellites. An integrated operational system for disaster warning has been set up in association with the India Meteorological Department.

Another set of modern facilities are the Automatic Weather Stations (AWS) deployed in various villages and forest areas, which collect the local weather data such as wind speed, humidity, temperature, pressure, etc., and relay them through satellites to a central location. They help make more accurate weather predictions for farmers in remote villages, thereby helping them to choose crops, plan farming activities and schedule harvests. The first AWS in

Kerala was set up in Noolpuzha, Wayanad District. Such stations need to be deployed all over India.

Space technology for national security has also been adequately used in India. Cartosat satellites are used to observe military movements across our borders and the movement of ships in the oceans.[3] The communication satellites provide critical connectivity. Recently, radar imaging satellites have been operationalized for reconnaissance in critical zones. Some of these assets have been handed over to the defence services for their day-to-day needs. An exclusive communication satellite for security needs was also launched recently.[4]

The Village Resource Centres (VRCs) was a new concept introduced by ISRO to integrate all rural development schemes. The VRCs are linked to the state centres for remote sensing applications. The services were provided using the remote sensing and communication satellites and included local weather forecasting, information for fishermen and farmers, mapping of local resources and planning for appropriate usage of land and water. The centres could also act as nodes for various digital data, including land records, tax collection, etc., and could double as focal points for tele-medicine and tele-education.

Dr V.S. Hedge was a key person behind the VRC and interfaced with user departments. S.K. Das's unstinted support was crucial in implementing these projects. He travelled to remote villages and met concerned officers, farmers and the common people. The projects were planned professionally and only after identifying the people's requirements. I, too, visited many locations on highly enjoyable trips. Das acquired a wealth of data about several places and could pinpoint the exact local needs. His book *Touching Lives* tells how ISRO's advanced R&D touches and enriches the lives of the common man in India, giving a convincing answer to those

---

[3]Choudhary, Srishti and Elizabeth Roche, 'Cartosat-3 Seen Adding Depth to India's Military Capabilities', *Livemint*, 20 January 2020, https://bit.ly/41Ydhx0. Accessed on 2 May 2023.

[4]Philip, Snehesh Alex, 'India Eyes More Military Satellites, Aims for Secure Communication & 24-Hr Border Surveillance', *The Print*, 23 March 2022, https://bit.ly/44gYoXX. Accessed on 2 May 2023.

who ask about the relevance of space research.[5]

Indian Space Research Organisation once undertook a scientific assessment in social and economic perspectives about the benefits of its projects for the country via the Madras School of Economics (MSE).[6] The MSE experts assessed the tangible and intangible contributions separately in detail, applying the yardsticks of social sciences and economics. The final assessment revealed that our society had benefitted by a factor of one-and-a-half times from the investments so far made by the government for the space programme. This was without accounting for the value of achievements in advanced technologies. The results of this study more than answers why the country should spend its resources on space instead of alleviating the sufferings of the poor.

ANTRIX: THE COMMERCIAL ARM OF ISRO

Launching satellites for foreign countries and organizations, selling remote sensing data to them and leasing transponders for private users in India are some activities through which ISRO makes direct income. We are able to launch satellites at a low cost compared to the international market. By the beginning of 1990s, there was a directive that such purely commercial ventures must not be carried out by ISRO directly. Thus, an autonomous company fully owned by the Government of India called Antrix Corporation Private Limited was born on 28 September 1992. 'Antrix' is the anglicized form of *antariksh*, the Sanskrit word for space. It operates out of the ISRO HQ campus. The chairman of ISRO acts as the chairman of the Antrix Board as well.

Remote sensing data from Indian satellites is sold to various countries, including the USA. Transponder capacity in satellites is leased for communication, TV broadcasting and for digital connectivity for businesses.

Antrix benefitted from the realization of the PSLV in 1994,

---

[5]Das, S.K., *Touching Lives—The Little Known Triumphs of the Indian Space Programme*, Penguin Books India Pvt Ltd, 2007.

[6]U. Sankar, *The Economics of India's Space Programme: An Exploratory Analysis*, Oxford University Press, 2007.

as the world noticed the reliable, low-cost launches it enabled. When I took over, Antrix was earning about ₹100 crore annually. I explored many avenues to increase its income. Contracts were signed with many foreign institutions for launching satellites and even for designing and building communication satellites for Europe. With our aggressive marketing strategy, the income had touched ₹1,000 crore mark by the time I left ISRO. The company acquired the 'mini ratna' status when K.R. Sridhara Murthi was the executive director. He later served as the managing director, too. It was solely due to his efforts that Antrix was able to scale such heights.

Indian Space Research Organisation was built from scratch, fuelled by the dreams of a handful of scientists. Dr Sarabhai, Professor Dhawan, Dr Kalam and the enthusiastic young people with them aimed for great heights, with only their engineering textbooks, old copies of journals and a few preliminary drawings on hand. People like me got the opportunity to be part of this dream and to work day and night. In later years, we have been able to pursue bigger goals like the PSLV and GSLV.

By the time I vacated the seat of the chairman of ISRO, almost all of Dr Sarabhai's dreams had been realized, and we could chalk out future programmes for the next 10 years covering human spaceflight, planetary explorations and advanced technologies for launch vehicles and satellites.

22

Treading New Paths

I was staying at ISRO's Bengaluru guest house after taking charge as the secretary to the DOS and chairman of ISRO. My wife Radha continued working at the VSSC in Thiruvananthapuram.

I used to reach my office by 9.00 a.m. My private secretary Yashoda and office assistant B.N. Padmanabha would be there before me and keep everything ready. Yashoda would give me a card with my day's appointments and a short description of each item. I, then, would turn to the files on my table and deal with all those where decisions had to be taken urgently. My policy was to not spend too long on administrative matters. I believe that scientists and technocrats holding higher positions must not deviate from their core areas.

By 10.00 a.m., I would commence interactions with the various technical groups in which the scientific secretary, programme officers and senior scientists would participate. The additional secretary and joint secretary would join for administrative matters and liaising with the government. Occasionally, video conferencing using our own satellite link was also used. I firmly believe in participatory management, and all decisions were taken only after elaborate reviews and discussions with all concerned. I gave clear instructions to immediately apprise me whenever issues cropped up at any centre. If everything went smoothly, there was no urgency in communication, but any problems had to be reported urgently. I needed to be in Delhi at least six or seven times every month. I would leave by the morning flight and catch the night flight back. I used to catch up on my reading and sleep on those flights!

The Delhi trips were mostly connected with my duties as the secretary to the DOS. I had to interact with the Cabinet and

Parliament to inform them about anything connected with space. I also liaised with the other ministries and state governments. Since the prime minister was also the Minister for Space, I interacted directly with him. This sometimes caused resentment among the other secretaries who were from the IAS cadre and were reporting to the Cabinet secretary and the concerned ministers. On a couple of occasions, I had differences of opinion with Cabinet Secretary B.K. Chaturvedi. However, I ensured that I never misused the links I had.

THE FIGHT FOR SCIENTISTS' CAUSES

My closeness with the prime minister helped take forward the interests of the scientific community. The recommendations of the sixth Pay Commission were being finalized back then. Initially, scientists were not given due consideration when fixing the grades. I spoke to the chairman of the Pay Commission many times. Dr Anil Kakodkar, then chairman of the AEC, also joined me in the battle. After exerting much pressure, the government agreed to review the pay and service rules for scientists. Finally, parity was brought in the wages of scientists with officers of other central government services, like the IAS. A scientist with 25 years of excellent service became eligible to draw a secretary-level salary.

At ISRO, scientists are not promoted against vacancies. Promotions are time-bound, based purely on merit. Even then, good scientific staff was becoming harder to retain, especially since the IT boom. I was able to bring in a performance-based incentive scheme as a measure to control employee attrition at ISRO. Under this scheme, additional increments up to a maximum number of six were given at the time of promotions. The number of increments was determined by the employee's knowledge and their contributions to the space programme. With this, many employees received up to 10 per cent hike in basic pay. Additionally, incentive schemes like yearly professional upgrade allowance and merit-based cash awards were also implemented. My goal was to remove the financial constraints for the ISRO staff. People who strive day and night to improve the nation's scientific knowledge and technical expertise must be able to lead a decent life. It is when this basic criterion is not fulfilled that corruption becomes an enticement.

Another issue was the relative difficulty of the administrative staff in getting promoted. Hence, we brought in a system to provide internal training to upgrade skills and to give more generous promotions.

Although many years have passed since I left ISRO, even now some colleagues tell me things like, 'Sir, due to the financial benefits you implemented, I was able to pay for my daughter's marriage', being able to provide better education to their children, build a house of their own, and so on.

Prime Minister Manmohan Singh supported these efforts. However, this was not the case with one of the senior ministers. He would behave haughtily, and even before we could open our mouths to say something, he would retort, 'I know, I know.' It was no doubt a reaction without understanding the matters on hand. 'What is the difference between an aircraft technician and a space technician?' he once asked.

'In the aircraft, imported equipment is integrated as is. The technicians get hefty pay packets for integration work. But in rocketry, the systems are developed indigenously and made operational, for which all the brain power and muscle power under one's command are to be used, with perhaps less than a quarter of the pay given by the airlines,' I answered. If we do not give enough encouragement, many excellent people may leave ISRO. I had received several job offers from the private sector during the SLV-3 period as well. A particular organization had offered me ten times the salary I had been receiving back then. But I did not go. Many others also had similar experiences.

The necessary approvals were obtained with great difficulty for the 'special pay package'. The NSA, M.K. Narayanan, played a crucial role in this achievement. Additional Secretary S.V. Ranganath was instrumental in overcoming the administrative hurdles.

Right from my SLV-3 days to even today, ISRO scientists are not permitted to publish the details of technology developments in journals outside ISRO. This means that we lose out on many accolades, including foreign ones. As the chairman, I introduced a programme to award meritorious people in ISRO. More than 130 people who have shown excellence in work are being given awards every year from 2008. Ten team awards are also given. The prize money is equivalent to the biggest scientific prize given in the country. In spite of initial government objections, Prime Minister Manmohan Singh gave the final approval for these special awards.

A FAMILY HOME IN BENGALURU

Radha retired from the VSSC in December 2003 with an 'SF' grade and came to Bengaluru. Thus, within a few months, we were together once again. A curious incident had happened some months earlier. She was due for a promotion and came to ISRO HQ for the interview. I was to chair the interview board as the chairman of ISRO but stepped aside that day since Radha was one of the candidates. I entrusted the responsibility to a senior member of the board. Radha did not clear the interview. Afterwards, one of the expert members accidently learnt about our relationship and admonished me, 'You could have just given an indication that she is your spouse!' The member did not think it unreasonable to consider such factors!

Both my sons were already employed in Bengaluru when I reached there. They were staying in an apartment. When Radha came to the city, we moved in with them and started searching for a more convenient house. We found one in Indira Nagar and all of us moved there. In 1996, my son Dileepan had married Sridevi from Kuttipuzha, a graduate in agriculture and the niece of Dr C.G. Krishnadas Nair, chairman of HAL. Their son Adithyan had been born in 1999. Radha was overjoyed to finally stay with her sons, daughter-in-law and grandson.

Dileepan was working at the DRDO after his degree in electronics and communication engineering from my alma mater. He was once called for an interview for a job at the VSSC. He refused to attend it, saying, 'If I get selected, people may say it was due to your influence. Hence, I do not wish to attend the interview at all!'

Sometime later, he left the DRDO and joined the multi-national company Hewlett Packard, where he is currently general manager. My younger son Jayakrishnan is the chief of HR department at an IT company in Bengaluru. He graduated in psychology and then underwent training at the Indian Institute for Personnel Management.

Our happy life with our children and grandchild did not last long. Sridevi fell ill. It started with her being unable to recognize any smell. Detailed investigations by experts revealed the issue—a fatal tumour, too advanced for any treatment to be effective. Sridevi's mother Chandrika Devi, who is a doctor, and all other relatives, reached Bengaluru. There was a turmoil within me. The toddler Adithyan was blissfully unaware of this. I could not help wondering whether the tragedy that had befallen me in childhood—losing my mother at an early age—was going to be repeated for him. The best medical attention was made available for Sridevi at Apollo Hospital, Chennai. Radha and I visited many temples and made offerings. Nothing could bring any solace. Sridevi left us in 2004. My mother had died when I was too young to really feel the depth of that tragedy. I had not encountered the death of anyone close to me after that, till the untimely demise of my daughter-in-law. I found it very difficult to bear the sorrow and pain of her death. We have no daughters of our own, and her death revealed how deeply we both had loved Sridevi.

We were living in a rented apartment and wished to build a house of our own in Bengaluru. However, we found it practically impossible considering the prevailing costs. One day, I was with Karnataka Chief Minister Dharam Singh at the inauguration ceremony for a tele-medicine programme for the state. I mentioned that I was thinking of moving back to Thiruvananthapuram once I retired from ISRO. He exclaimed, 'Karnataka needs scientists like you!' and immediately directed the chief secretary to provide me a piece of land at government rates. Within a month, a plot was allocated at a prime location in Hosur Sarjapura Road (HSR) Layout.

My father and father-in-law had looked after the construction of my first house at Sasthamangalam in Thiruvananthapuram. I wanted to construct the new house in the traditional *nalukettu* style of Kerala with a central courtyard inside.[1] It was made with

---

[1]Nalukettu is a traditional architectural style of Kerala, with a central courtyard

enough rooms, so that the entire family could stay together. The house was finished in 2007, and we started thinking about a name for it. Sridevi's death had filled my mind with memories about my mother Sarojam. We named the house 'Sarovaram' after her.

Two auspicious events took place at the rented house—Jayakrishnan's marriage and Dileepan's second marriage. Dileepan married Apsara from Palakkad at the Guruvayoor Temple. In September 2007, Apsara gave birth to a boy—Narayanan. Adithyan and Narayanan were my close companions in Bengaluru in those days. I had missed being with Dileepan when he was a child due to my busy office schedule. I tried to make up for it with the two grandsons. Jayakrishnan is more like a friend and philosopher to me. His passions are automobiles and cross-country races. His engineering skills are excellent, but it was perhaps fate that he ended up as a personnel manager.

Whenever I think about our new house in Bengaluru, thoughts about a great person who could not pay me a visit there fills my mind—Dr Kalam. I had informed him about constructing the house and he had promised to visit. He was then the president. One day, he was visiting Bengaluru and we were eagerly waiting for him. However, even after the scheduled time, there was no trace of our visitor! Then came Dr Kalam's call—it turned out that the president's retinue had gone straight ahead, missing the turning to my house, because it was not included in his official programme! It was too difficult for the entire vehicle entourage to return, and he promised me that he would come soon another day. But that never happened. I shifted from Bengaluru after my retirement from service.

FRIENDSHIPS AND FORESTS

M.K. Narayanan was the NSA when Dr Manmohan Singh was the prime minister. K.M. Chandrasekhar was the Cabinet secretary and T.K.A. Nair was the principal secretary. It was a time when many called the PMO a 'Malayali caucus'! But I am not sure whether Kerala used that golden opportunity. As far as ISRO was concerned,

---

which may or may not be covered, with rooms all around it.

I took the support of these people to realize many of my dream projects, cutting the often-encountered red-tape in the process.

One of the most memorable among those projects was setting up an academic institute at ISRO to attract talent and to absorb them into the organization after live training as part of their studies. Many talented students were being lured by the information technology (IT) boom back then. A few of our young engineers had left ISRO to accept more lucrative IT jobs. I knew that unless the issue was tackled fast, the future of the Indian space programme would be in jeopardy.

When I met the prime minister during the next DOS review meeting, I strongly highlighted this issue.

'I understand that you have a man-power crisis in ISRO?' Dr Manmohan Singh asked.

'Yes, Sir. The only solution is to establish a feeder training institute,' I replied.

I went on to say that students with potential can be provided with the best engineering education focussing on space and then be absorbed into ISRO as required. The scheme resembled the BARC training school, of which many seniors at ISRO, including me, were beneficiaries. That facility was lost when ISRO was detached from the DAE. The new institute would fill that gap. However, there was one difference: The BARC training school admitted graduates, but the space institute would take in students after the higher secondary level and train them, following the 'catch-them-young' philosophy of the armed forces. At the end of the four-year course, they would be awarded a degree equivalent to that available at the IITs. The prime minister liked the idea very much and directed T.K.A. Nair to prepare a detailed proposal the very next week.

It was 2005. Within three months, the required approvals for the project were obtained. There was some criticism about ISRO entering the field of education, which I ignored. As soon as the news spread, I began to get calls from chief secretaries, senior officers and ministers of many states. They offered to provide all the necessary facilities if the institute was set up in their state. Surprisingly, not even a single junior officer from Kerala contacted any of us regarding this project.

Thiruvananthapuram was the most appropriate location for the institute as some of the important centres of ISRO were located there. Hence, we did not consider the other offers and started our endeavour to find a suitable space. Even then, there was no affirmative move from the state government. Hence, ISRO tried to buy land directly and placed advertisements in many newspapers. We received six offers. A location in Kanakamala near Ponmudi seemed the most suitable one. Flanked by hills on three sides and with a view of the sea on the fourth, it was a pristine location. I was reminded of the Jet Propulsion Laboratory (JPL) in Florida, USA, situated atop a beautiful hill. We felt our institute could compete with it both in terms of natural beauty and scientific achievements!

The land in Ponmudi was part of the Merchiston Tea Estate, which was well past its heyday. After discussions, the price was agreed upon as ₹3 crore for about 80 hectares. As soon as the news was made public, a big controversy erupted! 'A concrete jungle is going to come up in an environmentally fragile location' was the allegation. Immediately, the Left Democratic Front (LDF) government, led by the Communist Party of India (Marxist) (CPM), intervened. V.S. Achuthanandan of the CPM was the chief minister and Binoy Viswam of the Communist Party of India (CPI) was the Minister for Environment and Forests.[2]

I made one thing very clear in our discussions with the government—only the most essential construction would be made, and that too after getting all the required permissions. Just about 10 acres of the land was deemed enough for the buildings. The rest, nearly 70 acres, was to be retained as forest land. However, many so-called 'environmentalists' with tunnel vision could not digest these arguments. Minister Viswam threw the biggest spoke in the wheel. After listening to all the discussions in the meeting, he would reiterate the same slogan—'The projected land is part of an environmentally fragile area, and no construction is permitted there.' One is helpless when emotional responses are made instead of balanced reviews and analysis!

---

[2]Radhakrishnan, M.G., 'Space Scam', *India Today*, 17 November 2017, https://bit.ly/44iYfDu. Accessed on 2 May 2023.

The 'Merchiston Estate controversy' continued to occupy centre stage in the media for some time. Finally, we found a way out. We decided to start the institute on temporary premises within the ISRO campus in Veli. Thus, the IIST was born in 2007.

The BTech courses were devised after the IIT courses, and students were enrolled into three streams, namely, aeronautics, avionics and space sciences. Expert teachers were also selected and appointed. Dr B.N. Suresh, who played a significant role in the development of the PSLV and GSLV, became the founding director of IIST.

We had not given up on the campus in Ponmudi. At one point, a date was fixed for laying the foundation stone by the prime minister. Again, Binoy Viswam intervened. Whenever I visited the place, the media somehow got wind of it and followed me. On one such occasion, one of the press photographers got a good 'photo-op'—I was drinking water from a water bottle. He caught me on camera, and the next day, the photo was printed in the newspaper with the caption—'ISRO Land Issue: Chairman Madhavan Nair Forced to Drink Water!'

I have always tried to proceed with projects regardless of the stumbling blocks. If one cannot go along the best way, take the next best path—this was my motto. We found that nearly 100 acres of land near the ISRO unit in Valiamala was a dense forest. We decided to build the academic infrastructure required for the institute on 20 acres there. We also met V.S. Achuthanandan and requested him to allocate another 20 acres adjoining the property. He was pleased and agreed to the suggestions. 'Mr Madhavan Nair, do not worry. Forget about the land in Ponmudi. We will give you land in Valiamala. If you require more, we will acquire and give you,' he promised. He subsequently sanctioned ₹20 crore for the purpose. There were some encroachment-related issues on 40 acres of land there, which the government could have easily solved. Since that land was not available, facilities like accommodation for the academic staff and recreational areas could not be set-up. As of 2023, it is understood that the state government has given the required clearances. I had to bear the brunt of criticism over this whole issue. None of these problems would have cropped up had we decided to set up the institute in another state!

Chief Minister Achuthanandan had made another offer too: There was some government-owned property on top of the Ponmudi Hills, and he offered to give 10 acres to ISRO. I accepted. We decided to set up some special laboratories and an Earth observation centre for the space institute at that location.

Now, every year, trained students from the space institute are inducted into ISRO. About 150 students who pass the Joint Entrance Examination (JEE) are admitted into the institute every year. Since there is good competition among the students to qualify for the IIST, only students who obtain ranks above 5,000 in the JEE can aspire to get a seat. All the expenses are met by the government. The only condition is to sign a bond to serve ISRO for five years after graduating with good grades, else a fine of ₹10 lakh is levied. I understand that the fee structure has been rationalized with that of the IITs now.

The central government service rules apply to ISRO's staff in scientific, administrative and auxiliary categories. The most important rule is the opportunity to remain in service till 60 years of age. When shortage of scientific staff was felt due to the IT boom during 1995–2005, increasing the age of retirement of scientific staff to 62 years was considered. Such a scheme would probably have been approved, but instead, we obtained approval for re-employment for two years of selected people who are efficient and have high technical skills. This scheme was enforced with a lot of care to ensure that only the right candidates are chosen. Later, alas, it sometimes got used as an easy way to extend the services of many undeserving persons!

23

Touching the Moon

On Independence Day in 2003, I was overjoyed to hear Prime Minister Vajpayee announce from the Red Fort in New Delhi, 'Our country is now ready to fly high in the field of science. I am pleased to announce that India will send her own spacecraft to the moon by 2008. It is being named Chandrayaan-1.'[1]

Normally, ISRO's projects do not figure in such lists. The name of the mission was another pleasant surprise. Sometime earlier, I had sent the prime minister a note seeking approval for a travel to the Moon. He had christened it Chandrayaan, meaning a craft for moon travel! The mission was announced as Chandrayaan-1, indicating that more may follow.

This announcement was the culmination of multiple previous presentations about possible missions to the Moon, first on the day of the first anniversary of the Pokhran blast, then later in front of a parliamentary committee.

This project always had a special place in Prime Minister Vajpayee's heart. Sometime later, he came to Sriharikota to witness a PSLV launch. He was highly appreciative of the professional manner in which the launch was organized and congratulated the entire ISRO community. As he was leaving, media persons surrounded him, asking about the progress of the project announced on Independence Day. He assured them that it was progressing well and that we would surely reach the Moon.

[1]'Prime Minister Shri Atal Bihari Vajpayee's Independence Day Address', *PMO Archives*, 15 August 2003, https://bit.ly/3WwvaiF. Accessed on 25 January 2023.

PLANS AND DESIGNS: THE TRICOLOUR ON THE MOON?

The task for the mission was to design a trajectory—a pathway—from the Earth to the Moon. Computing the velocity and position of the spacecraft under the complex dynamic conditions, with the gravitational pull of the Sun, the planets and the Moon acting on it, was the real challenge. The time, position and velocity for entering into an orbit around the Moon had to be calculated precisely. We decided to use the method of first placing the spacecraft in a long elliptical orbit around the Earth and then moving from that into an orbit around the Moon. It was possible to put the capsule in such an orbit using the PSLV-XL rocket, which has the maximum thrust at lift-off and uses six strap-on motors with additional propellant loading.

Dr K. Kasturirangan had constituted the Lunar Study Task Force, chaired by Dr George Joseph, to provide various options for the mission to the Moon. High-resolution mapping of the lunar surface and hard X-ray imaging were among the objectives that the committee recommended for the first mission. Nobody had made a high-resolution image database about the structure of the Moon's surface until then.

When I took charge as the chairman of ISRO in September 2003, I expanded the goals. The possibilities became clear after a couple of mission-review meetings. Since we were sending a spacecraft all the way to the Moon, the scientific objectives could be further extended to include a 3D-imaging camera, a laser altimeter and a hyper-spectral imaging payload. Even then, nearly 30-kg capacity was left over for other instruments. If we started developing new instruments, the launch would get delayed by a few years. Hence, we took it as an opportunity to bring in international cooperation.

During a visit to NASA's JPL, I had found that a synthetic aperture radar and hyper-spectral imager were waiting for a launch opportunity. We worked out a memorandum of understanding (MOU) with the JPL to carry these instruments onboard Chandrayaan. In the meantime, we received nearly 10 responses to our call for proposals, out of which four experiments complementing our mission objectives were selected. Thus, the mission became a truly international venture.

Space Applications Centre, Ahmedabad, realized a 3D-imaging camera under the guidance of Kiran Kumar, who later became the chairman of ISRO. The Laboratory for Electro-Optics Systems (LEOS) in Bengaluru developed a laser-ranging system.

While work on the mission progressed feverishly, a mid-course correction was introduced. Dr Kalam was the person behind that idea. A year had passed since I had taken up the job of the chairman of ISRO. A meeting to review the Chandrayaan configuration was coming up. Two weeks prior to the meeting, I met Dr Kalam in Delhi.

'Madhavan, what evidence are you going to show before the world that we reached the Moon?' he asked. 'When we carried out missions to Everest and Antarctica, we placed our flag there. In the case of the Moon mission, we are relying to convince the world with a lot of digital data. Don't you think that we should do something more?'

Such a simple question! We had never thought in that direction. Dr Kalam's interjections were always like this. He would ask some very simple questions. While searching for the answers, our entire perspective would get modified! On my way back, I was thinking about how a module inscribed with the tricolour flag can be placed on the surface of the Moon.

The very next day, I called a meeting with our mission team to discuss this topic. Some conservatives said that it was impossible to accommodate such a scheme at that late a stage within the tight budget and schedule constraints. But some adventurous youngsters agreed to take up the challenge. This included teams from ASMG and the Launch Vehicle Design Group at the VSSC. I held further detailed discussions with these teams. The VSSC showed readiness to build a module christened the MIP. Dr B.N. Suresh was the director of the VSSC then. Once the decision was taken, the extremists and conservatives came together. Everyone took up the challenge of realizing the probe and evolving a new mission strategy. That is indeed the 'ISRO style'.

The MIP, with the national flag inscribed on it, comprised three instruments—a mass spectrometer, a camera and an altimeter. A few instruments had to be jettisoned to accommodate the additional

35 kg into the payload. In spite of the additional work to include the MIP, we thought it was worthwhile. The significance of the mission and the resulting fame for the country were sure to skyrocket with that addition.

Dr M. Annadurai, a satellite expert, was the project director of Chandrayaan-1. Later, he became the director of ISAC, Bengaluru.

Dr P.S. Goel, the then director of ISAC, chaired the management council for the mission. Heads of different departments like Dr T.K. Alex, Kiran Kumar, Dr J.N. Goswami, Dr S.K. Shivakumar, M. Pichaimani, Dr Charles Elachi, Leo Jackson John, George Koshy, N.S. Hegde and Dr M. Annadurai were included in the council. Members of the JPL and ESA were also invited. Integrated mission reviews took place three or four times a year. As the chairman of ISRO, I chaired these reviews. Many crucial decisions had to be taken, one of them related to the deep space tracking network. We did not possess the antennae required for the network; the initial plan was to import them. But I felt that companies like BEL and the ECIL may be able to manufacture the items within the country. Many did not believe me when I first put forth the idea, but I was firm about striving for indigenization. In the end, the very complicated tracking network with huge antennae and a high-precision tracking system was realized without any support from external experts. At the heart of the network were the two antennae, 18 m and 32 m in diameter, set up in Byalalu near Bengaluru. This network has become the mainstay for all the interplanetary missions of ISRO.

The PSLV, with extended strap-on rockets having enhanced propellant loading, called PSLV-XL, would be able to take Chandrayaan along with the MIP module to an elliptical orbit around the Earth with an apogee of around 22,900 km. A liquid-engine rocket in the spacecraft would then be fired in five phases to take it further to the final elliptical orbit. Calibrating the trajectory parameters and assessing the influence of other celestial bodies like the Moon, Mars and the Sun had to be carried out at each phase. In the final leg, the required escape velocity would be imparted to the capsule to take it out of the Earth's orbit. The module would then move in outer space under the influence of gravitational fields from the Sun, Earth and Moon to reach a point only 500 km away from the Moon. Small rockets in the module would again be fired to reduce the velocity to 1.7 km/s. With that, the capsule would be captured by the gravitational pull of the Moon and start moving in an elliptical orbit around it. This was the plan.

Earth-based control systems for the spacecraft had to be set up. The most crucial facilities to be integrated included the Indian deep space network, mission operations centre and Indian Space Science Data Center.

CHANDRAYAAN BLASTS OFF

Huge trucks carried the rocket stages to Sriharikota three months before the launch date. The stages were then integrated vertically. The satellite was transported from Bengaluru. I had gone to Sriharikota at the beginning of the stacking and given the necessary directives. When I looked at the PSLV, I felt like a proud father looking at a son who has never failed, girding up its loins for the next battle!

Three weeks before the launch date, I conducted one more review. On 18 October 2008, I reached the SHAR for the launch. Radha was with me, as she is for most launches. We stayed at the guest house.

The review conducted that day was brief. Some of the other important technical reviews were planned for the next few days. A snag was reported in an old radar, and engineers had been trying to correct it for several days. The output power was not reaching peak levels. Experts from Bharat Heavy Electricals Limited (BHEL) who arrived at the SHAR also could not solve the issue. The topic came up for discussion during dinner after the technical review. Later at night, I went to the radar room with the scientist responsible for the system.

'Let me have a look at it,' I asked with my old enthusiasm for electronics.

I opened the console, looked inside and then voiced my doubt whether interference between the radio-frequency modulation circuit and the high-power stage was the issue. Detailed examinations soon revealed that the isolation between signal and power lines was not adequate. We discussed the solution. I went back to the guest house and had a sound sleep. The next morning, the engineers came and informed me that everything was working perfectly! The radar was operating at the full power of 1 megawatt.

The launch was scheduled for 6.22 a.m. on 22 October 2008. We got ready and reached the control centre early in the morning. The sky was full of rain clouds. Soon, it started to rain heavily, with strong winds blowing. Anxiety from the control room spilled into the overflowing visitors' and press galleries. The governors of Tamil Nadu and Andhra Pradesh had come to witness the launch. The situation was such that the question of whether to go ahead with the launch or not was now in the air.

'Should we postpone the launch, Sir?' the director of the SHAR asked me. The weather at the SHAR is always unpredictable. Experts had been evaluating data obtained from the radio sounding balloons sent up at specific intervals since the morning the day before. Now there was lightning and a little thunder, which could harm the rocket systems. I considered postponing the launch. But the next opportunity would only be after a month. The rocket and satellites could not be kept on the launch pad for such a long time. The fuel would have to be drained and the stages de-stacked, causing loss of money and also some prestige for the nation. My mind was prompting me to take the risk and proceed. Opportunities like this come rarely. Often, one has to take calculated risks for success.

I consulted the meteorological experts present. They reported that the rain had stopped and that there was no electrostatic activity. The sky would continue to be overcast and visibility would be poor. Only the radar data would show the rocket's trajectory. I decided to proceed using the special powers as the chairman of ISRO, even though the visibility was poor. If the launch failed, the whole country would take us to task! But the possibility of degradation of the liquid engines due to dismantling and storing was high.

The final countdown started. In earlier days, manual commands had to be issued every few seconds during the last phase of the countdown. Now everything was controlled by computers. The roll thrusters were ignited just four seconds before take-off to confirm their performance. Then the booster and strap-on motors were ignited, and the PSLV-XL rocket rose like a huge lighted tower, ejecting fire and smoke. Chandrayaan was safely ensconced inside the rocket. Crores of Indians witnessed the spectacle on television with hearts overflowing with pride.

We were sitting with our eyes glued to the computer monitors, too tense to even breathe. The signal confirming that the satellite had been placed into the 255 x 22,900-km elliptical orbit came at exactly 6.40 a.m., marking the completion of the first leg of the mission. We announced the news to the media.

I returned to Bengaluru. Further operations were controlled from ISTRAC station in Peenya. The spacecraft had to change orbits through a series of five manoeuvres to bring the capsule under the Moon's influence.

IN OUTER SPACE

Chandrayaan was indeed on a journey to unknown frontiers. As the distance from Earth increased, the Earth's gravitational attraction on the module decreased. Simultaneously, the pull of the Moon and the other planets increased. The exact influence of each couldn't be determined. The module's path had to be computed continuously and any deviation from the designated trajectory had to be corrected.

The Russians had not succeeded in their first four missions to the Moon. The USA had not succeeded in the first attempt either. We were trying a different approach of raising the orbit in steps, calibrating the performance of thrusters and ensuring we were on the right track. Our scientists carried out the operations to raise and change the orbit of Chandrayaan step by step, as per the planned timelines. A crucial manoeuvre was scheduled for 4 November. Rocket engines in the spacecraft were fired to provide an added impulse to enable its escape from the pull of the Earth, and the manoeuvre was successful. All of us heaved a sigh of relief. Our module had moved out of the Earth's orbit.

The next four days were spent in making the journey towards the Moon at around 10 km/s. If the same velocity continued, Chandrayaan would speed past the Moon and into deep space. Hence, the velocity of the module had to be reduced to 1.7 km/s. The tricky operation had to be achieved at the precise, pre-computed instant. We were also happy that our navigation and guidance system had performed well, and we could reach within a 10-km pill box close to the Moon.[2] The main spacecraft thruster operated in retro mode to decrease the velocity. The command for this was given from the deep space network at 4.51 p.m. on 8 November. The velocity of the module was reduced. It was attracted into the gravitational field of the Moon and began to go around it in an elliptical orbit with perigee of 500 km and apogee of 7,502 km. The next goal was to gradually reduce these distances to achieve a circular orbit around the Moon. Again, rocket engines in the spacecraft were employed in a manoeuvre similar to the one used for orbit correction of our communication satellites.

Once the spacecraft started orbiting the Moon in a circular orbit at the height of 200 km, the 12 instruments on board were checked to ensure smooth functioning. Each experiment was then started as per the requirements of the scientists concerned.

During the last leg of Chandrayaan's journey, pictures of the Earth were taken by orienting the cameras in the module to look at it from the lunar distance. The pictures were beautiful, just like the view we have of the Moon from the Earth. Instead of the grey and white of the Moon, the Earth had picturesque blue, white and green shades. Once the module was in the Moon's orbit, the cameras were commanded to take detailed stereo pictures of the Moon's surface. The first photos surprised everybody, as they showed deep, well-like craters flanked by steep mountains that were a few kilometres tall. A lot of data could be collected to prepare a high-resolution map of the Moon. This was the first major achievement of Chandrayaan-1.

TOUCHING THE MOON'S SURFACE

The D-Day for the next crucial event in the saga of the Chandrayaan was 14 November—the MIP's trip to the surface of the Moon. I reached Peenya by afternoon. Dr Kalam, who could not come to

[2]Pill box refers to the intended orbit parameters, with allowable dispersions to enable lunar capture.

the SHAR to participate in the launch, came down to Bengaluru just an hour before the commencement of operations. He was greatly excited and optimistic about the mission becoming a perfect success. The mere presence of my guru and guide was invigorating for us. His smiling face and encouraging words changed the atmosphere at ISTRAC and filled it with positive energy. Soon, we all took our places in front of the big screens. Some of the events I began this memoir with were about to take place.

The cuboid MIP was made of aluminium honeycomb, making it quite robust. It had to be detached from the Chandrayaan module and begin an elliptical trajectory to the surface of the Moon.

We wanted the MIP to drop near the south pole of the Moon. When the capsule reached a specific location in the northern hemisphere, the operations were initiated. The command to begin the action sequence was sent to Chandrayaan from the ground control centre at ISTRAC. The remaining operations were carried out by the computers onboard. Pyrotechnic igniters on the module were fired. The MIP got detached from the capsule. Retro motors were fired as in our earlier SRE, and these put the MIP on a ballistic trajectory carrying the Indian national flag to the Moon's surface. It was a free fall under the gravitational pull of the Moon. The instruments inside the MIP were operated as it was falling. The camera took closer pictures. The sensors tried to catch the chemical composition of the different trace gases in the tenuous atmosphere of the Moon.

The half-an-hour journey ended with the MIP impacting the Moon's surface near the Shackleton Crater, scattering dust all around. As the message reached the ISTRAC control centre, we all stood up, cheering and clapping with joy. Dr Kalam was grinning like a schoolboy.

I had a small model of the Chandrayaan capsule with me. I presented it to Dr Kalam. He was excited like a child with a new toy! The endeavour that he had started with the small SLV-3 had now reached the Moon!

Thus, India had the rare achievement of being the first nation to touch the Moon in its maiden attempt. Many memories come flooding into my mind of those joyous moments. Indians in the country and all over the world threw parties, celebrating India's success.

EVALUATING THE SUCCESS

The information gathered from the MIP was simply amazing. On analysis, the pictures from its camera revealed that the location of the fall was near the Moon's south pole. A big crater, 600-km long and 10-km deep, was seen nearby. Huge mountains of height up to a kilometre were seen spread across 200 m. High-resolution pictures from the orbiter clearly showed the marks left on the Moon's surface by the Apollo module of the USA, which had landed and moved across it in 1969. In fact, they looked like tractor tracks! Since there is no atmosphere and wind around the Moon, those marks hadn't been wiped out. Our cameras also captured some indications of other vehicles that had traversed the Moon's surface.

Many years later, when I was interacting with some school children and was asked the question, 'Did man ever land on the Moon?', I could say, 'Yes, I have seen the evidence through the pictures taken by our Chandrayaan-1!'

Data from the orbiter module, still in the 200-km circular orbit around the Moon, confirmed that everything was normal. That gave us the confidence to try and reduce the orbital height to 100 km above the Moon's surface to obtain higher resolution images. The necessary control systems were activated. However, something totally unexpected happened—an increase in temperature! Our understanding was that the Moon's surface was cool. But that was proved wrong. If only countries like the USA and Russia, which already knew this, had shared that information with us, we would not have ventured to the 100-km orbit and landed in trouble. The internal temperatures of some of the electronic modules increased worryingly. But we had already made very significant discoveries by then.

Data from the Chandrayaan confirmed the presence of water in the polar regions of the Moon. Craters at the poles of the Moon revealed tons of ice sheets below the surface. This was the most important reason why the world took note of the Chandrayaan mission. The presence of helium-3, a possible energy source for the future, was also confirmed on the Moon.

The instruments made some other discoveries: the impact of solar winds; a weak magnetosphere; presence of magnesium, aluminium, silicon, cadmium, iron, etc., in the free state; X-rays that originate when cosmic rays fall on radioactive materials; and so on. Along with photos of the Earth, about 90 per cent of the Moon's surface was mapped with the stereoscopic camera with 10-m resolution, perhaps being the best attempt so far. Several rocks that looked like carved sculptures were seen. There were indications of lava flow on the surface that could have occurred once upon a time.

A very important observation was made while the MIP was making its way to the Moon's surface—the presence of trace gases around the Moon. In addition to oxygen, the elixir of life, argon, helium and water vapour were also detected but in trace quantities. However, the mass spectrometer that recorded this data was not adequately calibrated and, hence, we could not announce it officially. The instrument had to be calibrated for at least three days to establish the baseline. We did not anticipate this, and it took several days to decipher the actual signals. Hence, we could not then confirm the correctness of the data. Later, our scientists, along with NASA, obtained some positive results using hyper-spectral imagery.

The heat resulting from the Sun's rays reflecting off the Moon's surface increased the temperature inside the module, designed to be below 40°C, to 50°C. Many efforts were made in vain over the next two weeks to reduce it. By January 2009, one of the power control systems shut down, forcing us to switch on the redundant unit. Finally, it was decided that Chandrayaan would go back to the 200-km orbit. On 19 May 2009, small rockets in the spacecraft were operated again till the distance increased to 200 km. In the middle of this, the star sensor used to compute the direction and location of the capsule stopped working, and redundant systems had to take over. A bi-static radar experiment scheduled for 21 August could not be attempted. In another week, signals from the spacecraft stopped completely. The last message was received on 29 August 2009 at 9.02 a.m. Detailed analysis of the data revealed that the redundant power control unit had also failed. Chandrayaan-1, expected to work flawlessly for two years, had to be declared non-operational after 10 months. The only consolation was that during this time, we had already received 90 per cent of the data targeted for the mission. In two years, we could have completed 100 per cent of the targeted data collection and many important parameters could have been verified once again.

The ₹600 crore sanctioned by the government for the Chandrayaan mission was only one-fifth of the cost incurred by similar American missions. News stories in the national and international media underscored the low expense of the mission.[3]

The American Institute of Aeronautics and Astronautics (AIAA) recognized the achievement and gave the AIAA 2009 Space Systems Award to Chandrayaan-1. Indian Space Research Organisation also bagged the National Space Society's Space Pioneer Award in 2009 for India's maiden Moon mission. Additionally, the International Academy of Astronautics recognized the Chandrayaan team for this big achievement and for making pioneering efforts towards international cooperation for planetary explorations.

[3]'Chandrayaan-1, India's First Moon Mission', *The Planetary Society*, https://bit.ly/3JcHkdw. Accessed on 25 January 2023.

24

Awards, Accolades and More

Chandrayaan-1's tremendous success was undoubtedly a result of the entire ISRO family's hard work over several years, toiling as a single coherent team focussed on the goal. It was also the fruit of the vision and spirit inculcated at ISRO by great visionaries like Dr Sarabhai, Dr Kalam, Professor Dhawan, Professor U.R. Rao and Dr Kasturirangan.

The mission successfully demonstrated the capabilities of Indian space scientists to the world. Many were surprised by the achievement made under severe constraints. Indian scientists became accepted as second to none in the world. But no amount of international acclaim can match the accolades from one's own country.

After the successful SRE mission, all ISRO employees were given a gold medal of one sovereign each in recognition of the special services they rendered. It helped to boost the spirit of oneness among employees spanning the entire organization's hierarchy—from the chairman to the last-grade workers. However, after Chandrayaan, we could only afford to give a gold locket half that weight. The money was taken from the profits of the Antrix Corporation—returns on the toil of ISRO team itself—thereby avoiding additional burden on the government. The positive attitude of the PMO towards ISRO helped enable such things.

I recall an incident that took place while I was at the PMO dealing with some official matters. Prime Minister Manmohan Singh was out of station. Two senior officials came out of a meeting. When they saw me, they started murmuring to each other. 'We keep toiling day in and day out tirelessly. What use! People like them are getting away with all the accolades and awards!'

I asked them what they were referring to, but received no answer.

We talked about other matters, and I returned to Bengaluru that evening. The next day, I received a phone call from the district collector of Bengaluru: I had been selected as one of the recipients of Padma Vibhushan for the year 2009—the second-highest civilian award of India! The government wanted to confirm whether I was willing to accept the award.

THE FIRST PADMA AWARD

I had received a similar phone call in 1998, when I was recommended for the Padma Bhushan. The district collector of Thiruvananthapuram had called me and, after confirming my identity, had asked if I was willing to accept the Padma Bhushan if selected. The success of the PSLV as a reliable launch vehicle had received international limelight and was the pride of the nation. Hence, I had not been surprised at being considered for the award. I assured the collector about my willingness. 'Keep this to yourself and do not share with anyone until the official announcement is made,' he had cautioned me.

The official announcement had come on the eve of Republic Day. With much jubilation in the house, I had started getting congratulatory messages from friends and relatives early in the morning. Many had been surprised about the Padma Bhushan without a Padma Shri preceding it.

Dr Kalam had called me that night. 'Buddy, you richly deserve it,' he had exclaimed. There is no greater prize for a shishya than being appreciated by the *guru*. In those days, Dr Kalam had been the scientific advisor to the prime minister. His book titled *Wings of Fire* had been published, and his fame had spread everywhere. He has described our relationship in that book.

The award ceremony had taken place after two months. We had been asked to report the night before. Radha and my accommodation had been arranged at the Ashoka Hotel with other Padma awardees. The officials had explained the details of the ceremony during a meeting at the Rashtrapati Bhavan the night before. How to conduct oneself when the president arrives; how to accept the award from him; how to walk to the ceremonial stand—we had been given step by step instructions.

The function had been at 10 o'clock the next morning. About 500 guests had assembled at the Ashoka Hall, including the prime minister. As soon as Dr Kalam had arrived, he had approached me, shaken my hands and said joyfully, 'This is only the beginning; keep it up!'

Indeed, his words have come true through a series of awards that I have received from state governments, universities and professional bodies. I have always felt his blessings for me. Even today, his memories surround me like a protective shield.

K.R. Narayanan had been the president at that time. I had met him earlier when he was the Indian ambassador to the USA. He had wanted to know the details of the different aspects of space research. Our political relations with the USA had been strained then, with American trade sanctions against us. He had explained his helplessness in solving the purchase problem but had promised to use his contacts to help us.

That day at the Rashtrapati Bhavan, as I had walked forward to receive the Padma award from the president, many memories had flashed through my mind. Of course, I had imagined no such prize when I had stepped into TERLS a quarter century ago. My only wish had been to demonstrate my engineering abilities. But God gave me the opportunity to become a co-traveller with many great men. I could participate in taking their dreams to greater heights and fructify them through hard work. We are but small men and women working as per the wishes of the creator of the universe. However, I have realized that dedicated efforts lead to results that defy even the wildest of aspirations. I bowed my head in humility and received the award. In the press meet afterwards, I dedicated my award to all members of the ISRO family who had always stood with me.

WITH DR KALAM AT THE RASHTRAPATI BHAVAN

The 2009 Padma Vibhushan was a great surprise to me. Dr Anil Kakodkar was also selected from the scientific field. In those days, the norm was to not consider people in government service for such awards, and both of us were still in service. Later, I learnt that the bold decision had been taken by the prime minister. Dr Manmohan Singh, who appreciated our contributions to atomic energy and space, respectively, and had obtained a waiver from the Cabinet.

This time, too, Dr Kalam was present at the award ceremony. He came to the Rashtrapati Bhavan as its former occupant.

'Sir, it was my desire to receive this award from your hands,' I told him.

He just smiled in reply. His tenure as the president of the country would definitely have been extended to one more term had he put in even a little effort in that direction. But he never brought that matter to the table. When the pressure to contest mounted, he publicly announced that he was not game for another term. The esteem of the position of the president rose higher through his actions.

I recall my visits to the Rashtrapati Bhavan when Dr Kalam was the president. On my maiden visit, he had first showed me the official bedroom—a room as big as a badminton court—set up with the most luxurious fittings. But Dr Kalam had refused to occupy it and had settled in another normal-sized room. He had not forgotten the old habit of hanging his shirts, like in the old lodge-room in Thiruvananthapuram. In those days, washing his clothes himself had been his Sunday chore. Though many helpers had been around, always ready to help, he would not let them. But at the Rashtrapati Bhavan, the orderly used to silently slip into the room and take away the worn clothes. A kitchen set-up to prepare dishes from cuisines across the world had been available. But the president enjoyed simple South Indian food, as always. Everything had been free and open for the president and his guests. But Dr Kalam used to demand a bill for the expenses incurred whenever he would have personal guests over, even if the 'guest' was his own brother and family. He would then sign the bill as 'private dinner' and pay from his pocket. I had learnt from his secretary that this was done during all of my visits except for official banquets.

Dr Kalam always introduced me in glowing terms to his VIP guests, like a proud teacher talking about his favourite student. Once, when the president of Ukraine had visited, Dr Kalam had invited me to come over. 'Look! He is the top-most specialist in rocketry in the country and my best friend'—this was how he had introduced me. I had been embarrassed by these superlatives. The Ukrainian president had also been an expert in rocketry. The three of us had a great time sharing notes on the old India–Soviet relations and new advances in rocket technology.

I also remember the first time I had met and spoken with L.K. Advani, the former deputy prime minister and a powerful leader. It had been at a reception hosted by the chief minister of Delhi. The PSLV had very much been in the news in those days.

'What is the difference between the PSLV and a missile?' he had asked me.

'Missile is a rocket designed to deliver warheads, whereas the PSLV is a big rocket system that carries satellites to orbits. In a normal configuration, it has the necessary mechanisms for taking satellites to precise orbits around the Earth. But if you reprogram its guidance system, instead of satellites, it can carry weapons. Then, the PSLV can be used to deliver them anywhere in the world.' I saw his face beam with pride over India's potential for defence applications.

OTHER AWARDS

The national media made much of the news of the Padma Vibhushan. Shekhar Gupta of NDTV invited me to his *Walk the Talk* programme, allowing me to elaborate on the achievements of the PSLV and other missions as well as my vision for the future of the Indian space programme.

I received many awards and prizes following the success of Chandrayaan-1. Many universities, both in India and abroad, conferred honorary doctorates upon me. The award ceremonies invariably became opportunities to interact with the students and academic communities. The International Lunar Exploration Working Group awarded the Chandrayaan-1 team the International Co-operation Award in 2008.[1]

I once mentioned my awards to Dr Kalam. He had already

[1]Bose, Praveen, 'Chandrayaan Wins Award for Global Co-operation', *Business Standard*, 29 January 2013, https://bit.ly/3WKKKsH. Accessed on 1 June 2023.

received honorary doctorates from 31 universities. I had 15. After becoming the president, he had refused all such recognitions. He said jokingly, 'In rocket technology, the disciple has outsmarted the teacher. The same should happen in the case of doctorates too.'

The annual session of the Indian Science Congress was held in Chidambaram, Tamil Nadu, in 2007. Usually, the prime minister inaugurates the session, a protocol begun by Pandit Nehru, who was the president of the very first Science Congress. The Science Congress is an event held in high esteem by the Indian scientific community. I, too, received an invitation to attend the inaugural session then. Busy with many commitments, I had not been planning to go. But a call came from the PMO asking me to attend the meeting, and, hence, I attended it. It was at the end of the event when the prime minister awarded me a gold medal; I was taken by surprise! I also felt very humbled.

I was able to play a significant role in the Science Congress in 2010 in the campus of University of Kerala, Thiruvananthapuram. I proudly remember the humble contributions that could be made to that prime institute of learning as the president of the Science Congress whenever I pass by the campus.

There is also a painful memory in connection with awards. The French government had decided to confer their highest civilian title, Knight of the National Order of the French Legion of Honour, on me. Normally such awards are handed over by the French ambassador in India. Back then, I was already retired and was the Vikram Sarabhai Professor at ISRO. Hence, I had to obtain official permission to receive such awards. A letter was sent to the prime minister, but he was not in Delhi at that time and may have missed it. But I heard that some officials at ISRO and the PMO had done some mischief. I learnt that the French embassy was told by someone to not give me the award in the context of the Devas Scam. That award ceremony never took place.

ADMINISTRATIVE PROGRESS

Regarding work, I was deeply committed as the chairman to accelerate the growth of ISRO. My focus was on schemes to raise personnel morale and increase their dedication to the organization. I tried to increase the compensation amount paid to dependents of employees who die while in service. Earlier, only ₹1.5 lakh was given to the family as per the government norms.

In 2004, there had been a huge explosion in the propellant plant in Sriharikota. Six employees had burnt to death and many had suffered injuries.[2] I had rushed to meet the families and console the dependents. That was the time when many realities had become clear to me. The ₹1.5-lakh compensation was insufficient as permanent succour for the families. The realization had pained me greatly. I met the prime minister and apprised him of the circumstances. He readily agreed to increase the compensation amount to ₹10 lakh.

For a permanent solution to the issue, a series of discussions were initiated with insurance companies. My goal was to set up an insurance policy at a very low premium for accident victims. Finally, one company agreed to a scheme with just ₹10 contributed by the staff member and the government per month. This ensured any accidental death during work would get compensated with ₹10 lakh. I was also able to implement a plan for handling employees' and their dependents' medical expenses and extend the scheme to include retired employees as well.

The trust placed in me by the prime minister and higher officials in the government enabled me to do many such things. The prime minister never unnecessarily intervened in my activities. A friendly atmosphere prevailed during every review meeting, where I would take senior ISRO scientists with me. The UPA Chairperson Sonia Gandhi had a positive attitude towards the DOS. She never failed to send a congratulatory message after every successful mission.

I always believed that more power must be given to the directors of individual ISRO centres to ensure the smooth functioning of the organization. One of the most important factors was to increase the financial powers. The maximum sum that each director could spend independently had a ceiling of ₹1 crore. I raised it to ₹10 crore to speed up project implementation. A completely computerized system

---

[2]'Sriharikota ISRO Blast Kills Six,' *The Times of India*, 24 February 2004, https://bit.ly/3Vtg5Q5. Accessed on 3 May 2023.

was also established to oversee spending. The central government acquired a similar setup only a decade later.

The National Remote Sensing Agency (NRSA), though no different from any ISRO centre, was then working as a registered society. I thought that the agency should be taken over by the government. My efforts in that direction finally fructified. The takeover allowed greater financial support for the agency. A system was also set up, through Antrix, to sell the data collected by our remote sensing satellites. About six contracts were signed with different countries. The major one was for the supply of IRS data to the American agricultural department. This also helped Antrix's revenue to reach ₹1,000 crore.

During my tenure, we had eminent industrialists like Ratan Tata, Jamshyd Godrej and Ravindra Reddy among Antrix board members. They helped the company cultivate a high professional standard. Antrix was also granted the mini ratna status as a central public-sector enterprise. The central government was the only shareholder in the company, with an investment of ₹1 crore. Antrix could give threefold dividends in the last couple of years during my tenure as the chairman of the board.

I wish the people who, in later years, killed the goose that laid golden eggs cared to look at what Antrix has contributed to space commerce.[3]

[3]Basis the annual reports of Antrix Corporation (not available in public domain).

25

Beyond the Borders

As ISRO's chairman, I also focussed on expanding and strengthening its international collaborations in space exploration.

Thumba Equatorial Rocket Launching Station was started in 1963 as an international collaborative programme, taking help and contributions from various countries. Cooperation with Russia, the USA, France, Japan and others initially helped our space programme to grow. Those ties needed to be further strengthened to progress. We had ongoing cooperation with only six or seven countries when I took charge, but by the time I left ISRO, we had entered into MOUs with 25 countries for cooperation in the space sector. Today, we have achieved the capacity to build and launch satellites for all those countries.

Even though the USA turned unfriendly after the launch of SLV-3 as they seem to have perceived it as a stepping stone to developing missiles, I once got an opportunity to visit the JPL. Dr Charles Elachi was its director back then. We toured all their laboratories, where I saw a proto model of the Mars Rover. I also noticed a few instruments that could not be launched into orbits. The reason cited was lack of funds. Their space budget was being spent on building and maintaining the Space Station—at nearly US $150 billion, I felt it was a white elephant. Their Space Shuttle programme had to be wound up. Astronauts were then being taken to the Space Station with Russian help. If only India had succeeded in its mission to send people to space, we could have captured the American market.

I was convinced that we must successfully take humans into orbits around the Earth to start with. Voyages to the Moon or

Mars could be planned afterwards. However, the then government perceived such missions as an extravagance. 'Why should a poor country like India waste so much money for a space programme,' they asked. I think we are sometimes asked to walk backwards based on the misconception that we are depriving the poor. Most such comments, however, are made without understanding the societal benefits brought in by space-based resources and the long-term goal of being at par with the developed countries. Only by creating wealth can poverty be eradicated. Modern technologies play a vital role in creating wealth in every country. The history of ISRO and the improvements brought to rural lives clearly show how beneficial the investments in the space programme have been. But if people occupying responsible positions are determined to act blind even though they have eyes to see, then the future of the country is sure to be bleak. Absence of political support put our dreams of human spaceflight programme in cold storage.

We have commercial launch contracts with the French space agency for launching our heavy communication satellites. It is not easy to enter into such agreements with the USA, mainly due to the stringent conditions the Americans insist upon. In Russia's case, the huge cost acts as a deterrent. The Ariane rocket of the French agency has turned out to be affordable and most reliable.

INTERNATIONAL FRIENDS

I had excellent personal relations with the heads of international space agencies. The president of CNES, Yannick D'Escatha, is a close friend. The good relations helped to take our bilateral cooperation to new heights. Experiments like Megha Tropiques for the study of tropical weather conditions and building satellites jointly came out of it. D'Escatha was even ready to send French experts for our review meetings, virtually amounting to technology transfer. Their assistance was useful for us in analysing the GSLV's failures.

When examining the international trends in space research, China attracts our attention the most. So far, we have not been able to build any cooperation with them in this area. In spite of a few invitations to visit China over the years, I could not go. Finally, in 2014, I went to Beijing to attend a conference of the IAA. I was the president of IAA at that time, having been elected as the first non-American president of this body in 2010.

Professor Liu Jiyuan, former president of the Chinese space agency, was the vice president of the IAA during my tenure. He was a close confidant of the Chinese government. In a first for an Indian, he showed me around the Chinese space research facilities. I found the Chinese facilities to be as good as those in developed countries. Their investment in this area was five times India's. Space research and aircraft development were under the same agency, which proved beneficial in many ways. I saw their old rocket and satellite integration facility as well as the new ones, which looked as good as those at NASA. In India, we have two 'clean-rooms' for satellite integration; in China, a sixth clean-room was under construction! Each was the size of a tennis court.

The space assets of the country are used for various civilian and military operations. Hence, protecting these assets is vital. India is a signatory to the Outer Space Treaty, which declares that outer space is the common heritage of humankind and has to be preserved and not weaponized. However, our space resources need to be protected from hostile satellites. We should think about the detection and destruction of any such hostile objects. The recent anti-satellite experiment is a forerunner in this direction.

When discussing international relations in space, the organization called UN COPUOS needs to be mentioned. Headquartered in Vienna, it meets twice a year; I had participated in the meetings from 1998 as the leader of the Indian delegation. Most of the discussions centred on the weaponization of space and the danger posed by defunct satellites and other space debris. India could play a major role as a moderator among the differing American and Russian blocs. Dr Sarabhai, Professor Yash Pal and Professor U.R. Rao had earlier made important contributions in this forum.

The international community meets in Paris quite often, and it is the place from where we coordinate with other European countries. ISRO has presence there in the form of the ISRO Technical Liaison Unit (ITLU), which works in association with the Indian embassy. That vibrant office was managed by Dr Radhika Ramachandran when I was ISRO's chairman. Ranjan Mathai was the Indian ambassador to France then and wholly supported space-related activities. Along with Yannick D'Escatha, Jean-Yves Le Gall, chief executive of Arianespace, and Professor Jean-Jacques Dordain, head of the ESA, were my close friends.

Arianespace used to charge heavily for launching our communication satellites. After we successfully realized the GSLV, they began giving us some reductions. It was in our interest to maintain good relations with them. I would remind Dr Radhika every now and then about this. She would meet the heads of the space agencies in Europe in person and maintain the contacts. She was tremendously helpful in handling the IAA and UN COPUOS affairs. I recall that a reception was organized at the ITLU after the Chandrayaan-1 launch. It turned out to be a big event showcasing ISRO's achievements to the European community. Among others, Yannick d'Escatha was there and spent nearly two hours showing solidarity with us!

Dr Radhika is a top scientist in atmospheric research and has made significant contributions in atmospheric modelling. She has also acted as a technical liaison officer in Delhi—a very complex and challenging job of coordinating with the PMO and other departments. Later, she returned to scientific work and retired as the director of Space Physics Laboratory at Thiruvananthapuram, which was nucleated by Dr Sarabhai himself. Dr Radhika is a fine role model for female scientists at ISRO.

26

ISRO: People and Culture

The ISRO family is nearly 15,000 strong, 40 per cent of whom are expert scientists and engineers. Technicians make up 30 per cent, and the rest are administration and support staff. An equal number of people from industries also participate in the programmes. Selfless commitment of all the team members is the mainstay of ISRO's success story.

In the mid-1960s, Dr Sarabhai attracted Indian scientists working in the USA and Europe to head the technology developments in space in India. Professor U.R. Rao, who returned after working with NASA, was already at the PRL. Dr M.K. Mukherji, Dr D.S. Rane, Dr S.C. Gupta, Dr A.E. Muthunayagam, Dr V.R. Gowarikar and Dr Y.J. Rao were among them. These senior scientists were asked to set up laboratories in their respective fields in Thumba. Scientists picked up by Dr Sarabhai included M.R. Kurup, D. Eswaradas and R. Aruvamudan from the BARC and Dr Kalam and H.G.S. Murthy from the defence labs. As mentioned already, Murthy set up TERLS and became its founder director.

SUCCESSION AND STAFF

A leadership crisis had occurred with the unexpected demise of Dr Sarabhai, the founder director of the SSTC. None of the seniors was willing to accept the other as the director. So, a management council was set up with five members, with each taking turns to chair it.

This was the situation when Professor Dhawan took charge of ISRO. He convinced Dr Brahm Prakash, who had just retired from the BARC, to take charge of the SSTC. The unassuming and calm metallurgist brought peace and harmony among the warring factions. He integrated all the units of Thumba, giving equal importance to both foreign-returned scientists and home-grown technologists.

Sometime later, the Satellite Systems Development group headed by Professor U.R. Rao moved to Bengaluru. Dr Y.J. Rao was given charge of setting up a launch complex at the newly acquired land at the southern tip of Andhra Pradesh. Dr Kalam was entrusted with developing SLV-3. The troika of Professor Dhawan, Dr Brahm Prakash and Dr Kalam has to be given credit for the inclusion of India in the exclusive space club. In 1979, due to failing health, Dr Brahm Prakash handed over directorship of the VSSC to Dr V.R. Gowarikar. The big propellant plant in Sriharikota as well as the development of HTPB-based propellant count among his contributions to ISRO.

Professor Dhawan believed that all the development in propulsion systems should be under one centre because of commonalities in the technologies.

Liquid propulsion activities were being carried out in Bengaluru as well at the VSSC in Thiruvananthapuram, with testing being done in Mahendragiri. Considering the need to consolidate and strengthen the activities, the decision to form the LPSC was taken.

Leadership changes in ISRO have sometimes created heartburn. When Professor U.R. Rao was appointed as the chairman, Dr Gowarikar, the main contender, went on a sabbatical and later moved to Delhi as secretary to the Department of Science and Technology. Dr K. Kasturirangan took over as the chairman of ISRO after Professor Rao. The former had been the project director for Earth observation satellites. Indeed, he can be called the father of remote sensing satellites and application programmes in our country.

Dr Kasturirangan's appointment disappointed many. Whispers were heard about the disappointment of Dr Muthunayagam and P.P. Kale, who were the contenders for the post of the chairman. Later, Dr Muthunayagam moved out as the secretary to the newly formed Department of Ocean Development. Kale was elevated to the post of director of the VSSC.

All these leaders have done full justice to the various technical activities in a friendly and cooperative spirit at ISRO. The challenges regarding technology have always been the binding force among all.

Dr S.C. Gupta, who took over the reins of the VSSC from Dr Gowarikar, deserves mention. Dr Sarabhai had brought Dr Gupta to India from a major instrumentation company in the USA. His expertise was in areas like precision navigation, gyroscopes, guidance and control. He was also an institution builder, proponent of systems engineering and expert in nurturing new talents such as N. Sridharan Dhas, N. Vedachalam and Dr B.N. Suresh. He founded the IISU at Vattiyoorkavu in Thiruvananthapuram, which Vedachalam built up to a full-fledged facility. Dr Gupta settled down in Thiruvananthapuram and passed away very recently.

P.P. Kale was the director of the VSSC for only nine months. He had been the director of the SAC in Ahmedabad, and the shift to Thiruvananthapuram did not suit him. He took voluntary retirement and was succeeded by Dr S. Srinivasan, the world-class rocket designer. Dr Srinivasan had led the design of all ISRO rockets, starting from SLV-3 to GSLV Mark II. He is not with us today. I, Dr Suresh, Dr K. Radhakrishnan, S. Ramakrishnan, P.S. Veeraraghavan, M.C. Dathan, Dr K. Sivan and S. Somanath later held the responsibility of the director of the VSSC. S. Somanath, the blue-eyed boy who had worked with me from the very beginning of the PSLV project, is the chairman of ISRO now. Dr S. Unnikrishnan Nair took over as the director of the VSSC from Somanath.

Dr A.E. Muthunayagam was the founding director of the LPSC and led the developments in liquid engines until 1994. When the spy scandal broke out, he had to move out. He can be credited with the infrastructure development in Mahendragiri and the development of liquid rocket engines for the PSLV as well as the INSAT series of satellites. He had strong lieutenants like Nambinarayanan and Sridharan Dhas with him. He moved to Delhi, and I took charge of the LPSC during the most difficult of times. I am thankful that I could contribute to the development of India's first cryogenic engine. I cannot forget the contributions of N. Sridharan Dhas, M.K.G. Nair, V. Gnana Gandhi, D. Gunasekharan, K. Kasiviswanathan, M. Annamalai and several others. Dr Vasantha, R.V. Perumal, M.K.G. Nair, N. Vedachalam, S. Ramakrishnan, M.C. Dathan, K. Sivan and S. Somanath steered the LPSC in later years. Now, Dr V. Narayanan holds the position. His rise from being a simple mechanical engineer to become the top-most expert in cryogenic engines in the country is commendable.

Professor U.R. Rao crafted ISAC in Bengaluru into a world-class centre. Dr K. Kasturirangan took charge after him. Dr P.S. Goel demonstrated stellar performance as the director. He is an expert in satellite technology and control systems and later served as the secretary to the Ministry of Earth Sciences. ISRO Satellite Centre has now been rechristened as the U R Rao Satellite Centre (URSC).

Dr Y.J. Rao was the founding director of the SHAR. He later returned to the USA. Col N. Pant and M.R. Kurup took over and made the island facility truly world-class. R. Aravamudan, Dr S. Srinivasan, Dr S. Vasantha, R. Jeyamani, K. Narayana, M. Annamalai, M.C. Dathan, Dr M.Y.S. Prasad, P. Kunhikrishnan, S. Pandian and now A. Rajarajan have provided much-needed continuity.

The director of the LVPO at ISRO HQ interfaces between ISRO's chairman and the launch vehicle centres at the VSSC, LPSC and SDSC-SHAR. Srinivasa Shetty held this position during the tenures of Professor Dhawan and Professor Rao. D. Narayana Moorthi, a leader in the SLV-3 team, took over later. He was the director of the LVPO during the entire period when I was the director of the LPSC and VSSC. We used to have consultations on technical and administrative matters almost daily. He still held that position when I became the chairman of ISRO. His specialty was that for every issue, he would invariably have a very uncommon perspective. He was an officer who combined technical expertise on launch vehicles, excellent management skills and the benefit of a long association with Dr Kalam. Even after Narayana Moorthi's retirement from ISRO, Dr Kalam used to call him to the Rashtrapati Bhavan when he was president of India to work together on projects. Narayana Moorthi continues to be a good friend and advisor to me.

Dr P.S. Sastri took charge as the LVPO's director after Narayana Moorthi and played a significant role in ISRO's efforts to collaborate with Israel. He also made major contributions in realizing contracts for cryogenic technology and ion propulsion with the Russians. D.R. Suma held that position when I left ISRO. Her comprehensive knowledge of launch vehicles, long working experience at the VSSC and the ability to interact with senior scientists both in and outside the country proved very useful. She contributed to evolving the 2020 vision for ISRO. She took the initiative to consolidate inputs from various groups at all ISRO centres and formulated a blueprint about what ISRO must do in the next decade. Today, that plan is being implemented with Dr Somanath's initiative. Suma rose to the position of founder chairman and managing director of the newly formed NewSpace India Limited, which undertook ISRO's commercial activities.

Women make up 20 per cent of the ISRO community. In India, these many women working in an science and technology organization is rare. I have been asked many times about why more women have not come into top leadership positions in the organization. I have found that generally women display better performance than their male counterparts in the initial stages of their careers. But, I believe that once they get married and have children, a lot of their time is spent in caring for the children and the family. I think this is why they are sometimes not able to apply their full attention to official matters. Promotions at ISRO are given based on one's performance. Women fare badly on some occasions, and I think this is one reason for it. But many have later overcome setbacks and risen to higher positions. During my tenure, the promotion committees were instructed to encourage women employees, and many became group directors, programme directors and project directors. T.S. Ramadevi and Dr V.R. Lalithambika at the VSSC and Dr T.K. Anuradha at ISAC are examples of the women who rose to hold management positions.

A DRIVEN WORK CULTURE

Many people believe that working towards well-defined goals at an R&D organization is difficult. But at ISRO, all activities are planned well in advance and undertaken in a time-bound manner. Everything is planned ahead of schedule—what to do, how to do it and when to do it. Most scientists are engaged in such developmental activities. A few focus on fundamental science and are engaged in space exploration, which may not be time-bound. Indian Space Research Organisation has always encouraged innovation.

Suited up for the clean-room at the ISRO Inertial Systems Unit (IISU), c. 2008. Some of the people in the photo are P.S. Veeraraghavan (second on my left) and Dr P.P. Mohan Lal (second on my right).
Courtesy: ISRO Archives

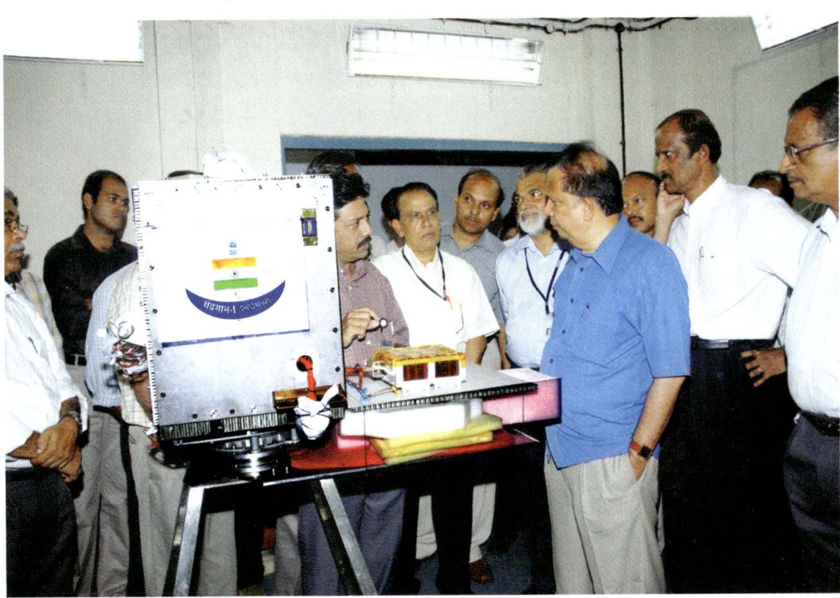

Inspecting the Moon Impact Probe (MIP) at the VSSC during the Chandrayaan-1 development in 2008. From left: M. Mohan, Ashok Kumar, Dr K. Radhakrishnan, I, John P. Zachariah and S. Ramakrishnan.
Courtesy: ISRO Archives

Chandrayaan-1 with the MIP at the environment test facility at ISAC in 2008
Courtesy: ISRO Archives

Reaching for the Moon: PSLV-C11 rocket lifts off from Sriharikota with Chandrayaan-1 spacecraft in 2008.
Courtesy: ISRO Archives

Moon's surface captured by the camera in Chandrayaan-1
Courtesy: ISRO Archives

Dr Kalam shares the excitement of the MIP touching the Moon's surface at the control room at ISRO Telemetry, Tracking and Command Network (ISTRAC), Peenya, Bengaluru, in 2008.
Courtesy: ISRO Archives

Celebrating with colleagues in the control room after the MIP impact on the Moon in 2008
Courtesy: ISRO Archives

Presenting a picture captured by Cartosat-2A to Prime Minister Dr Manmohan Singh at the prime minister's residence in 2008. M. Krishnaswamy is on my right. S. Ramakrishnan is on the extreme right.
Courtesy: ISRO Archives

With 'Guru' Dr Kalam at ISTRAC control centre, Peenya, Bengaluru, in 2008
Courtesy: ISRO Archives

With Narendra Modi, the chief minister of Gujarat, after the Chandrayaan-1 mission at the Physical Research Laboratory (PRL), Ahmedabad, in 2008

Courtesy: ISRO Archives

Signing a memorandum of understanding (MOU) with the French space agency Centre National d'Etudes Spatiales (CNES) in 2008. French Foreign Minister Bernard Kouchner (bottom right), Prime Minister Dr Manmohan Singh (top left) and French President Nicolas Sarkozy (top right) are seen.

Courtesy: ISRO Archives

A national honour: Receiving the Padma Vibhushan from the President of India Pratibha Patil in 2009
Courtesy: ISRO Archives

Flanked by the chairman of Atomic Energy Commission (AEC) Dr Anil Kakodkar (my right) and Mukesh Ambani (my left) in New Delhi in 2009
Courtesy: ISRO Archives

At the inaugural function of Dr Vikram Sarabhai Space Foundation along with Dr Kalam and other dignitaries in Kochi in 2010
Courtesy: G. Madhavan Nair

With Radha during a visit to the Great Wall of China in 2013

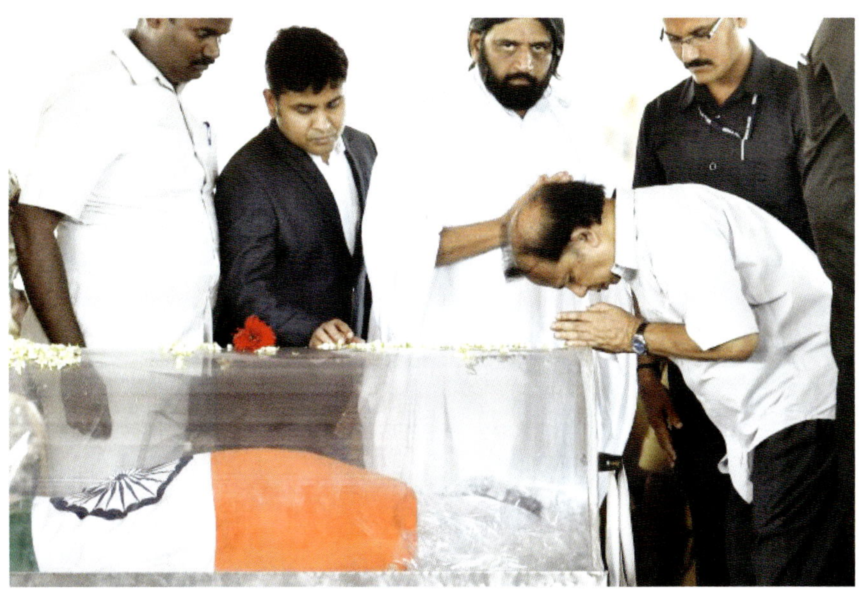

Paying respects to the mortal remains of Dr Kalam in Rameswaram in 2015
Courtesy: G. Madhavan Nair

With some good friends: At an international conference with the president of the CNES Yannick d'Escatha (front left), Dr Anil Kakodkar (centre, back row) and others in Kochi in 2016

Courtesy: G. Madhavan Nair

At the tenth convocation of Indian Institute of Space Science and Technology (IIST) on 17 December 2022, where I was the chief guest. Seen from left in the foreground: Dr S. Unnikrishnan Nair, Director, IIST and Director, VSSC; Dr B.N. Suresh, Chancellor, IIST; S. Somanath, Chairman, ISRO and Secretary, Department of Space (DOS); and Dr V. Narayanan, Director, Liquid Propulsion System Centre (LPSC).

The scientists are provided with the necessary facilities to work independently on their projects, the progress of which are critically examined on a periodic basis and necessary directions are given. Whenever issues crop up, expert committees are set up to assess the situation and decide the way forward. This is the unique working style at ISRO.

Clear vision, goal-setting, careful planning and meticulous reviews, coupled with a relatively independent working environment in the organization, has enabled ISRO's excellent performance. I wish such systems were put in place in other departments as well.

27

Turning the Page

The retirement age of central government personnel is 60. I took charge as the chairman of ISRO a few weeks before my superannuation date. The appointment was initially for two years. The government extended the service subsequently twice for two years each time. Dr Kakodkar also had a similar privilege as the chairman of the AEC. I understand that such decisions are made by the Cabinet based on our performance. It was during my third term that the Chandrayaan-1 mission was successfully completed. Following the saying that it is better to stop singing when the voice is still good, I communicated to the prime minister that I wished to step down from active service.

I had joined the space programme as an engineer 42 years earlier. Getting groomed by people like Dr Sarabhai, Dr Kalam and Professor Dhawan; growing to take responsibility for the development of India's workhorse launcher PSLV; and culminating in implementing the Chandrayaan-1 mission—this had indeed been a highly rewarding period. It also gave me great pride that I could play a significant role in the indigenous development of cryogenic engines.

I formally met the prime minister and senior officials like T.K.A. Nair and M.K. Narayanan at the PMO and expressed my gratitude for the great opportunities and support extended to me. Afterwards, I addressed the ISRO employees for their unstinted cooperation and sincere contributions.

I had submitted to the prime minister a panel of three names to be considered for succeeding me a few weeks before my retirement. In organizations like ISRO, the practice has been to select a chairman based not only on seniority but individual professional capabilities as well. The panel included Dr T.K. Alex, the director of ISAC in Bengaluru; Dr R. Navalgund, the director of the SAC; and Dr K. Radhakrishnan, the director of the VSSC. There was a selection committee composed of senior officials and scientists. I happened to meet one of the members, Professor C.N.R. Rao, on the evening flight to Bengaluru. Though the results had not been officially announced, he mentioned to me that the committee had given a lot of weight to my views and Dr Radhakrishnan was the first choice.

The order appointing Dr Radhakrishnan was issued while he was performing at a music concert in Guruvayoor. He immediately took a copy of that order and placed it at the feet of Lord Krishna, seeking his blessings.

TRANSFERRING CHARGE

I was supposed to hand over the charge on the afternoon of 31 October 2009. I chose the VSSC for that function. I reached Thiruvananthapuram from Bengaluru in the morning and, as usual, reviewed a few activities at the VSSC. Dr Radhakrishnan was the director of the VSSC at that time. We chose noon as the auspicious time for transferring charge. All the necessary papers were prepared by Yashoda, my trusted secretary. Immediately after the formal signing of papers, a meeting of the VCMC was convened with all the senior officers of the VSSC and my colleagues from ISRO HQ.

I had informed everyone that I did not wish for any send-off function. Symbolically, Dr Radhakrishnan adorned me with a traditional Kerala-style shawl and presented me with a silver lamp. While handing these over, he quoted the famous words about bowing to a teacher, '*Gurur Brahma, Gurur Vishnu, Gurur Devo Maheshwara; Gurur Sakshaat Para Brahma, Tasmai Shri Gurave Namah*' (Guru represents Brahma, Vishnu and Shiva—the gods of creation, sustenance and destruction. Guru is the absolute Lord. I salute such a Guru). He added respectfully that I was his guru and then accepted the power transfer orders.

Prime Minister Manmohan Singh had inaugurated the IIST campus in Valiamala a while ago through teleconference. His principal secretary T.K.A. Nair had been a great support in getting approval for that project. We thought it was appropriate that Nair inaugurate the Ponmudi campus of the IIST. Immediately after lunch, we travelled to Ponmudi, a hill station about 40 km from Thiruvananthapuram. After going around the site, the foundation stone was laid. My wife also accompanied us. During a tea party at the LPSC, my wife had a short conversation with Nair. Later, I learnt that my wife had requested him that I be spared from any arduous work after my retirement!

Dr Radhakrishnan reached ISRO HQ the same evening and signed the report about him taking charge as the chairman. The next day, I reached Bengaluru by afternoon and directly went to my house at HSR Layout, instead of driving as usual to my temple, ISRO HQ.

Dr Radhakrishnan requested me to continue as the Vikram Sarabhai Professor at ISRO. I was happy to continue to contribute to ISRO's programmes as an expert. It was also heartening that I was the first beneficiary of the programme of appointing retired experts as visiting professors or consultants.

The next day onwards, Dr Radhakrishnan began interactions on the various ongoing projects, receiving briefings from all top officials. Bhaskara Narayana, the scientific secretary, was one of the top-most specialists in satellite communication in India. Technically excellent, he was also good at conducting managerial interfaces with other departments. That is why I had retained him as the scientific secretary even after his superannuation. He had drawn up a master plan to nearly double the satellite transponder capacity within five years. He was absolutely honest in his working habits, and it was surprising that he was charged with corrupt practices later in the Devas Scam. V. Jayaraman, the programme director for Earth observation systems, was not only an expert in remote sensing satellites but also in evolving various application programmes for agriculture, fisheries and forestry. D.R. Suma, the programme director for launch vehicles, had given a lot of thrust to the launch vehicle development programme. K.R. Sridhara Murthi, the executive director of Antrix, was a leader with excellent foresight who multiplied Antrix's business fivefold during my tenure. Though Dr Radhakrishnan used them to understand the intricacies of space activities, he soon dropped these people one by one from their positions on some pretext or the other.

Dr Radhakrishnan came to my house that evening and spent a lot of time discussing ISRO's future programmes and seeking guidance on several matters. I was happy that he was considering my guidance even after I had stepped down from office.

VARIOUS PROJECTS

After a few days, I received an invitation from the Bhutan Remote Sensing Centre to review their programmes and make recommendations. They received me as a State guest. Bhutan really is paradise on Earth. Within the short period of stay, I could gauge the cool, confident and peace-loving nature of the people there. I cannot describe the serene beauty of nature I saw, unspoilt by human intervention. You have to see to believe the abundance of fresh trees, gardens and flowers. History sleeps in the monasteries and palaces built thousands of years ago. No wonder that a global study has rated Bhutan first in quality of life.

As the Vikram Sarabhai Professor at ISRO HQ, I had taken up with the prime minister the need for India to develop a passenger aircraft for civilian applications. He agreed in principle and formed a study team under the banner of the National Civil Aircraft Development (NCAD) programme. I had the opportunity to chair this committee. We assembled a hundred-member team with a mix of senior experts retired from agencies like HAL, NAL, DRDO, etc., and freshly recruited young scientists. A full-fledged design office was set up, with a powerful computing facility as well as design tools. We could complete a market survey and evolve the configuration of a 90-seater aircraft to meet the connectivity requirements between small towns and metros. A report containing all the technical specifications was submitted to the government within the stipulated one year. The implementation was proposed in public–private participation mode with cost-sharing on a 50–50 basis, with a total outlay of around ₹10,000 crore. Dr A.R. Upadhya, the director of NAL, gave unstinting support for this activity. Several experts from NAL like Shyam Shetty and Yogesh Kumar, an ex-HAL senior executive, were of great help.

After an extensive review of the report by the Planning Commission as requested by the prime minister, Vice Chairman Dr Montek Singh Ahluwalia recommended that such a project was very much needed by the country. The investment cost was justified thanks to the large financial gain that would accrue from selling the aircraft. National Aerospace Laboratories, under CSIR, was entrusted with processing the project for approval. But somehow, Dr Brahmachari, then director general of CSIR, who was himself a member of the NCAD team, developed cold feet, stating that CSIR had no background of handling such large projects. Later, the government issued an order stating that a joint team under NAL and HAL may initiate the activities with ₹10 crore as seed money. But somehow, even after several years, the National Civil Aviation Project has not taken wings.

MANGALYAAN

There is yet a long road ahead to realize technology for recoverable and reusable launch vehicles. Japan and the USA had already made strides in this area. The basic technology we were targeting was much more advanced than theirs. The first goal was to fly a small model using an SLV-3 booster. Many systems had to be developed from scratch—hypersonic aerodynamic control, re-entry technology and autonomous flight management system. A full model was prepared, and it was possible to test it in a year's time. But there was a retreat, perhaps fearing failure, which is always a possibility when new things are attempted.

Let me clarify my views on the Mars mission. While work on Chandrayaan-1 had been ongoing, concurrent efforts were being undertaken for the follow-on mission Chandrayaan-2. Preparations for the second mission had been mostly completed by the time I left ISRO. All those subsystems were diverted to Mangalyaan, the mission to Mars, which could be achieved within a year as a result. The required technology was similar to that of the Moon mission. We had already learnt how to control the trajectory of the rocket accurately. The additional requirements for the Mars mission were to simulate the trajectory on ground computers and feed the speed and direction of the spacecraft at the end of the launch. When the spacecraft reaches near Mars, if its speed is reduced by operating the rocket engine in the spacecraft, it will automatically get pulled into an orbit around Mars. This was exactly what was done during Chandrayaan-1.

A mission to Mars was already in ISRO's plans for the next decade, since opportunities for reaching Mars's orbits come only once in two years. Initially, the mission intended to obtain scientific knowledge from Mars, which would benefit the entire scientific community. During the first review meeting, I had emphasized the need and importance of including a number of specific payloads. Even though some countries had already carried out missions to Mars, there were many important aspects that none of them had attempted so far. We wished to pioneer those areas. A rocket as capable as the GSLV was required for launching such a spacecraft.

However, since the GSLV was not yet ready, the Mangalyaan was launched using the PSLV after inevitable modifications in the mission plan. Many compromises were made due to the mass constraint. The Mangalyaan carried a less than 10 kg payload when it was launched, and only a few instruments could be accommodated inside it: a camera and three payloads, which were actually leftovers from the Chandrayaan-1 mission. This was really disappointing, considering the amount of time, effort and money invested into the mission. In contrast, Chandrayaan-1 had carried 10 instruments, five from ISRO and five from other nations.

Since the PSLV's capability to carry the spacecraft to Mars was limited, Mangalyaan could not carry enough fuel to achieve a respectable orbit. The Mangalyaan's orbit was not circular, but elliptical, with the nearest distance to Mars being 385 km and the farthest 80,000 km. Consequently, even good-quality photographs could not be taken. It may be recalled that Chandrayaan-1 was placed in a 200-km circular orbit around the Moon. Previous missions to Mars by other agencies had sent back photographs covering the whole surface—that too pictures of very high quality!

Not much information has been gathered so far using the other three scientific instruments aboard Mangalyaan either. Even though a lot of money, around ₹450 crore, was spent, it is doubtful whether the mission has given adequate returns.[1]

Many of my successor's actions in dropping flagship projects conceived during my tenure paved the way for bureaucratic control of the organization, resulting in the annual expenditure of ISRO being cut to nearly half of what it was in the previous years. The nationally important programmes of tele-medicine, tele-education and village resource centres were virtually closed down. The biggest tragedy was not pursuing the human spaceflight programme, which got revived only in 2016 after Dr Sivan took over as the chairman.

[1]'Mangalyaan's Cost Wasn't Rs 450 Crore, Austere ISRO Returned ₹2.61 Crore', *IndiaTimes*, 18 November 2016, https://bit.ly/3NYtGgP. Accessed on 5 May 2023.

28

A Step Backwards

The date 15 April 2010 was a tragic one for ISRO, when the maiden launch of the indigenous cryogenic stage onboard GSLV Mark II failed. It was the fourth launch of the GSLV Mark II rocket and the first one with the indigenous cryogenic engine. I was present at the mission control centre at the SHAR for the launch, and we were all heartbroken. It seemed like the repetition of the curse of failed first launches—SLV-3 and the ASLV. The PSLV had also tasted failure in the maiden mission. The only exception was the first mission of GSLV Mark II with a Russian-made cryogenic upper stage, which was a success. The second mission failed and was followed by success in the third mission. Now in its fourth flight, the rocket with the indigenous cryogenic stage had ended up in the Pacific Ocean. The decade-long efforts of thousands of engineers and other ISRO staff to master cryogenic technology could not be proven through flight. It was a highly disappointing and demoralizing moment.

This launch, like most geostationary launches from Sriharikota, was conducted in the evening. The core stage and the second stage had performed precisely. Then, at the beginning of the cryogenic stage, the mission had come to an abrupt end.

The initial data about the flight's performance could be collected by the late evening. At the customary press meeting, Dr Radhakrishnan only made a one-line statement: 'The mission was not successful, and we are investigating the reasons for the failure.' Neither he nor his colleagues responded to the media questions.

Immediately after this, the post-flight analysis meeting started. Individual teams substantiated how their subsystems and the ground stations had performed well. When the ignition command for the cryogenic stage was given, it had started picking up thrust. Suddenly, the thrust had fallen to zero. As a result, no further addition to the velocity and altitude required to achieve the intended geo-transfer orbit had occurred. The cryogenic stage, along with the spacecraft, had landed in the ocean.

The cryogenics development team had some preliminary ideas about the failure. As soon as they began their presentation, Dr Radhakrishnan stated that everyone was tired and, hence, there need not be any further discussions on the day. This was quite unheard of in ISRO culture. The team normally forgets tiredness and toils all night to discuss such matters. I raised this concern. I wanted to continue the meeting but was overruled. I could see a fear of facing failure in the new chief. I was seeing this for the first time at ISRO.

Failures shatter the hopes of many, but the lessons learnt from failures are the foundations for future successes. This philosophy is ingrained in everyone at ISRO. Quite often, even complex technology solutions emerge from such failures.

THE DEVAS SCAM: FIRST STIRRINGS

A failure-analysis committee was constituted as usual. I was asked to chair it and I gladly accepted. In the preliminary meeting, I asked the members to specifically go through the performance and design details of each subsystem. Millions of bytes of flight data were deciphered and the performance of every subsystem during the flight was verified by the respective specialists.

The next meeting of the failure-analysis committee was scheduled for 31 May 2010 at the VSSC, the lead centre for launch vehicle development. It was a great experience to listen to the specialists and the differing viewpoints about reasons for the deviation in performance. Quite often, the arguments are similar to that in courtrooms with surprising inputs. The initial presentations confirmed accurate performance of the lower stages. The signature of ignition of the cryogenic stage was also confirmed.

During the meeting, I received a message to get in touch with the prime minister immediately.

I came out of the conference hall and rang up the PMO. Without any delay, Prime Minister Manmohan Singh came on the line. I was surprised to find him unusually disturbed. He asked me whether I had seen the news related to the spectrum sale by the DOS in the media and asked what it was all about. I was totally in the dark, since I had not seen that day's newspapers. I was aware of the stories related to the '2G scam' where the Minister of Communication A. Raja had allegedly sold spectrum to various telecom companies, causing losses to the government. Various related investigations and court cases were ongoing.

The prime minister enquired about an agreement between Antrix, the commercial wing of ISRO, and a company called Devas in 2005. He said that a much bigger scam than the 2G was being reported, alleging that ISRO has caused losses to the government in spectrum sale to Devas. Though I had not seen the media reports, I explained to the prime minister the difference between spectrum sale for terrestrial use as opposed to lease of transponder from a spacecraft working in the S band. He wanted to know the factual situation and directed me to give him a report within 24 hours. I replied that I would get back to him within a few hours. I had to suspend the failure-analysis meeting and turn my attention immediately to what came to be called the 'Devas Scam'.

I went through the day's newspapers. The leading national newspapers, *The Hindu* and *The Economic Times,* had reported that the DOS was involved in another spectrum scam and had caused loss to the public of ₹2.8 lakh crore by cheaply selling precious S-band spectrum to a private company—a bombshell compared to the almost ₹1.8 lakh crore attributed to the 2G scam![1] Since the DOS was directly under the prime minister, the report was targeted at him. No wonder the PMO was alarmed.

Sitting in Thiruvananthapuram, I could not access the relevant files. I contacted a few of my colleagues in Bengaluru and dug into my memory. Within a few hours, I could put together the facts about the issue into a four-page note that I faxed to the PMO. Antrix

[1]'A ₹1.76 Lakh Crore Scam—Just Notional?', *The Hindu*, 29 December 2017, https://bit.ly/44uFKfr. Accessed on 5 May 2023.

had signed an agreement with Devas, a company owned by a team of ISRO ex-employees. Apparently, the issue had now cropped up based on an audit query to the DOS, which would normally be replied to in due course. Instead, some interested parties within the department seemed to have leaked it to the media.

I sought an appointment with the prime minister to explain the entire issue and to point out how the media reports were incorrect. It was immediately granted for the day after. I rushed to Delhi and met Prime Minister Manmohan Singh, spending almost an hour with him.

I explained, at the outset, both through the note and in person, that ISRO has not sold any spectrum to anybody. I clarified ISRO's roles and responsibilities. The organization does not deal with spectrum sales. Its responsibility is only to provide transponder capacity to users and to collect leasing charges. The Department of Telecommunication (DOT) approves spectrum use. In this case, Antrix's agreement with Devas was only to lease S-band transponder capacity from a satellite being built by ISRO. The leasing charges were similar to that for other transponders.

The user is responsible for getting appropriate licenses from the DOT for using the spectrum after paying the required license fee. The DOT fixes the spectrum charges after considering different aspects like revenue earning capacity, data rate, coverage, etc. The user has to pay the necessary license and monitoring fees to the DOT. This process is equivalent to spectrum sale for terrestrial use.

I also clarified that the valuation of spectrum used for space and for terrestrial networks was different. Because of the large quantity of reuse, the terrestrial spectrum earns nearly a thousand times more revenue compared to the use in spacecraft, where reuses are limited. The audit comment was based on the wrong assumption of same charges for both the uses.

The prime minister seemed convinced about my arguments. But things did not end there.

I did not know then that this was the start of a series of events that were to haunt and hurt me for years and continue to do so even today, after 10 years. I shall continue that story in the next chapter.

BACK TO THE CRYO-FAILURE ANALYSIS

While these events were unfolding, the failure analysis of the first indigenous cryogenic stage was completed. The details collected during the initiation of the stage made it abundantly clear that the engine had ignited as planned. The turbine speed and thrust had built up normally. After a few seconds, the turbine had stopped rotating. There could be several reasons for this. The probability of each was considered. Finally, it was narrowed down to either loss of high pressure in the helium tank or some debris getting caught in the bearing of the turbine, causing a seizure. The gas bottle pressure had been normal. Hence, seizure of the turbine due to entrapment of some foreign particle was considered as the most probable reason.

Another gas bottle fabricated with the flight unit was available at the centre in Mahendragiri. Detailed examination of this unit revealed lots of metallic particles left behind from the welding process of the tank. The downstream filter was not fine enough to stop the particles. I was shocked to realize this fact as it was very similar to the scenario during the failure of the first SLV-3 flight.

The corrective action in the present case was straightforward and simple: Adopt a tighter procedure for cleaning the gas tank and introduce a finer filter. We could have realized the next flight within a year. However, several simulation tests, including vacuum ignition trials, were carried out before the next flight.

29

Facts that Illuminate

Before we discuss details of the Devas controversy, let us understand some relevant technical details and revisit the development of satellite communication, which has become a part and parcel of daily life in India today.

Dr Sarabhai saw the benefit of providing connectivity to every corner of this vast country using geostationary satellites. To further this vision, he laid the foundation of the INSAT. Since we did not have the capability to realize such satellites then, a collaborative agreement was made with Ford Aerospace to design, manufacture and launch them. The first satellite of this series, INSAT-1, made as per our specification, was launched in 1982. It had a short life. Same was the case with 1B too, in 1983. With corrections to address technical issues, INSAT-1C and 1D were launched in 1988 and 1990, respectively. Using these satellites, services like telecommunication, TV broadcasting and weather forecasting schemes were implemented in India for the first time.

TRANSPONDER TECHNOLOGY AND BANDWIDTH

Transponders are the key instruments onboard a communication satellite, used to receive and retransmit radio frequency signals. Frequencies in the S, C and Ku bands were used in the past. In the recently launched satellites, several transponders operate in Ku band (around 11 GHz) and Ka band (up to 30 GHz). Availability of electronic components operating at higher frequencies enabled the use of Ku-band transponders, which operate at lower speed, for direct-to-home (DTH) transmission of TV programmes, and Ka band, which operates at high speed, to provide high-speed digital connectivity.

Communication satellites are placed in orbits around the equator at a height of 36,000 km. Orbital slots for satellites and operating frequencies are allocated by the International Telecommunication Union (ITU). The requirements of each country and spectrum availability are considered, and the allocation is done ensuring that it is used for specific purposes without causing interference for others. Each country is allotted specific slots of 2.5 degrees each on the equatorial plane.

India has five such allocations. Indian Space Research Organisation coordinated with the ITU for spectrum usage exclusively for space-related applications. We obtained specific allocations in very high frequency (VHF), S band, C band, Ku band and Ka band for satellite communication in the mid-1980s. This was a far-sighted action by ISRO, and the resource is now owned by the country. Our satellites are placed only at the allotted locations.

Since the whole issue of the Devas Scam is related to spectrum, let us examine the use of radio spectrum, especially for mobile communication. We have come a long way since Motorola's first handheld mobile in 1983. The point to be noted is that there is no clash of frequency bands between space and cellular services as allotted by the ITU. In India, some conflict came up in 2008, when some trials were made for WiMAX services. This was successfully resolved, with the DOT allocating 40 MHz out of the space segment for terrestrial use. However, WiMAX services did not pick up in India, and the allotted spectrum lies vacant. The S band used for satellite and mobile communication are well separated.

The DOS and ISRO had coordinated with the ITU for use of the S-band spectrum 2,500–2,690 MHz for various purposes. Out of this, there were separate allocations for defence (80 MHz), telecom (40 MHz), broadcasting (70 MHz) and two-way communications (20 MHz). The bandwidth allotted for terrestrial mobile communication is around 2,100 MHz.

Terrestrial towers can only provide coverage in approximately 10-km radius using the S-band or microwave frequencies. The towers then have to be repeated at a distance of about 20 km, and the same bandwidth could be reused at least a thousand times, providing that many more connections. Theoretically, a few thousand terminals can provide coverage over entire India. In contrast, from space, the entire country can normally be covered with a single beam. The bandwidth can be utilized only once. However, with large deployable antennae, five spot beams can cover different parts of India, effectively multiplying reuse by five times, providing that many more connections. Hence, the revenue-earning capacity of space-based systems is a thousand times less than that of terrestrial use of spectrum.

The first INSAT satellite used an S band and some VHFs for weather monitoring and disaster management. Many of our Doordarshan channels were initially carried in the S band. The C bands were used for various telecommunication purposes. Later, by 2000, Doordarshan migrated to C band. With the need for higher bandwidth and more channels, ISRO developed Ku-band transponders. These are quite popular now for DTH and very small aperture terminal (VSAT) connectivity. By 2005, most of the communication had shifted to C or Ku band, mainly because the S band needs large antennae of about 3-m diameter. They are expensive and difficult to maintain. On the other hand, Ku band needs antennae of less than 1 m. The net result was that the S band spectrum allotted for space-based broadcast service was lying vacant.

ROLES, RESPONSIBILITIES AND REGULATIONS

Managing the development, deployment and introduction of space-based services is solely the responsibility of ISRO/DOS. So is creating transponder capacity in geostationary satellites and making it available to the government or private users. The DOS has been following a transparent and streamlined procedure for this.

Till 2000, when the new satellite communication policy was announced to encourage private participation in satellite communication, the main users of satellite services were government agencies. The INSAT Coordination Committee was formed, with secretaries to the DOT, Information and Broadcasting (I&B) and Science and Technology departments as members, to review the programme implementation, advise on technical matters and resolve conflicts, if any. Over time, several private users emerged, and the

Committee continued functioning in an advisory role. The DOS submitted a comprehensive proposal on the policy to be followed in satellite communication, especially considering the needs of private players (satellite communication policy), which was finalized in 2002. Here, too, the DOS is vested with the prime responsibility to provide communication transponder requirements, and has to ensure 100 per cent satisfaction for all the users. The INSAT Coordination Committee has the role of advising on policy matters and resolving technical conflicts.

Based on the satellite communication policy, ISRO-DOS-Antrix has put in place well-defined procedures to allot satellite transponders. Indian Space Research Organisation has to provide the space-based transponder capacity after collecting leasing charges as per the DOS norms. It is the nodal agency for receiving requests from the government or private players. Requirements of all private users have to be met exactly. The required satellite capacity has to be made available from ISRO's existing or to-be-developed satellites. In case this is not feasible, ISRO has to provide the necessary transponder capacity from other sources, leased through Antrix. To fix the leasing charges, the DOS considers factors like the international market price and whether it is adequate to cover the costs of building the satellite, launching it and operating it continuously from its control centre. The entire cost has to be recovered over a period of five to six years. It also has to be ensured that ISRO gets adequate returns on its investment. Additionally, the stipulation at that time was that the allotment has to be made on a first-come-first-served basis.

After getting the transponder capacity allocated by the DOS, a user has to approach the DOT for an operating license by paying the spectrum fee and monitoring charges. The DOT ensures whether the specified service is authorized as per the rules and regulations of the country. They get the opinions of the Wireless Planning and Coordination wing of the DOT and I&B department. The DOT also fixes the spectrum charges and monitoring fees as per guidelines issued by the Telecom Regulatory Authority of India (TRAI). The charges vary depending on the revenue potential of specific users. This process is equivalent to 'spectrum scale for telecom services' by the DOT.

As you can see, transponder leasing and spectrum sale are two separate, independent activities, and the responsibility of the DOS and DOT, respectively. In the case of the Devas MOU, the DOS-Antrix had agreed to provide the transponder capacity in the GSAT6 satellite being developed, based on mutually agreed leasing charges, ensuring adequate return on investment.

Further, Antrix's business activities are controlled by its board of directors. The government is represented in the board by the member (finance) and additional secretary. The secretary to the DOS is the chairman of the board. Decisions made by the board do not need any further approval by the government.

ANTRIX'S MOU WITH DEVAS

Antrix is fully owned by the government, with the primary goal of leasing transponder capacity to users, providing launch services for satellites and marketing remote sensing data globally. A modest beginning of ₹100 crore in 2005 grew to ₹1,000 crore by 2008. The company obtained several international contracts for marketing earth observation data from Indian satellites and communication services through geostationary platforms. It also took up the challenging job of building two communication satellites for European customers using ISRO's facilities. Taking into account its excellent performance, the government granted it mini ratna status.

During ISRO's initial years, all development activities were carried out using in-house facilities, but as the programmes expanded, industrialization became a major thrust area. However, not many industries in the country were willing to venture into the high-tech area requiring large investments, involving high risk and providing low returns. To overcome this, ISRO encouraged new ventures founded by senior technocrats who could take long leave or retirement from ISRO to take up space-based commercial activities using the technologies developed by ISRO.

Dr M.G. Chandrasekhar, who was the scientific secretary under Dr K. Kasturirangan, and D. Venugopal, an ex-employee of ISRO working in the satellite communication office, utilized the opportunity. They initially joined *WorldSpace Radio,* a satellite-based entertainment channel broadcasting music all over the world. However, I think that the scheme did not succeed commercially for several reasons and was wound up. Later, from what I know, Dr Chandrasekhar, along with R. Viswanathan and D. Venugopal, constituted the core team of a company called Forge Advisors LLC in the USA.[1]

In May 2003, a high-level team headed by the then chairman, Dr Kasturirangan, along with members of the Antrix Corporation, visited the USA. Forge Advisors had submitted a proposal to form a joint venture with Antrix. They claimed that they had access to critical technologies related to direct broadcast of audio and video signals from space to cover large terrestrial areas. At that time, space-based systems were used for similar applications in the USA and Japan primarily for broadcasting to mobile platforms in cars, trucks and railways. Indian Space Research Organisation found that it was advantageous to adopt similar systems for Indian users too. Hence, taking advantage of technical and commercial strengths and with a long-term perspective, an MOU was signed between Forge and Antrix to explore the feasibility of a joint venture for commercializing space-based products and services globally. Dr Chandrasekhar represented Forge Advisors as the lead person.

In September 2003, I took charge as the chairman of ISRO from Dr Kasturirangan. It was a sudden transition, and we couldn't discuss current and future activities in detail before the transfer of charge. I tried to ensure that all the activities and programmes initiated by Dr Kasturirangan were pursued undiluted. In the case of the MOU with Forge Advisors too, I wanted to pursue the decision taken by my predecessor.

Antrix and Forge Advisors had some interactions based on the MOU. As part of implementing it, Antrix received a detailed proposal on the technical details and requirements for the joint venture company in April 2004. Sometime later, during my visit to Vancouver for the International Astronautical Congress (IAC), Forge Advisors made a presentation on the proposed joint venture

---

[1]Based on internal documents of Antrix Corporation, which the author had access to as chairman of the board.

and handed over a hard copy of their presentation. I immediately marked it to Sridhara Murthi, the executive director of Antrix, for further action.

This proposal was discussed by the Antrix board of directors. The board wanted some more clarity on the technical and managerial aspects and appointed a high-level committee chaired by Dr K.N. Shankara, then director of SAC, Ahmedabad. The Committee assessed that if we proceeded with the joint venture, the high business risks in implementing a new concept would have to be shared. Additionally, such an action would violate the mandate of Antrix. So, the Committee recommended that Antrix should take up only the limited liability of leasing transponder capacity from a satellite being developed by ISRO on standard commercial terms. The Committee's recommendation came up for discussion during the Antrix board meeting in December 2004. After detailed discussions, the board accepted the recommendations of the Shankara Committee unanimously and gave directions to proceed further.

Forge Advisors formed an Indian company called Devas Multimedia to pursue the actions. The Antrix–Devas agreement reserving transponder capacity in a satellite being developed by ISRO was a result of this action.

The Devas agreement was no different from the lease agreements Antrix had made with various service providers like Tata Sky, Zee TV, Sun TV and other users. The agreements were only for making the required transponder capacity available to the users. It was the responsibility of the users to get the operating licenses from the DOT. As in the case of DTH or VSAT operators, the responsibility of developing technologies for the receiving ground equipment and the software belonged to the service provider—in this case, Devas.

Success of this mode of operation had already been demonstrated in the DTH revolution brought in by several operators, where agreements were signed based on operational satellites or just before the launch of new ones. The only difference with the Devas agreement was that the satellite development had only started and launch was aimed in about three years.

Since the capacity was being booked in advance and new technology would have to be developed, as a safeguard, Devas was asked to pay ₹58 crore in advance as reservation fee. The risk of developing the satellite was taken by Antrix. In case Devas failed to establish an operational system in terms of technology and equipment for handheld communication, the lease agreement would be cancelled and the advance paid would be forfeited. Conversely, if ISRO failed to provide the transponder capacity, the penalty payable to Devas was US $5 million (about ₹30 crore). Such safeguards are perfectly in line with international practices.

GSAT6 SATELLITE DEVELOPMENT PLAN

Satellite technology development takes three to five years, and ISRO has always taken the initiative to introduce new schemes with a long-term vision. The standards of broadcasting and communication using geostationary satellites and corresponding technology have evolved in the country concurrently with satellite technology.

During the early 2000s, the global needs of satellite communication to handheld devices were being met through the foreign satellite company Inmarsat, operated by an international agency, and Thuraya, owned by Indonesia. India also depended on these. Since the system was controlled by foreign agencies, there were security issues, and the need for our own system was felt. Hence, ISRO took up a feasibility study on satellite-based communication to handheld devices. Since there was no allocation from the ITU for L band in India, which the Indonesian satellites used, the only option was to use the S band allotted to ISRO.

Using the S band required the development of a high-power S-band transponder and a large (10-m diameter) antenna that can be deployed in space to provide connectivity to handheld units as well as multiple beams, enabling frequency reuse. It would have been a first of its kind for India. The proposed satellite operating in the S band was expected to facilitate broadcast services, namely, for beaming multimedia content to handheld mobile platforms. The satellite was intended to be used for developing the much-needed two-way communication through handheld devices throughout the country.

Development of the advanced satellite technologies required for such a mission was initiated in 2002. Using pre-project funding, the large deployable antenna and high-power S-band transponder was being developed at ISAC, Bengaluru.

Once we were confident that these subsystems could be developed indigenously and after extensive internal reviews, a project report was submitted in early 2005 to the government for approval by ISAC. The project envisaged an S-band satellite for beaming video, audio or digital data for two-way communication from handheld devices. Initially, the satellite was designated as INSAT-4E but was later rechristened as GSAT6 as it was to be launched using the GSLV.

The GSAT6 satellite development was part of the programme to be implemented in the approved five-year plan. The required funding had also been included in ISRO's budget. The project was intended for gaining experience and demonstrating the country's capability to provide handheld communication through satellites all over India. Space Applications Centre in Ahmedabad was entrusted with developing the associated software and hardware for proving the technology.

This was the period in which discussions were taking place between Antrix and Forge Advisors. Though the proposal from the latter was for a joint venture, on practical considerations to reduce the risk, the Shankara Committee had recommended against it and proposed leasing 90 per cent of the satellite capacity for commercial operations. The MOU did not mention that the GSAT6 satellite was going to be used.

The S-band communication satellite and associated systems would have been developed even if some private party had not come to utilize it. We can compare this with the development of the Ku-band satellite by ISRO. When that satellite was conceived and was launched four years later in 2004 based on a study of international trends, private players came forward and leased the capacity for DTH services. When ISRO began the development of the Ku-band satellite, there was no technology or standards for DTH in the country! The standards evolved in parallel. The applications evolved subsequently, mainly with the participation of private players.

The GSAT6 was developed after surveying domestic needs

and international trends. Considering the pressing need, the basic technology for handheld telephony was developed by ISRO (the service provider's responsibility was to develop technology for multimedia broadcasting). Studies had indicated that about 10 MHz of bandwidth would be needed for ISRO's technology development for satellite phones. The balance capacity of 70 MHz was set aside to meet any other requirement of broadcasting to handheld devices. Users could choose to use the transponders for any form of content—whether audio, video or digital—in analogue or digital form, subject to the user getting the necessary clearance and license for operation from the DOT.

After extensive discussions and review within ISRO as well as scrutiny of the project report by the member (finance) of the DOS as well as the finance ministry, the report about the GSAT6 satellite being developed by ISRO was discussed during the Space Commission meeting in June 2005. A major part of the capacity was ear-marked for leasing to private users. The proposal for undertaking the development of GSAT6 and the necessary funding was processed. Among the members, Dr K. Kasturirangan (as a member of the Space Commission), Dr P.S. Goel and Professor Roddam Narasimha actively participated in the review of the technical aspects related to the GSAT6 development plan and its usage. Satisfactory answers were provided by ISRO to queries raised by these members on issues related to uncertainties in the technology, potential military and civilian applications, reasonableness of the schedule and budget requirements. Dr Kasturirangan had been directly involved in the technology development plan since 2002, and his participation had eventually led to the MOU between Antrix and Forge Advisors.

Dr Goel, as the director of ISAC, was the author of the project report for GSAT6 development. As mentioned, 90 per cent of the transponder capacity was to be leased to private players, but their names weren't specified as per the precedence, since the decision-making authority on the choice of parties and the lease agreements is with Antrix. Additionally, there is always the possibility of a party who shows interest in the initial phase not taking up the transponder later.

It has never been the practice to record verbatim the views of the members during Space Commission meetings. Only the final decision and recommendations to the government are recorded in the minutes. The proposal to the Space Commission elaborated on the technological challenges and advantages of the new system for providing multimedia services from space to handheld/mobile units. The new system proposed to utilize the S-band spectrum allotted for such services, which was lying vacant. A 10-MHz spectrum outside the broadcast band was to be used for providing mobile communication.

A point to be noted that became relevant for the Devas case later was a query raised in the meeting: what was the contingency plan in case the contractor failed to provide the ground equipment and software? It was clarified that in such a case, the plan was to use the technology being developed by SAC.

The Space Commission meeting discussing the technology for the GSAT6 was also attended by the principal secretary, Cabinet secretary and finance secretary. Hence, it is very clear that the apex body of the Indian space programme, namely, the Space Commission, was fully informed about the technical aspects of the GSAT6 when it recommended the development and utilization plan of the GSAT6 satellite to the government. The Space Commission approved the project report based on technical merits and the need for the new technology in the country.[2]

Since the cost of the project exceeded ₹150 crore, Cabinet approval had to be obtained. Based on the approval by the Space Commission, a note for the Cabinet was prepared by the DOS.[3]

It may be noted that Cabinet approval was sought for pursuing advanced technology for satellite-based broadcast services to mobile devices and not for the lease agreement for transponder utilization. It had also been clarified that SAC, Ahmedabad, was already working on the end-to-end technology demonstration.

Based on the approval of the project proposal by the Cabinet, the

---

[2]'ICC International Court of Arbitration, Case No. 18051/CYK, DEVAS MULTIMEDIA PRIVATE LIMITED (India) vs/ ANTRIX CORPORATION LIMITED (India)', *Devas Facts,* 13 January 2021, https://bit.ly/3MEScRs. Accessed on 4 April 2023. p. 12, para 49.e.

[3]Ibid. p. 18, para 72.

GSAT6 project activities were taken up on priority. The proto models were developed and put through various qualification tests, and the spacecraft integration was almost completed by September 2009. In about three months, the satellite would have been ready for launch. It was supposed to onboard GSLV Mark II, which unfortunately encountered a failure in April 2010.

30

A Sordid Drama: The Devas Scam

By mid-2010, a totally unexpected turn of events cast aspersions on my actions, and false allegations were raised against me, causing me unprecedented agony. The major issue was the Devas Scam, which I briefly touched upon in the previous chapters. Let me delve a little more into those events and explain my analysis of the same.

To recap, I was at the VSSC in Thiruvananthapuram on 31 May 2010, chairing a failure-analysis meeting for the GSLV's indigenous cryogenic stage. In the middle of the meeting, I was interrupted and was asked to urgently call the PMO. Dr Manmohan Singh came on the line and asked me about reports in the media alleging that the DOS had caused a loss to the government of ₹2.8 crore through short selling of spectrum to a private company called Devas. He directed me to immediately give a detailed report about the facts of the matter, which I submitted within a few hours. I also sought and obtained a personal appointment with him.

While I submitted a report on the matter to the PMO, the then chairman of ISRO, Dr Radhakrishnan, along with the former chairman, Dr K. Kasturirangan, gave a press conference in Delhi on the Devas issue. Unfortunately, the technicalities of the deal and the financial aspects could not be explained properly, and several questions from the media were left unanswered. Apparently, they had not studied or understood the details of the issue and had not bothered to discuss it with the few people in Bengaluru, including myself, who had directly dealt with the matter.

I rushed to New Delhi the next day and spent almost an hour with the prime minister. I explained at length about the agreement with Devas, the difference in spectrum usage in space and on ground, the technical and financial aspects of the project and how there was absolutely no financial loss to the government. I also explained that in the press conference, these points had not been clarified properly. The prime minister seemed convinced of my arguments. He gave me permission to meet the press and explain the situation. As I was about to leave, he asked why Dr Radhakrishnan could not explain the facts. I replied that it may be due to the fact he had not dealt with the GSAT6 until then and lacked proper understanding about the intricacies of the issue. He had not consulted any of us who were associated with the matter either. After a pause, the prime minister chided me, commenting, 'He was your choice, wasn't he?'

Yes, Dr Radhakrishnan had indeed been my choice as my successor. He had joined the VSSC in 1970 and was with ISRO until 2002. In his role in monitoring and budget control at the VSSC, he used to interact with me extensively. Later, he moved to ISRO HQ as the director for budget and planning. We continued to interact often for various project activities and financial matters. One day, I heard that he had to move to the NRSA, Hyderabad. He then quit ISRO to join as the director of the Indian National Centre for Ocean Information Services, under the Ministry of Earth Sciences. This was when I took over as the chairman of ISRO. I brought him back to ISRO, initially as the director of NRSA and, within one year, as the director of the VSSC. It had created some buzz. I had to overrule some senior scientists who had also been closely associated with me as part of the launch vehicle programme. I had the grand plan of him taking over from me, and I was grooming him to be the director of ISRO's largest centre. Later, I played a key role in his selection as the chairman of ISRO, despite facing apprehension from many of my senior colleagues, who expressed concerns over priority being given to a person who had once left ISRO.

In the last month of my term as the chairman, during preparations for a PSLV launch at the SHAR, Dr Radhakrishnan presented me with a copy of ISRO's 'Vision 2020' document and sought my blessings to see that the programme gets implemented smoothly. The document had been prepared by ISRO after extensive discussions under my guidance. It detailed the future road map and activities such as recoverable and reusable launch vehicles, radar imaging satellites, hyper-spectral imaging systems and advanced communication systems. I was extremely happy to see that my successor had accepted this document as his bible. The future programmes of ISRO were all enshrined in it and, if implemented, would have brought a lot of new technologies and glory to India. I had promised him all my support for the successful implementation of the same.

THE BUILD-UP TO THE CONTROVERSY

At the end of the meeting, the prime minister also directed me to meet two senior bureaucrats at the PMO, namely, the principal secretary and the NSA. I did so immediately. I had known them both personally and officially for a long time, and the meeting was friendly. But I felt that some of the questions asked were like those of an investigating agency. After a couple of hours, they concluded that whatever I had explained made sense. But strangely, they advised that I should not speak to the media and go public with the facts. They were afraid that it may look like a war between two Malayalis or two Nairs. Dr Radhakrishnan had already given a statement more or less supporting the report in *The Hindu*. In hindsight, I think it was a mistake not to have given a proper explanation to the media then. Perhaps, I should not have listened to the advice of those officers. Later, I came to know that the authorities had projected that the agreement was established by violating rules and procedures and that it was a case of corruption. God knows from where they got such information.

Let us look at the sequence of events leading to the controversy.

The development of the GSAT6 satellite had progressed well, and Devas was pursuing its contractual obligations with Antrix. On 31 October 2009, Dr Radhakrishnan took over as the chairman of ISRO after me. It is understood from the relevant file at ISRO HQ when I was there as well as from the basic International Chamber of Commerce (ICC) award proceedings that, within a few weeks of my retirement, Dr S.V. Kibe, who was then programme director of satellite navigation at ISRO HQ and associate director of the satellite communication programme office, gave a note to

Dr Radhakrishnan, claiming that there were many irregularities in the Antrix–Devas agreement, which was immediately passed on to the joint secretary in charge of vigilance at the DOS for investigation.[1] Concurrently, a single-man committee with Dr B.N. Suresh was appointed to go through the technical and commercial aspects of the agreement.[2]

The whole issue happened in the context of the 2G scam involving A. Raja. Since 2G cellular services in the S band (2,100 MHz) were gaining popularity, several companies wanted to corner the licenses for operation. Without many players in the field, the DOT, in 2005, adopted the policy of first-come-first-served. Apparently, A. Raja (then minister in charge) as well as some politicians and bureaucrats colluded to sell the spectrum licenses at low prices. The CAG highlighted in his report a loss to the exchequer to the extent of ₹1.7 lakh crore. This news became explosive, leading to Raja's resignation. Later, there was a CBI inquiry on the issue, and it was clearly established that the spectrum had been sold at a much lower price, causing loss to the exchequer and gain to the minister and his associates. Even today, related court cases are ongoing.

On 31 May 2010, *The Hindu* and *The Economic Times* put out the explosive news of a much bigger scam than Raja's. The trigger point for the media report was an audit query raised in 2010 to the DOS by the CAG on the spectrum valuation in the Devas agreement. The query highlighted that the DOS had caused a presumptive loss of ₹2.8 lakh crore on account of the deal with Devas by short selling the spectrum. Since the DOS was directly under the prime minister, some people saw this as an opportunity to corner him. Even before the DOS gave a reply to the audit query, *The Hindu* built up a story based on the matter. Within a day, other media also started echoing it. The PMO immediately formed a shield around the prime minister to save his image. I don't think there was any meaningful analysis or attempt to provide proper

[1]'ICC International Court of Arbitration, Case No. 18051/CYK, DEVAS MULTIMEDIA PRIVATE LIMITED (India) vs/ ANTRIX CORPORATION LIMITED (India)', *Devas Facts,* 13 January 2021, https://bit.ly/3MEScRs. Accessed on 4 April 2023. p. 22.

[2]Ibid.

answers to the audit query by the people at the DOS. Instead, they also joined the bandwagon and aggravated the issue.

The B.N. Suresh Committee's report was submitted in June 2010. It concluded that there was no anomaly in the Antrix–Devas agreement and that it was, in fact, beneficial to ISRO.[3] However, one paragraph was added later, which said that the S-band spectrum is precious, and its utilization plan may be reviewed considering future needs. But no such review took place.

In the meantime, for reasons unknown, instead of pursuing the vigilance inquiry, I understand that files related to Kibe's original complaint and the Suresh Committee Report were taken over by Additional Secretary G. Balachandran. The Suresh Committee's report was never made public for reasons unknown. It is very clear that something was cooking behind the scenes.

Normally, such reports are reviewed by the secretary to the DOS and further actions are taken. Without completing the action items, an urgent meeting of the Space Commission was organized within weeks, in June 2010, to discuss Devas-related issues. Surprisingly, in the meeting, instead of presenting the Suresh Committee's report and subsequent actions, Dr Radhakrishnan and the additional secretary presented a totally different picture, suppressing many of the facts. It is understood from private documents that they claimed that there had been numerous violations of procedure while establishing the agreement, and, hence, it needed to be annulled.[4] The meeting was attended by the Minister of State, principal secretary and the NSA, among others. Looking back, it is strange that the Space Commission took a snap decision without considering the recommendation and conclusions of the Suresh Committee and that it directed the DOS to cancel the agreement with Devas. The members must have had the 2G scam at the back of their minds and might have taken the statement made by the secretary to the DOS at face value. It is understood from private conversations that the action taken was mainly to protect the highest echelons of government.

---

[3]Ibid. p. 23.

[4]Ibid. pp. 27–8, para 111.

My main grievance with Dr Radhakrishnan was that he did not have the courtesy to consult Dr K. Kasturirangan and me, who were part of decision-making in the Devas agreement. Only one brief meeting was held with me on the subject before the Space Commission meeting. He only sought clarification on how a correction was made in the Cabinet note seeking approval for the GSAT6 project. I told him that I had not seen the file recently, but it can better be reviewed by S.K. Das and Ramana Reddy.

After the Space Commission meeting, Dr Radhakrishnan informed me that a decision had been taken to cancel the agreement. I told him that I did not agree with the arguments put forward for the cancellation. However, I believed that once a decision was made, we should implement it without fail. Additionally, during the discussions, I pointed out provisions in the agreement that could be used to make Devas the defaulters for the cancellation and that would not involve paying the penalty on cancellation. As I learnt from conversations with various people, instead of making use of such provisions, he contemplated a decision to proceed based on force majeure, meaning that unforeseeable circumstances had prevented the fulfilling of the contract.

I have learnt about the details of the subsequent events only through the media and the report of the ICC award. These are given henceforth.

Though the Space Commission had recommended cancellation of the Devas agreement citing procedure deviations, the chairman of ISRO made it a secondary issue and took the matter to the Cabinet Committee on Security (CCS) in February 2011. The reason quoted for cancellation was that the S-band spectrum was required for meeting the needs of some defence applications and for critical societal needs. This again shows lack of understanding that there are separate allocations for frequencies within the S band for its use for defence and broadcast purposes. The allocation is made by the ITU. *The S-band spectrum allotted by the ITU for broadcast from satellite cannot be reallocated for any other purpose.* This point is supported by recent reports, which indicate that the assertion that the S-band spectrum was planned to be used for security and societal applications was not entirely accurate. The GSAT6 satellite was finally launched in 2015, and barely 20 per cent of the capacity has been used by anybody so far.[5] The second satellite GSAT-6A did not succeed.[6]

Moreover, the DOS tried to get the opinion of the DOT, the defence users and the legal department, after the decision was made by the Space Commission in July 2010. Several inputs from these agencies contradicted the stand taken by the DOS in the Space Commission meeting. The matter was taken to the CCS only after a long wait of eight months. Additional Secretary Balachandran, who was the secretary to the Space Commission, had pointed out certain corrections that needed to be made in the proposal to the CCS. These suggestions were also ignored.

The actions of some personnel of ISRO/DOS and some politicians in Delhi could create a lot of doubt in anyone's mind. If, for whatever reasons, the Space Commission takes a decision to cancel an agreement, it is mandatory that the intentions are communicated to the party and are implemented through mutual discussions on a possible settlement. However, Devas was not informed of such an intention.[7] Meanwhile, serious discussions were progressing between ISRO and Devas on possible launch options, since the satellite was ready![8] After the Space Commission had already made the decision to cancel the agreement, why was the matter kept hidden, and how did such discussions take place?

In February 2011, the prime minister announced the CCS's decision to cancel the agreement. Eight months had passed since the Space Commission's decision.[9] Immediately afterwards, the

---

[5]'GSAT-6 Satellite Launched in 2015 Largely Unutilised: Centre's Auditor CAG', *NDTV*, 20 December 2022, https://bit.ly/3oEseFH. Accessed on 24 April 2023.

[6]D.S. Madhumathi, 'We Averted a Possible Debacle: ISRO Chairman', *The Hindu*, 11 August 2018, https://bit.ly/3zCwLdL. Accessed on 6 April 2023.

[7]'ICC International Court of Arbitration, Case No. 18051/CYK, DEVAS MULTIMEDIA PRIVATE LIMITED (India) vs/ ANTRIX CORPORATION LIMITED (India)', *Devas Facts*, 13 January 2021, https://bit.ly/3MEScRs. Accessed on 4 April 2023. p. 31.

[8]Ibid. p. 29–30.

[9]The report stated: 'On 30 June 2010 the DOS provided a note to the Space Commission concerning the termination of the Devas Agreement.' See ICC International Court of Arbitration, Case No. 18051/CYK, DEVAS MULTIMEDIA

CCS's decision was officially communicated to Devas by the DOS, terminating the agreement unilaterally and returning the reservation fee amount.

Though Devas subsequently attempted to hold a high-level discussion with Antrix, it was not agreed upon. If such a discussion could not converge to a satisfactory conclusion, there was provision for appointing an arbitration team. Devas requested for arbitration on the matter with the DOS, but that was not agreed upon either.[10] Consequently, Devas took the matter up with the ICC for appointing an arbitration council. The DOS did not cooperate even in this, and the ICC appointed a member representing Antrix to the arbitration council.[11]

Devas made an astronomical claim of US $1.6 billion as damages. I understand that no meaningful counterarguments were made by the DOS. The ICC accepted the argument that the reason for cancellation was that the S-band spectrum was needed for security applications and force majeure could be applied. It is understood that inputs given by the DOS about requirements of defence and other user needs led to the ICC's decision to compensate to the extent the capacity was for civilian applications, which came to US $562 million![12] The case was against Antrix, but not a soul from Antrix was even called in as a witness! The net result was that the Antrix/DOS stand was not properly justified during the arbitration procedures, and the case was lost. I am afraid Additional Secretary A. Vijayanand failed to defend the government's action adequately. These actions gave rise to the doubt whether the cancellation was stage-managed to benefit Devas!

In 2015, the ICC issued an order of compensation to Devas to

PRIVATE LIMITED (India) vs/ ANTRIX CORPORATION LIMITED (India)', *Devas Facts,* 13 January 2021, https://bit.ly/3MEScRs. Accessed on 4 April 2023. p 27.

[10]Ibid. p. 34.

[11]Thomas, K. Thomas, 'Did Fighting the Wrong Battle Cost Antrix the Devas War?', *The Hindu BusinessLine*, 22 January 2018, https://bit.ly/3nMFXcQ. Accessed on 4 April 2023.

[12]'ICC International Court of Arbitration, Case No. 18051/CYK, DEVAS MULTIMEDIA PRIVATE LIMITED (India) vs/ ANTRIX CORPORATION LIMITED (India)', *Devas Facts,* 13 January 2021, https://bit.ly/3MEScRs. Accessed on 4 April 2023. p. 95.

the extent of US $562 million against the perceived loss of future business opportunities due to the unilateral cancellation of the agreement and the DOS not following proper procedures or rules complying with international norms.[13] Normally, the government would have inquired into this matter that has brought such a heavy financial burden to the country. But no such action has been taken so far.

The court has since set aside the ICC award issued in 2015. The National Company Law Appellate Tribunal has directed the liquidation of Devas, and the latter may not be able to get the award implemented. But as time passes, the interest burden mounts, and today, it turns out to be US $1.2 billion.[14] The legal expense itself has mounted to an astronomical sum.

A BALANCED ASSESSMENT

The events following the CCS's decision to cancel the agreement show many actions where the cart was put before the horse. After cancelling the agreement in February 2011, a high-power review committee was appointed by the government to look into all aspects of the Antrix–Devas deal with B.K. Chaturvedi, ex-Cabinet secretary, and Professor Narasimha, Space Commission member, as members. Normally, such reviews are conducted by the Space Commission *before* taking a major decision. The committee went through all the relevant files and interviewed several officials involved in the project before submitting its final report in March 2011. Its main conclusion was that there had been no spectrum sale and, hence, no loss to the government.[15] The committee also concluded that, on the contrary, if the agreement had been implemented as planned, the government would have received high returns from the project, possibly higher than any other public-sector undertaking. The new

---

[13]Ibid. p. 95.

[14]Singh, Surendra, 'Devas Wins 9-Year-Old Legal Battle against Antrix as US Courts Awards It $1.2 Billion Compensation', *The Times of India*, 30 October 2020, https://bit.ly/3LrV9pu. Accessed on 24 April 2023.

[15]Chowdhury Shubhadeep, 'No Vendetta Against Nair, His Team: ISRO Chief', *The Tribune*, 7 February 2012, https://bit.ly/3IQhhc9. Accessed on 17 January 2023.

technology of handheld digital communication using satellites was very much needed for the country to become self-reliant.

The committee further stated:

> Concerns of cheap selling of spectrum to Devas have no basis whatsoever. Space spectrum is not comparable to terrestrial spectrum. Devas was required to obtain licenses from DoT/I&B for providing services to customers, and would have to pay, apart from transponder leasing charges, other charges which would be determined by the Telecom Regulatory Authority of India (TRAI) based on their consultation mechanism.[16]

That would have led to a huge financial gain to the government.

However, the Committee cited certain procedural lapses and wanted those to be corrected in the future. For example, the report pointed out that the government had not been kept informed about the agreement with Devas. It also recommended that efforts should be made to consolidate the spectrum requirements for military and societal applications and that ISRO should make efforts to augment the spectrum available for such applications. The Committee emphatically stated that no spectrum sale had been carried out by ISRO. If only the Space Commission had had access to this report and the Suresh Committee Report before its meeting, the entire course of events could have been different.

I believe that since the conclusion of the Committee's report did not justify the action taken for cancellation, and it seems with the sole intention of finding a scapegoat, in May 2011, yet another panel headed by former Vigilance Commissioner Pratyush Sinha was appointed.[17] Strangely, Dr Radhakrishnan himself sat as a member on the new panel, which is unusual.

One of the members who resigned from the panel midway has stated that many of the suggestions were forced on the panel, citing

---

[16]Ibid.

[17]'Statement on High Powered Review Committee and High Level Team on ANTRIX-DEVAS Agreement: Status of Follow Up Actions', *ISRO*, 4 February 2012, https://bit.ly/41zbxdk. Accessed on 24 April 2023; 'New Probe Ordered into Antrix-Devas Deal', *The Hindu*, 18 June 2011, https://bit.ly/41zbEWi. Accessed on 24 April 2023.

external interference. I wanted to make a deposition before this panel. After a lot of effort, I got a half-an-hour meeting with the chairman of the panel. He did not show any inclination to listen to my views. I later sent him a detailed note on some of the major issues.[18] He did not show the courtesy to take note of, seek any clarifications about or hold discussions with me on the points I had raised. It is my belief that the report was conditioned to justify the decisions already made and implemented by the DOS.

All the three committees that reviewed the Antrix–Devas deal concluded that there had been no spectrum sale and only a lease of the S-band transponder. They also recommended that the new technology for communication from satellite to handheld devices is absolutely needed for the country.

The Pratyush Sinha Panel came out with a new finding—that the action of Antrix–DOS helped Devas make an undue gain of ₹575 crore by selling shares in the international market.[19] If one examines the concerned file, the above amount was brought in by Devas to make use of foreign equity participation as per the prevalent government norms. Also, in Devas's application for foreign investment approval to the Foreign Investment Promotion Board (FIPB), there was no reference to the deal between Devas and Antrix. Prior to approving the investment by the FIPB, the views of the DOT were sought, but not of the DOS or Antrix. The FIPB approval was given based on the Internet Protocol television services license issued by the DOT. It is surprising that the Pratyush Sinha Panel concluded that the so-called undue gain by Devas is caused by an 'act of omission' and commission by Antrix and the DOS officials that included four scientists and four IAS officers and recommended action under service rules or pension rules![20] Later actions, including the CBI inquiry, were based on this wrong notion.

---

[18]'Statement on High Powered Review Committee and High Level Team on ANTRIX-DEVAS Agreement: Status of follow up actions', *ISRO*, 4 February 2012, https://bit.ly/416PnOZ. Accessed on 5 April 2023. p. 2.

[19]'CAG Rips into ISRO for Devas Deal, Clears PMO', *The Times of India*, 16 May 2012, https://bit.ly/3QS37cw. Accessed on 17 January 2023.

[20]Gandhi, Divya, 'Report Hints at "Collusive Behaviour" in Antrix-Devas Deal', *The Hindu*, 6 February 2012, https://bit.ly/3m5GXIR. Accessed on 6 April 2023.

As per central government service rules, when such an accusation is made, specific charges will have to be framed against each of the officers, and all of them must be given a fair opportunity to defend themselves. Only if the explanations are unsatisfactory can the department take any punitive actions. If the accusation is proved, then punishment has to be recommended. In this case, the action was taken well before even the preliminary inquiry reports were in place! In the case of secretary-level persons, such actions require the approval of the appointing authority, the president of India. However, without following any such rules and procedures, the DOS meted out punishment in February 2012 to only the scientists, including me, by debarring them from any government jobs, while no action was taken against the IAS officers.[21] The DOS has no power to do such things. This is a clear case of high-handed action, taking law into the hands targeting a few of us, and the intention was to harm the reputation of scientists who had spoken against the wrong decisions of the UPA-II government.

THE BAN IS IMPOSED

When the ban order was suddenly issued by the DOS debarring me, Sridhara Murthi, Bhaskara Narayana and Dr Shankara from participating in any government activities, I was the Vikram Sarabhai Professor at ISRO and was contributing to various technical and managerial reviews. This was totally unprecedented and issued without following rules and procedures.

The ban orders were sent to all government departments and even to state governments. But not even a copy of the order was served to us. I got a copy from a friend in the media. The next evening, a letter was sent to me through a messenger, terminating my term as the Vikram Sarabhai Professor at ISRO. I had to resign from the post of president of the Patna IIT Governing Council and from some boards of public-sector undertakings of which I was a member.

---

[21] 'ISRO Report Indicts Ex-ISRO Chief, 3 Others', *Nagaland Post*, 5 February 2012, https://bit.ly/3L9MvKW. Accessed on 24 April 2023.

There was a public uproar about the DOS's autocratic decisions and actions. The media called foul and echoed it for several days. Senior scientists like Professor C.N.R. Rao, Dr Anil Kakodkar, Kiran Karnik and so on expressed their disagreement in public.[22] But the strongest protest was made by Professor Narasimha, who had been a member of the Chaturvedi Committee. He met Dr Manmohan Singh, explained the factual situation and told him that the action taken was wrong. As an act of protest, he resigned from the Space Commission.[23]

Dr Kalam was touring Sri Lanka at the time. When he returned, I met and apprised him of the issue. I could convince him of my innocence. He advised me to approach the Supreme Court. He also told me that he would recommend one of his friends, a senior counsel in the Supreme Court, possibly at a reduced fee. Upon enquiry, I was told that I may have to shell out a huge sum of money. That would mean my entire life's savings received as retirement benefits! I could not afford that and, hence, did not pursue that course of action.

Some of my friends also advised me to seek legal recourse. I approached the Central Administrative Tribunal (CAT) in Kochi. But my experiences with both the CAT and High Court of Kerala were highly disappointing. After keeping the petition idle for more than a year, the tribunal washed its hands off the issue, saying that only pension-related matters came under their purview. In my case, the issue was about service matters, particularly my service after retirement as the Vikram Sarabhai Professor. I challenged that decision in the High Court of Kerala. After a year, I was told that the matter did not come under their jurisdiction as the event had taken place in Bengaluru. They gave me the option of approaching the Karnataka High Court. But I was told that it may take several years for the

---

[22]Azriel, Merryl, 'ISRO Controversy Continues to Roil Indian Space Community', *Space Safety Magazine*, 29 February 2012, https://bit.ly/4354ZEr. Accessed on 5 April 2023; Narain, Sunita, 'Indian Scientists: Missing in Action', *Centre for Science and Environment*, https://bit.ly/3ZKFjKa. Accessed on 5 April 2023.

[23]Azriel, Merryl, 'ISRO Controversy Continues to Roil Indian Space Community', *Space Safety Magazine*, 29 February 2012, https://bit.ly/4354ZEr. Accessed on 5 April 2023.

case to be heard there. Nearly three years had already passed! I thought it would be a waste of time and money and left it at that.

A legal remedy seems to be a mirage. We all know that Nambinarayanan had to wait for 25 years before he could get justice.

THE CBI INQUIRY

During the arbitration proceedings, the UPA-II government was told that if a criminal conspiracy was established, the award by the ICC could be blocked, and it initiated a CBI inquiry just before it left office in 2014.[24] It seems to me that the CBI inquiry was initiated to apparently protect the persons responsible for bringing the hefty ICC award upon ISRO. As a part of the inquiry, an FIR was filed against Antrix and the DOS officials as well as executives of Devas on alleged irregularities in the Antrix–Devas agreement.[25] There was no further progress for almost six months. Then suddenly in May 2015, a team landed at ISRO HQ in Bengaluru. They began collecting files from Antrix and ISRO as well as taking statements from various people.

I got a call to appear at the CBI HQ in New Delhi. When I reported there, a four-page questionnaire was awaiting me. Since I had not recently seen the FIR or the concerned files, I had to reply to the queries, relying on my memory for details. In certain instances, the CBI showed me some of the files seized from Antrix. I got the impression that the officers were satisfied with my explanations. Between the discussions, two legal persons from the CBI also joined and asked for some clarifications about differences in spectrum valuation for terrestrial and space applications. I could give satisfactory answers to these queries too. I thought that was the end of the matter.

I was invited to lunch with the deputy inspector general in charge of the investigation. He was an Indian Police Service officer who had got motivated by following my achievements and contributions

---

[24]Rao, Veena S., 'The Antrix Devas Deal: A Fall Gal's Story', *Governance Now*, 29 August 2017, https://bit.ly/3nM7BH7. Accessed on 5 April 2023.
[25]Ibid.

to ISRO. I pointed out to him that there had been no spectrum sale or financial loss caused to the government and absolutely no indication of corrupt practices. At the end of our conversation, he stated that all the papers submitted by the DOS seemed to indict me in the case. They seem to have been files prepared specifically for that purpose! Later, I learnt from reliable sources that just before the CBI team arrived at ISRO HQ, some of the relevant papers revealing the facts were removed, and only the negative inputs were kept in the file! Additionally, the conclusions of the Pratyush Sinha Panel were projected as the major evidence, suppressing many of the technical and managerial findings in the Chaturvedi Committee Report. The CBI had been fed selective data by the DOS, which did not accommodate the fact that the real loss was on account of means adopted for cancelling the agreement.

By the end of 2016, the CBI filed a charge sheet in the Patiala Court at Delhi. Since the officers had seemed satisfied with my answers, I was shocked to see my name listed as one of the major accused in the charge sheet, picturing me as the mastermind behind the alleged scam!

The CBI court raised the question whether, as per Section 197 of the Code of Criminal Procedure, necessary permissions had been obtained from the government, since we were all former central government servants. Consequently, the process of obtaining this sanction was initiated. Normally, especially when a secretary-level person is involved, the charges and allegations are mandatorily examined by a senior committee comprising a few secretaries from different departments. Recommendations of the committee must then be placed before the minister in charge, which, in this case, was the prime minister. Apparently, no such action was taken by the DOS. My attempt, using the provision of the Right to Information Act, to obtain a copy of the file related to issuing sanctions under Section 197 did not succeed. The department refused to share the details, citing that the matter was under investigation.

Later, the CBI produced 18,000 pages of various files related to this case before the court along with a preliminary charge sheet. Scrutiny of those papers has raised many questions in my mind. However, I cannot delve into them in this book since the matter is sub judice.

Though the charge sheet was presented in the court in 2016, neither has it gone beyond the stage of document verification nor is there any indication as to when hearing will start. I am really surprised at the pace at which the legal machinery works in the country, even when the government itself was interested in closing the case at the earliest. Reviewing nearly 20,000 pages of notes about the case as well as examining more than 60 witnesses and the nine accused may take several years. I wonder if I will be able to prove my innocence within my lifespan. But my conscience is clear—I have not done anything wrong or ever indulged in any corrupt practices. It is only as the fallout of some ill-informed and perhaps corrupt persons trying to hide their wrongdoings that I am being victimized. I remember the ordeal Nambinarayanan went through due to the notorious spy scam in 1994. He had to go from court to court and spend lakhs of rupees for nearly 20 years before he could get justice. I don't know if I will get justice in my remaining years.

Whatever I have written above are facts. Several of these issues need detailed technical clarifications.

SOME MORE FROM BEHIND THE SCENES

As stated earlier, the revenue-earning capacity of space-based systems is a thousand times less than that of terrestrial use of spectrum. So, projecting a pre-emptive loss of ₹2.8 lakh crore was totally erroneous.

The CAG understood this mistake later and corrected it. In this context, the concluding remarks on the Antrix–Devas Scam of the then CAG Vinod Rai as given in his autobiography titled *Not Just an Accountant* are worth quoting: 'It is a different story that after a closer examination of the audit report, we in the Headquarters felt that the loss figure had no basis and dropped it.'[26] No financial loss to the government was reported in the final audit report by the CAG. What was included was their version of procedural lapses without specifying any details.

---

[26]Rai, Vinod, *Not Just an Accountant: The Diary of the Nation's Conscience Keeper*, Rupa Publications, 2014, p. 118.

Initially, as a disciplined ISRO employee, I kept quiet and shared my views only with the chairman, Dr Radhakrishnan. I thought that he understood the points and would use them to defend ISRO and refute the allegations. Since that did not happen, I had to take a stand and explain the difference between valuations of ground spectrum and space spectrum publicly. Many major journalists understood the points and published them. I heard later that rumours were going around that I was fighting against the government, and I would have to pay a heavy penalty for that.

I was told that a team of central ministers had been set up to shield the prime minister, immediately after the news on the scam broke out. If only the DOS had carried out a detailed investigation and analysis, they would not have supported the media's depiction of the scam. I do not think the DOS could effectively explain the issues to the team of ministers or to the prime minister. Perhaps this was the reason for the snap decision taken by the Space Commission to cancel the agreement like dropping a hot potato.

Looking back, I think some people may have played mischievous roles to achieve their personal goals. I remember feeling that Kibe was a discontented person. He was due to retire in November 2009, so he may have wanted the favour of continued service and wished to please the new chairman. It had come to my notice that both of them seemed to harbour a dislike for Sridhara Murthi, managing director of Antrix, as well as for Bhaskara Narayana, the director of the satellite communication programme office and Kibe's boss. So, it seems to me at least possible that Kibe used this opportunity to malign them and earn the favour of the then chairman of ISRO. That could be the motive behind making a baseless complaint in November 2009 on the Antrix–Devas agreement. I cannot comment on what role Dr Radhakrishnan may have played in this, and whether he was even directly involved.

Additional Secretary Balachandran seemed to have a very strange relationship with Dr Radhakrishnan. Initially, they worked hand-in-glove on various issues, but later, I heard that they had fallen out over some issues. Balachandran did not show anything openly, but it might be that he had an agenda to somehow fix Dr Radhakrishnan. All the subsequent events are a result of this complex dynamics between a few individuals. Given the host of rumours flying around, it is hard to determine what to believe. I even heard at one point that there were rumours that the additional secretary was working with Minister A. Raja and that the audit query had been deliberately leaked to the media to help Raja and dilute his case.

A HOST OF ALLEGATIONS

One of the allegations made was that Devas made an undue gain of ₹575 crore, but this financial gain was through getting foreign investment into the company at two stages. The company was registered as an Internet service provider with the main activity of developing software and hardware. They obtained a licence for information processing and technology (IPT) services from the DOT. Their application to the FIPB for receiving foreign investment quoted their development plan and was not based on the agreement with Antrix. Initially, they got clearance for receiving 24 per cent foreign funds. Subsequently, a change was made by the government in the norms for foreign investment, which raised it to 74 per cent. Using this provision, Devas again sought FIPB clearance. This application also did not cite the agreement with Antrix. This process took place between 2006 and 2009. The FIPB had sought the opinion of the DOT while deliberating on this application. As mentioned earlier, none of the DOT, FIPB and Devas had consulted or asked for any clearance or approval from Antrix or the DOS. Hence, blaming the Antrix–DOS team for facilitating the foreign investment is baseless. Clearly, the foreign investment was brought into the country by Devas for developing software and hardware for IPT services and was not based on the satellite lease agreement with Antrix.

Yet another allegation was that one person holding multiple roles led to corrupt practices at ISRO. This custom was the result of a unique management structure evolved by Dr Bhabha, nurtured by Dr Sarabhai and pursued by all who successively became the chairmen of ISRO. It enabled ISRO to become the top-most performer among the R&D organizations in the country. A totally open and transparent decentralized management system is practised at the units and centres. The chairman of ISRO is never a dictator in such a democratic management system. During my tenure, there was no occasion when any of the review committee recommendations were overruled.[27]

Several facts of this case have been brought to light by the ICC arbitration. Apparently, based on the charge sheet I have received, the investigating agency had not taken note of many of these details presented to the international court, condemning the actions of the UPA-II government with respect to the ICC award.

One of the stories making the rounds was that the entire drama may have been enacted to help Devas. Even though the concept of satellite-based handheld devices for multimedia services was attractive in 2005, by 2008, telecom services in India had advanced significantly and similar services were being provided by terrestrial mobile operators in 3G and 4G. Devas may have feared that its scheme would not lead to commercial success under those circumstances. To provide such a satellite-based service augmented through the ground segment, it would have had to shell out a heavy licence fee on par with that of terrestrial operators. This would have made the project totally unviable economically and would have caused heavy losses to Devas. This may have been the reason why it wanted the agreement with Antrix/ISRO to be cancelled. If it was cancelled as per their request, they would have to forgo the advance booking charges of ₹58 crore. However, if Antrix cancelled the same, the advance would be refunded to Devas. So, it is possible that some people with vested interests may have influenced the DOS to cancel the agreement.

One question that is not yet answered by anybody is the following: the CBI inquiry is limited to the period from 2004 to 2009, when I was the chairman of ISRO. But the source of the issue is the MOU signed under the guidance of Dr K. Kasturirangan, my predecessor. The cancellation and consequent damages had occurred during 2010–11, when Dr Radhakrishnan was the chairman. Why weren't these periods scrutinized as well?

Further, why was a New York-based law firm nominated to argue the case from India's side?[28] Why was not a senior lawyer from India

---

[27]A statement in the Pratyush Sinha Panel Report.

[28]'ICC International Court of Arbitration, Case No. 18051/CYK, DEVAS

designated to represent the Government of India at the international court? This remains a mystery! In contrast, Devas used a top Indian lawyer to argue their case. The entire drama of cancellation of the Devas agreement and the subsequent events in the international courts leaves many doubts unexplained and is shrouded in mystery.

I find it unfortunate that some actions under the advice of the DOS have put the entire nation in a difficult situation. I get the feeling that biased opinions of some of the DOS officials may be misleading the government on the fight to block the penalty. Unless there is a comprehensive review, especially on the cancellation of the contract, the facts will not come out.

At the centre of these events is Dr Radhakrishnan. Even though I had played a crucial role in him becoming the chairman of ISRO, after assuming charge, he somehow started developing a hostile attitude towards me. It was perhaps due to professional jealousy and wrong advice given by the coterie that surrounded him. I have gathered from some personal discussions that he seems to have privately expressed the view that the cancellation was to save face. Later, I was told by various people that he is one person who cannot stand any criticism from others. Putting all these points together, it seems to me that the ban order and the CBI case were acts of witch-hunting and vendetta. It is difficult to understand the behaviour of Dr Radhakrishnan. After leaving ISRO HQ forever, I have avoided meeting or communicating with him.

One redeeming fact is that even today, much respect and love towards me seems to be left in the minds of many people in the country, including children and scientists. That is all thanks to the challenging tasks undertaken by me at ISRO and the benefits made available by the government for all the employees. I am really proud to have been a part of this great organization and of having done at least something useful for our country. The love and affection of the people wipe out all the agony and trauma caused to me by my successor.

MULTIMEDIA PRIVATE LIMITED (India) vs/ ANTRIX CORPORATION LIMITED (India)', *Devas Facts*, 13 January 2021, https://bit.ly/3MEScRs. Accessed on 4 April 2023. p. 3.

31

Gurave Namah

I could easily overcome the failures due to the technical problems I encountered during my career with determination and hard work. But the turbulence caused by certain events after my retirement shook me up. My analytical approach to problem-solving ultimately helped me to recover and stabilize my life. Behind everything was the confidence in myself that I have done nothing wrong in my official capacity or in my personal life. Various inquiry committees that looked into the Devas issue invariably gave me a clean chit. However, the court case is still ongoing. It continues to be a small irritant in my life.

Indian Space Research Organisation severed connections with me, and I returned to Kerala. The house that I had built in Sasthamangalam had to be cleaned up, and my wife and I settled down at our favourite old abode.

DR KALAM'S PASSING

The day 27 July 2015 turned out to be a very sad day. There was nothing unusual at first. It began normally. I was organizing an event for launching a new centre to address developmental issues of Kerala. The organizers entrusted me with inviting Dr Kalam for the inaugural function. Usually, I call him in the evening hours. I attempted to reach him on his mobile phone. Even after several attempts, all I could hear was: 'The person you are calling is not reachable.' It never occurred to me that I would not be able to reach him ever after.

A few minutes later, my telephone rang—it was a Press Trust of India (PTI) representative in Thiruvananthapuram. He spoke softly, asking, 'Have you heard the sad news?' I had not heard any special news that day and nothing had appeared on TV either. After a pause, he told me that Dr Kalam was no more. I could not believe my ears. I thought it must be fake news. But the PTI representative went on to explain that while Dr Kalam was preparing to address the students at Indian Institute of Management (IIM) Shillong, he had collapsed on the stage and had to be rushed to a hospital. Though the official declaration had not come, it was known from reliable sources that he was no more—he had passed away due to a cardiac arrest.

I could not digest this shocking news. Just a week earlier, we had had a lengthy chat over the phone. When I had enquired about his health, he had mentioned that he had had a thorough check-up done at the military hospital in Delhi and no health-related problems had been reported. He had been following his hectic daily schedules as usual.

After my conversation with the PTI representative, I talked to Dr Kalam's personal staff in Delhi. They, too, were dumbstruck.

The news put me in a deeply depressed mood. Thousands of fond memories of my guru, starting from the days of working at the bishop's house adjoining the Mary Magdalena Mariam Church at TERLS to the strolls in the Mughal Gardens at the Rashtrapati Bhavan flashed through my mind. Reminiscences of the many challenging moments of failures and successes flooded me. I recalled the last message from him while we were walking on the lawns of his residence in Delhi. 'The main challenge before the country is how the quality of life of the common man can be improved. Poverty, ill health and illiteracy are haunting those less privileged. People like us should seriously consider taking up socially relevant projects to lift them up by making use of modern technology,' he had commented.

An official announcement came after a few hours, but there was still no confirmation about when the body was to be brought to Delhi and where the cremation was to take place. There were indications that his mortal remains may be laid to rest at his birth place in Rameswaram. I was waiting for the confirmation, so that I could go and have a final glimpse of my guru.

EARLIER THAT DAY

Technical officer Janpal Singh had accompanied Dr Kalam to Shillong along with his personal assistant, Sheridon. After landing at the Guwahati airport at noon, they had travelled to Shillong by road. Dr Kalam never wasted even a single moment. He had shared his concerns with Singh, saying, 'As president, I saw two different regimes at the centre. Recently, I witnessed the chaotic behaviour of people's representatives in Parliament. I do not know how to make these parliamentarians understand behaving properly and focussing on the real issues in the development agenda for the entire nation.' Dr Kalam had framed three questions to the students of IIM based on these thoughts, asking for their suggestions on remedial measures. He had wanted to engage in a debate on the issue with the budding leaders.

Dr Kalam had reached IIM a short while before the event was scheduled to start. The management suggested that he rest for some time before starting the function. He had enquired whether the students were ready and had said that he did not want them to wait. So, after freshening up quickly, he had rushed to the conference hall. His assistant had set up the computer screen and tested the mic. Dr Kalam had just begun his address to the students, but even before completing the first sentence, he had collapsed on the stage. He had been rushed to the military hospital without any delay, but he had already taken his last breath before reaching there.

The doctors could not make any formal announcement about the demise of the former president of India and the great scientist revered by the global community without completing elaborate official procedures. As soon as the official declaration came, Dr Kalam's older brother Kunju Marikkar made a request through the district collector that his mortal remains be buried in the soil of his birth, in Rameswaram. Prime Minister Narendra Modi accepted the request despite the logistical problems for the dignitaries who wished to participate in the funeral.

Since no post-mortem was conducted, one can never be certain about the exact reason behind his death. But sometime later, I had an opportunity to visit IIM Shillong to address the students.

The impressive campus is located on hilly terrain. Except for the main administrative block, the other facilities are built at different heights of the hillock, connected with steep steps. I had to deliver the lecture in the same hall where my guru had breathed his last. It has the height of nearly a three-storeyed building, and there is no option other than to walk up the winding steps. By the time I reached the conference hall, I was breathless. It took me several minutes to catch my breath. Imagine the plight of Dr Kalam, who had travelled from Delhi to Shillong, taking about six hours for the journey, and then climbing the steps in one stretch to the conference hall. I am sure that must have put pressure on his heart. I wonder whether that was the trigger for his massive heart attack.

On 27 July, Dr Kalam's body was taken in a helicopter from Shillong to Guwahati and from there to Delhi in an Air Force aircraft. President Pranab Mukherjee and Prime Minister Modi were at the Delhi airport to receive his body. The next day, the mortal remains were placed for public view in Delhi. The burial was planned in Rameswaram.

Normally, the government builds huge bungalows for retired presidents at the place of their choice. However, Dr Kalam chose to live in an old two-storey bungalow with a huge garden built during British times. He did not want to own a palatial building at government expense. This shows how simple his habits were. It was in that compound that his mortal remains were placed for public view. People from all walks of life and political parties as well as ambassadors from various countries lined up in front of 7, Rajaji Marg, to pay their last respects. Ambassadors representing the heads of the USA, Russia and France as well as the UN Secretary General placed wreaths on Dr Kalam's body and recorded their condolence messages. Since the display was for only one day, several people had to go back disappointed.

On the next morning, his body was airlifted by an Air Force aircraft to Madurai as per schedule. The local army contingent received it and proceeded to Rameswaram. The road was lined with people from all parts of the country who had come to have a last darshan of the Missile Man of India.

IN RAMESWARAM

I had decided to be in Rameswaram for a final darshan of my guru and had reached the previous evening. I was waiting with the dignitaries from the state and central governments when the body arrived. The government had allotted two acres of land for the final burial and building a memorial. Elaborate arrangements had been made for receiving the governors, chief ministers, foreign dignitaries and people's representatives who arrived for the event.

Chief Minister of Kerala Oommen Chandy had tried to bring the mortal remains to Thiruvananthapuram, considering the fact that Dr Kalam had spent nearly two decades of his life there and had thousands of followers at ISRO centres there. However, due to a shortage of time for making elaborate security arrangements, he could not implement the plan.

I can never forget the last few moments that I had with Dr Kalam's embalmed body lying within a glass cage. I touched his feet and prayed. His face was smiling as always. I felt as though he was telling me that it was time for him to leave this world, but I have a mission to translate many of his ideas for societal uplift into fulfilment.

I visited Dr Kalam's ancestral house. A large crowd was trying to console his brother Marikkar. I could see that he was heartbroken. He was lamenting that it was too early for his brother, 10 years younger than him, to leave this world. Dr Kalam had not visited Rameswaram in several years. However, he used to contact his elder brother telephonically quite often.

By evening, the incessant flow of the crowd that had gathered to get a last glimpse of Dr Kalam in Rameswaram caused huge traffic blocks. The trains were overflowing. The chief priest of the Shiva temple and leaders from all religions were among the crowd to pay their last respects.

As per Islamic practice, the body had to be taken to the family house for the family members to perform the last rites. Accordingly, the armed forces team responsible for funeral arrangements took the body of Dr Kalam there. After completing the rituals, his body was taken to the mosque at Rameswaram, where he used to pray regularly during his childhood. The priest and other senior members of the community had assembled to conduct the last prayers before wrapping Dr Kalam's mortal remains with the traditional green cloth. The army spread the tricolour on top of that. This was followed by Dr Kalam's last journey of 2 km to the burial ground.

The funeral procession passed through the narrow roads of Rameswaram, past Mandapam Panchayat Union Elementary School where Dr Kalam had learnt the alphabet. The students and teachers stood in front of the school with lighted candles. While the old school building is not there anymore, there is a marble plate in the renovated block with the inscription:

His Excellency Dr. A.P.J. Abdul Kalam
The President of India
Studied in this School.

Prime Minister Modi, senior ministers from the central and state governments as well as several foreign dignitaries had assembled on the ground to pay their last respects. After giving the traditional guard of honour, Dr Kalam's body was finally lowered into the ground. Once again, mullahs and close family members performed their rites and the pit was filled with soil.

It was immediately declared that a monument would be built in Dr Kalam's memory on the ground where his body had been laid to rest. Initially, the state government took the responsibility of implementing it. But since there was not much progress after a year, the DRDO, with which Dr Kalam had spent half of his career, took it up. Now, there is a simple structure at the spot in the name of Dr Kalam, with an exhibition hall, a library, a conference facility and a few working spaces for researchers.

The place has become yet another holy place for the pilgrims coming to Rameswaram, especially for children and students.

REMEMBERING KALAM

Dr Kalam has left me and many others with lots of memories. He never believed in astrology. He never accepted the concept of predicting the future based on the position of planets and stars.

However, he respected the technical knowledge present in the various Vedas and Puranas. We used to wonder how the ancient rishis had in-depth knowledge of some of the topics related to the solar system and the universe, comparable to the modern findings in astrophysics. Often Dr Kalam and I would engage in discussions related to religions, ancient sciences and human civilizations. I was amazed at his deep knowledge of Islam, Christianity and Hinduism. During the early days, he did not pursue Islamic prayers or other routines, but in the latter half of his life, he was meticulous in following the discipline during the month of Ramadan. During the whole month, he would not touch even water during the daytime and would perform namaaz at least three times a day as specified in the Islamic texts. However, he avoided the luxurious food habits followed by many for breaking the fast at the end of the day.

During Ramadan, there was a custom of organizing a huge feast for invited dignitaries at the Rashtrapati Bhavan. During Dr Kalam's tenure as president, he instructed his office to stop the practice and to use the savings (about ₹20 lakh) to serve food packets to the poor in the city.

That was quintessentially Kalam!

32

New Pastures

I had a very close relationship with Dr K. Kasturirangan. We travelled abroad together many times. We used to discuss several matters, including missions to send humans to space. When Dr Kasturigrangan got appointed as vice chairman of the IAA, he nominated me as a member. It was my first step into the international professional body. Later, when he left that position in 2004, I became the vice chairman.

INTERNATIONAL INVOLVEMENT

The academy meets once every year at its Paris HQ. A second meeting of the year is at the IAC, a major event with more than 2,500 participants, including many of the global personalities among the space community. Being one among them was no simple matter! The meeting was conducted in India twice, the first time in Bengaluru in 1988. In 2007, I organized the meeting in Hyderabad under the aegis of ISRO. I was then elected as the president of the academy—the first non-American president of the IAA.

In the midst of all the controversies around the Devas Scam, the international space community stood with me. Some of my colleagues from ISRO had complained to the IAA about me. However, Yannick d'Escatha, the then head of the CNES, exposed the wrong actions taken by ISRO and supported me, as did Jean-Michel Contant, the secretary general of the IAA. I was consequently re-elected as president of the IAA for two more terms, up to 2016.

I am happy that several studies on advanced space systems could be completed under the banner of the IAA during my tenure. Space solar power was one among them. The idea was to collect solar energy from space using large solar panels in outer space and transfer it to the Earth through microwaves. Another study was about using a 'space elevator' instead of rockets to take satellites or instruments to outer space. A space elevator is an escalator-like structure extending over 100 km in height and is made using advanced lightweight materials like carbon nanotubes.

A major achievement was gathering the global space agencies for a technical meet. Heads of 26 space agencies met in Washington, D.C., under the banner of the IAA in 2010. Discussions were organized on four major thrust areas for space exploration—human presence in outer space, robotic exploration of other planets, climate change and technologies for disaster management and mitigation. The resulting ideas were taken up by several space agencies as part of their programmes. Additionally, an international conference on climate change was organized in Thiruvananthapuram in 2014. I am happy that several recommendations related to mitigating climate change were presented and were accepted in the subsequent conference at Paris.

At present, I am engaged as the president of the management council of the Environment Resource Research Centre (ERRC) set up in 1991 in Thiruvananthapuram by well-known scientist Dr P.K.K. Nair. The ERRC is engaged in consultancy for the Kerala government and Government of India. Government funding in this area has reduced, and presently, my efforts are focussed on diversifying the activities and achieving economic stability.

In 2010, with advice and support from Dr Kalam, a centre for propagating science and technology, called Vikram Sarabhai Science Foundation was set up by Dr Indira Rajan under our guidance in Kochi. She had visited NASA as part of a student interaction programme, along with Dr Kalam, and that was the motivation for this venture. Dr Rajan is a dynamic person who has been active in the field of education. She has set up a small space museum and conducts science talent search programmes to attract young children to science and technology. It is her dream to set up a school and a large science and technology exhibition to identify talented children, expose them to the challenges and opportunities in scientific explorations and enable them to pursue scientific careers.

As a mentor, I provide guidance. I also spend a lot of time trying to motivate children in schools associated with the foundation.

After returning to Thiruvananthapuram, my schedule has been fairly leisurely. Once in a while, I travel to other parts of Kerala and to major cities in other states, mainly to interact with students. My wife is happy since most of our relatives are in Thiruvananthapuram. She is able to visit them regularly. She often joins me on my trips to the Kochi area, so that we can have a darshan of Guruvayoorappan.

THE WORLD AROUND

I was fortunate to visit several foreign countries through official engagements. The only continent that I could not visit was Australia. Though the visits were short, I always tried to absorb as much as possible about the modern technologies and the way of life there.

One thing that I noticed about the people of many countries was their discipline and hard-working nature. Perhaps their way of life has been shaped by the hardships they went through during the World Wars. In Russia and China, the communist regimes induced a high level of discipline through the party machinery. The polite behaviour and dedication to work of the Japanese greatly impressed me. I found them to be highly quality-conscious in all undertakings. The hostile surroundings and scarce natural resources combined with patriotism has driven the Israelis to rare heights of innovation and high productivity. The refined attitude, patriotism and self-dependence of the French and the technical excellence of the Germans also impressed me a lot.

Some of my most memorable trips were undertaken as part of the prime minister's delegation to Russia, the USA and France. Atomic energy and space being the flagship achievements of the country, Prime Minister Manmohan Singh used to include Dr Anil Kakodkar and me in the delegations. Flights with the prime minister's team were unique, with ample opportunities to interact with Dr Singh. Entry and exit from the foreign countries were without the hassles of immigration and customs formalities. Witnessing the guard of honour welcoming our prime minister to the host country was always fascinating. In many of the interactions, both Dr Kakodkar and myself were able to make active contributions for strengthening bilateral cooperation. Discussions between India and Russia involved the development of cryogenic engine technology. With France, the focus was launching heavy satellites and building several subsystems, including the Vikas engine. With the USA, it was India who helped scientists from the JPL to fly their instruments to the Moon in our Chandrayaan-1.

Europe

India closely cooperated with the Soviet Union, starting from the 1960s when M100 rockets were launched every week to measure upper atmospheric winds. The huge volume of data collected has been extremely valuable for getting a clear understanding of the tropical monsoon phenomenon. Later, the Russians partnered with ISRO by providing cryogenic rocket engines for the developmental flights of the GSLV. Even today, they provide training to the Indian astronauts for our Gaganyaan mission.

Indian Space Research Organisation had the opportunity to work with the CNES right from the beginning of TERLS. The bilateral relations became the strongest while d'Escatha was the president. The joint project Megha Tropiques is a fine example of Indo-French collaboration.

German scientists worked with their Indian counterparts in sounding rocket experiments in the early stages of TERLS. Later, the collaborations were limited to exchange of scientists and using the German satellite tracking and control centres for tracking ISRO satellites.

China

Though China is one of the space powers, ISRO has had very little interaction with the Chinese so far in this domain. I was once invited to participate in a conference there in the 1980s, but I could not get a Chinese visa. However, I met several specialists from the Chinese space agency during the Vienna secession of the UN COPUOS. In spite of their friendliness, they never parted with any technical details about their space programme. As the president of the IAA, I established close contacts with Professor Liu Jiyuan, vice president of the IAA, who was earlier the president of the Chinese space agency.

The Chinese were the first in the world to use rockets for fireworks. In modern times, they aimed to place a satellite in orbit by 1959 to celebrate the tenth anniversary of the People's Republic of China. By 1970, China had fully established the capability of orbiting satellites around the Earth. (At this time, India's first satellite launch vehicle was on the drawing board, leading to a successful mission in 1980.) Concurrently, a programme for a manned capsule was officially declared in 1971 and the design of Shuguang spacecraft was initiated.

A new heavy-lift satellite launch vehicle had made its maiden flight in 1971. The CZ-2A launcher, originally designed to carry the Shuguang-1 spacecraft, was initially tested in 1974. It had carried China's first recoverable satellite, but the mission had failed. After some redesign, the modified CZ-2C rocket successfully launched a recoverable satellite in orbit on 26 November 1975.

The 2C series had a payload capability of 2,400 kg into low-Earth orbit, while the 4C could carry 4,200 kg of payload (the PSLV and GSLV are comparable to these launch vehicles). Development is in progress for the LM-5 series, which can take 25 tons to low-Earth orbit (double the capacity of GSLV Mark III). Further, the Chinese have plans for a heavy-lift launcher called LM-9, capable of carrying up to 130 tons to orbit.

All along, the Chinese space programme has focussed on achieving manned mission capability, and many laboratories and universities have been working towards it. I understand that Chinese capabilities in missiles and satellite launching technologies are nearly as advanced as that of the Russians.

Due to the potential of space technology for military activities, China was on the embargo list for a long time and unable to get any technology from the Western world. They consequently accelerated their internal efforts. The net result is that today China is a leader of satellite launches in the Asia Pacific region and has the upper hand in manned missions.

The Chinese initiative to develop a civil aviation aircraft with 90-passenger capacity impressed me greatly. This was similar to the idea I had nucleated in India in 2011. If we had started that programme then, we could have had a prototype flying by 2015.

The Chinese initiative was started in 2009, and the first flying model was already ready by 2015. The Chinese aircraft manufacturing agency had set up a huge complex for integration, design and development as well as some limited production, all under one roof. Further plans were progressing for the development of a 200-seater aircraft. It is sad that India lost a great opportunity in that area.

I once had the privilege of staying in a room once used by the great Chinese leader Mao Zedong. It was a simple building with two bedrooms like any common man's abode. What a simple lifestyle Mao Zedong had adopted, compared to the pomp and luxury of the earlier emperors!

The balanced mix of the strict discipline of communist regimes coupled with a capitalistic management style and profit sharing with all team members is the primary reason China has emerged as a global manufacturing hub. Investments in universities and research laboratories are also paying rich dividends; several universities have risen to the top 100 universities of the world.

After being a poverty-ridden country lacking in significant industrial base, China has emerged as an economic power that has attracted foreign investment.

Israel

I visited Israel in the mid-1980s, when the government wanted to establish contact with the aerospace industries there for developing mutually beneficial programmes. I had to travel with a private passport since India did not have diplomatic relations with Israel then. I had useful discussions with the Israeli space agency and aerospace industries. They gladly shared the details of their latest developments, and we were amazed to see the most advanced optical imaging systems, radar imaging systems and very compact satellites for Earth observation developed by that small country.

Just as we helped the Israelis launch RISAT-1, several inputs from the Israelis have helped us in perfecting our radar imaging satellites. We also had Israeli support for modernizing our semiconductor-fabrication facility in Chandigarh. I had the opportunity to interact closely with the Israeli space agency chief Dr Isaac Ben-Israel and to collaborate in various joint space projects.

My next visit to Israel was in 2012 for an IAC meeting in Jerusalem. The capital had shifted from Tel Aviv to Jerusalem by then. During my first visit, I had seen a small township with a desert-like landscape, surrounded by the famous places of worship of Jews, Christians and Muslims. The second time, I found Jerusalem a well laid-out city with all modern facilities, including several luxury hotels and conference facilities built without affecting the ancient historic monuments. My wife, who joined me on this visit, and I had sufficient time between the conference meetings to explore the nearby locations. The driver-cum-guide shared details about old Israel and the modern state during our journeys. It was amazing that a small country with population of less than a crore could do such wonders in converting the desert land into one full of greenery.

The progress in aerospace and advanced technologies by the small nation, which was totally destroyed during World War II, is amazing. The hard work and innovations of the Jewish community, which migrated to this small country while facing many adversities along with animosity from all the neighbouring countries, speak volumes about their courage and perseverance. When people are driven to a corner, the best performances emerge. Israel is a good example of that.

In spite of the excellence achieved in science and technology, the Israeli people lead a simple lifestyle and still follow ancient Jewish traditions. An example is their belief that no one should operate any device or equipment during Saturdays. Hence, even in the five-star hotel we were staying in, we had to be satisfied with cold sandwiches and fruit juice that day! The lift was in automatic mode—it stopped at every floor and closed the door without the need for touching any button. This felt very strange to us, but one has to be a Roman while in Rome!

The USA

Indian Space Research Organisation closely cooperated with NASA, starting from the early 1960s, but interaction practically came to a standstill after the launch of SLV-3 and during the period of embargo. Recently, closer ties have been restarted with cooperation for the Chandrayaan-1 mission and in radar satellites for Earth observation.

When Ford Aerospace was building our INSAT-1 satellite, I had a chance to visit the USA as part of the INSAT-1 review team. I could visit the launch facilities of the Delta rocket and the spacecraft integration facilities and familiarize myself with NASA's state-of-the-art facilities. Delta was a versatile launch vehicle being used to put satellites in geostationary and low-Earth orbits. I was supposed to look only at the spacecraft and its interface with the rocket. But I took the opportunity to understand as much as possible about the rocket, launch installations, procedures for filling liquid fuels as well as the command and control centre for managing the launch operations. These inputs came in handy later, when we were designing the PSLV launch vehicle as well as setting up the launch installations including our own control centre at the SHAR.

In those days, interactions with NASA's technical teams were quite friendly. As India progressed in space activities, the Americans started seeing us as a competitor and became more and more secretive. Immediately after the launch of SLV-3, we saw the potential danger of an embargo. A high-level team led by T.N. Seshan, then additional secretary to the DOS, was sent to procure as many components and materials as possible on an on-the-spot basis of purchase. I was part of this team. We successfully negotiated and placed orders for several items for the SLV-3 rockets.

On visits to some of the manufacturers, I absorbed as many details as I could. Moog was a company engaged in the manufacture of electro-hydraulic servo systems. Though our aim was to procure simple servo valves, I could gather many details on hydraulic actuators used in rockets. I passed on this information to N. Sridharan Dhas and also arranged a visit for him to Moog. It enabled us to develop a secondary injection thrust vector control system for our solid rockets. The time spent there was utilized not for sightseeing or personal entertainment but for technology absorption.

After that, for almost two decades, I did not visit the USA. As part of the embargo, Indian scientists were denied opportunities to participate in technical activities related to space or atomic energy. A partial relief came 2005 onwards, thanks to the initiatives of

Prime Minister Manmohan Singh and President George Bush to re-establish cooperation in such high-tech areas.

With the development of new-generation space transportation systems, space tourism and planetary exploration will get a real boost. These private ventures have built upon the technology developed for NASA's earlier missions and the refurbished facilities of the Saturn rockets.

In the SpaceX model, an individual's initiative that looks at the long-term perspective, clubbed with personal funding, has emerged as a successful model for space transportation systems. The effort has taken more than 15 years. Many of the modules developed since the Apollo mission have helped in completing the development of the new systems. Elon Musk had hired several veterans from NASA and the aerospace industry in the USA. All the activities, starting from conceptual design to detailed engineering, fabrication of hardware, integration and testing, are carried out under one roof, with Chief Executive Elon Musk holding the reins of the entire organization. This was indeed the model evolved and practised by ISRO for over five decades and also the main reason for the success story of the Indian space programme! Long-term vision coupled with an organizational structure that gives autonomy of functioning and ensures unity of command is the main reason for the success of the Indian space programme. Recently, there has been some attempt to take away this successful working model and to give thrust to industrialization instead.

THE FUTURE

Compared to global standards, ISRO's programmes today are lagging behind in several areas. The first is the ability to fly humans to space and bring them back. The Gaganyaan programme is a small beginning, and we have to chalk out how we can send people to the Moon and Mars. Certainly, more powerful rockets are needed, and the time has come to concentrate on eco-friendly fuels and semi-cryogenic rockets. In the Earth observation scenario, better resolution and day-and-night observation systems have to be developed. Observation platforms from geostationary orbits and high bandwidth connectivity from space to mobile devices are immediate priorities. The recent focus on commercialization has virtually paused innovation and adventurous future programmes.

European countries are now concentrating on commercial launches of communication satellites as well as developing aircraft. The Russian programme is not progressing much because of the lack of funding. The net result is that China is emerging as the global power in space.

India also had similar opportunities, but I feel that lack of initiative and imaginative programmes over the last decade have really let India down. It is not that we do not have the ideas; it is not that we do not possess the technical capabilities; it is not that we do not have the right kind of manpower—but the lack of inspired leadership is affecting the Indian space programme.

However, political will and visionary leadership can reverse the trend. If India wakes up and puts its best foot forward, utilizing its large resource of highly talented personnel, well-equipped laboratories and accumulated knowledge, we can still emerge as the global power in space exploration and in providing space-based services. Though the National Democratic Alliance (NDA) government under the leadership of Prime Minister Modi has taken lots of initiatives, a lot more needs to be done.

THE JOURNEY CONTINUES

After leaving office, I have been making efforts to popularize and propagate science. I spend most of my time imparting the knowledge acquired through my experience to the new generation. I visit colleges, schools and universities, giving talks and engaging with the students. My schedule includes at least one such meeting a week. I try to explain the challenges associated with space exploration and the adventures of scientific research. I have really enjoyed these activities, and till date, I have interacted with close to one lakh students across various parts of the country. I have found that sometimes the students are more informed than me in some of the latest developments. In that case, I return home and read about the topics, so that my understanding of the subject also improves. On the whole, sharing knowledge has been a rich experience for me. During the peak of Covid-19, too, this habit continued through webinars. That also became a new and pleasant undertaking for me.

Often people ask me why I do not get into politics. I feel that one should not enter politics just for the position or fame, but only if one can utilize 100 per cent of their time to be of service to the people. Only then does it have any meaning. I have served the people of this country for nearly half a century through the space programme, and I am satisfied with the outcome of my efforts. It has been a highly fulfilling career, and I do not want to dilute my happiness by getting involved in the political mess of today, especially in Kerala. I would rather spend my time teaching and motivating the next generation.

Today, India certainly has the potential to emerge as a strong economic, knowledge and military leader in the world. We have plenty of natural resources and, above all, the largest youth population in the world. Our youth have already penetrated academics, research and commerce fields in several countries, especially in the USA. Many of these countries depend on India for highly qualified young people for driving their science, technology and growth machineries. Indian youth have high intellectual and practical capabilities. The challenge before us is to empower them with the knowledge and skills they can use for the benefit of humankind. Sadly, our educational system is not tuned towards this objective. A drastic change is needed, promoting skill development and knowledge application. As I write this, the New Education Policy has been declared by the government, and I think it addresses many of the issues related to learning and equipping the youth.

The country's youth is our real power. Enthusing them and guiding them to face the challenges of the world using science and technology is the need of the hour. I consider it as a highly satisfying mission for the remainder of my life.

One thing that fascinates me is the fact that even after 10 years of leaving office, often at airports or other public places, people bump into me asking whether I am the chairman of ISRO. That is always very nice to hear. I have to patiently explain to them that I left office several years ago! They engage me in discussions about

ISRO's achievements and social contributions during my tenure. I think it is the practical applications of space technology for the benefit of the common man and the Chandrayaan mission that made me popular. I must thank the media and the public for that.

I am happy that I have been able to follow the footsteps of our founding father Dr Vikram Sarabhai and be a true disciple of Dr A.P.J. Abdul Kalam, the Missile Man and the first technocrat to become the president of India.

I believe that whatever happens, happens for the best. So be it.

Index